FINAL ACTS

FINAL ACTS

The Creation
of Three Late O'Neill Plays

JUDITH E. BARLOW

THE UNIVERSITY OF GEORGIA PRESS
Athens

© 1985 by the University of Georgia Press
Athens, Georgia 30602
All rights reserved

Designed by Kathi L. Dailey
Set in 10 on 13 Linotron 202 Caledonia
The paper in this book meets the guidelines for
permanence and durability of the Committee on
Production Guidelines for Book Longevity of the
Council on Library Resources.

Printed in the United States of America

90 89 88 87 86 85   6 5 4 3 2 1

Library of Congress Cataloging in Publication Data

Barlow, Judith E.
Final acts.

Bibliography: p.
Includes index.
O'Neill, Eugene, 1888–1953—Technique. 2. O'Neill,
Eugene, 1888–1953. Iceman cometh. 3. O'Neill, Eugene,
1888–1953. Long day's journey into night. 4. O'Neill,
Eugene, 1888–1953. Moon for the misbegotten. I. Title.
PS3529.N5Z564 1985   812'.52   84-16260
ISBN 0-8203-0759-9

CONTENTS

Acknowledgments   vi

A Note on Transcription   vii

Introduction   1

CHAPTER ONE   *The Iceman Cometh*   8

CHAPTER TWO   *Long Day's Journey Into Night*   63

CHAPTER THREE   *A Moon for the Misbegotten*   112

Postscript   157

Notes   163

Selected Bibliography   193

Index   209

ACKNOWLEDGMENTS

O VER THE DOZEN YEARS I have been researching this book, I have been aided immensely by the staffs of the Beinecke Library at Yale University, the Princeton University Library, the Cornell University Library, the New York Public Library at Lincoln Center, the Houghton Library at Harvard University, and the Monte Cristo Cottage in New London, Connecticut. Special thanks must go to the fine people at the Beinecke, particularly David E. Schoonover and Donald Gallup, present and past curators, respectively, of the American Literature Collection, and librarians Anne Whelpley, Stephen Jones, Mary Angelotti, Aldo Cupo, and Julie Campbell. I am also deeply indebted to Gerald Weales, who patiently read and thoughtfully criticized the many drafts of this book; Michael Kaufman, who first inspired and later encouraged my interest in O'Neill; Richard Goldman and Jeffrey Berman, who provided valuable criticism; and Winifred L. Frazer, who helped me track character sources in *The Iceman Cometh*. The Research Foundation of the State University of New York provided me with a grant that partly supported my research.

Permission to quote from and reproduce unpublished materials in the Eugene O'Neill Collection and Theatre Guild Collection, Collection of American Literature, the Beinecke Rare Book and Manuscript Library, Yale University, has been granted by the Yale University Library. Gerald E. Stram has granted permission to quote from Carlotta Monterey O'Neill's letters and diaries at the Beinecke. Letters from Eugene O'Neill to George Jean Nathan, in their Nathan Collection, Department of Rare Books, are quoted by permission of the Library Board of Cornell University Library. Letters from Eugene O'Neill to Julian P. Boyd, in their Eugene O'Neill Collection, and from O'Neill to George C. Tyler, in their George Crouse Tyler Papers, William Seymour Theatre Collection, are quoted by permission of the Princeton University Library.

A NOTE ON TRANSCRIPTION

HANDWRITTEN DOCUMENTS

Unless otherwise indicated, all quotations from O'Neill's handwritten documents are based wholly on my own transcriptions. A bracketed question mark means I am unsure of my reading of the preceding word. Two bracketed question marks indicate that I have omitted a word that is illegible. If a few words are completely obliterated (canceled by O'Neill) without ruining the sense of the sentence, I have silently omitted them. For notes and scenarios, I quote exactly—without supplying missing connectives and articles—and simply eschew the cumbersome *sic*. For full pencil drafts, where revisions are significant, angle brackets (⟨⟩) enclose words O'Neill inserted either above a line or in the margin. These words usually constitute additions, although in a few cases O'Neill may be reinserting words previously erased. I have silently corrected obvious misspellings and a very few punctuation errors, but otherwise the transcriptions are as close as possible to exact renderings of O'Neill's words, with the noted limitations.

TYPEWRITTEN DRAFTS

When the typist's errors are so minor that they do not affect meaning—usually in cases of omitted or altered minor words or variant spellings of slang terms—I quote exactly from the typescript. When the typist's errors are significant—usually in cases of accidentally skipped lines or altered major words—I supply the corresponding manuscript passage and indicate I am doing so. I have silently corrected obvious misspellings and a very few punctuation errors.

INTRODUCTION

W HEN EUGENE O'NEILL died three decades ago, *The Iceman Cometh* had found only moderate success on Broadway, *A Moon for the Misbegotten* had closed on the road before reaching New York, and *Long Day's Journey Into Night* lay sealed in a Random House vault. It was not until 1956 that José Quintero's revival of *Iceman* and his subsequent American premiere of *Journey* won these plays the attention they deserve, and *Moon* had to wait until 1973 before a fine production introduced O'Neill's last drama to a wide audience. Today, frequent revivals, movies, and television films keep these works continually in the public eye and contribute to the rise in O'Neill's reputation that has proceeded unabated for more than a quarter century.

Critical analyses of these dramas have kept pace with increased popular interest, but none has fully utilized a vital source of information: the notes, scenarios, and drafts O'Neill wrote as he created these works.[1] O'Neill began in his notes and outlines with ideas for themes and rather broad conceptions of character. It is fascinating to watch his creative imagination at work focusing themes, delineating character, transforming vague elements into a dramatic whole. Examining these manuscripts is one way to begin to understand the working of the playwright's mind.

The present investigation of *Iceman*, *Journey*, and *Moon* is not intended simply as a technical account of O'Neill's composition method in his later years, although it is in part that. We can see how, and how much, the playwright modified his dramas from their first appearance on paper to their finished form, as well as what kinds of revisions he made at each stage. The once-popular image of O'Neill the tormented artist spilling his words wantonly on the page as he relived his past traumas is a romantic fiction or at best an incomplete picture; O'Neill was also a meticulous craftsman who shaped and edited his work carefully. He rarely took kindly to others' suggestions about how to revise his plays, but he listened to the internal critic every good writer must possess.

This study treats each play individually, from early notes to finished text. Ultimately, of course, the dramatic significance of a play resides in the final version the author presents for publication and production; the preliminary drafts do not alter the drama itself. However, knowledge of those early drafts can appreciably enhance our critical understanding of the completed play. By examining how O'Neill modified his work through successive drafts, we can see what he sought to emphasize, what he labored hardest to convey to his audience. Further, O'Neill often states more baldly in notes and drafts what is conveyed only obliquely on the printed page or the stage. This is the essence of drama; a play is not a thesis. But seeing the themes and characters presented bluntly in initial manuscripts can help us understand the later, less direct presentation. Knowing from what materials the playwright began may also illuminate why a dramatic piece does or does not "succeed." A play's weakness may grow out of the dramatist's failure to develop fully the ideas from which he began or may reflect the limitations or contradictions in those ideas. Finally, studying how O'Neill built his dramas forces us to look closely at important aspects of the finished works that might otherwise be overlooked. In the conclusion to the first volume of his treatise on Shakespeare's sources, the critic Kenneth Muir comments, "There are . . . occasions when the knowledge that Shakespeare deviated from his known sources will cause us to ask questions which may lead us to a true interpretation of the play."[2] This is especially valid with *Iceman, Journey,* and *Moon* because the "sources" themselves are O'Neill's work. "Why did the playwright make that change?" may be a key question that unlocks the mysteries of the finished text.

Iceman, Journey, and *Moon* have their roots in O'Neill's early work and his personal experience, and occasionally in plays by other dramatists. Each of the following chapters begins with an investigation of these origins. Since in his notes and outlines O'Neill regularly refers by name to people he knew, some discussion of these figures is essential, but biography is here considered only when immediately relevant to the drama at hand. Although O'Neill certainly mined the ore of personal history for these plays, they must be recognized as the fictional dramatic creations they are.

O'Neill's Work Diary, his letters, the manuscripts themselves, and his wife Carlotta's diary provide the information necessary for dating these dramas. Establishing when O'Neill labored on each play yields information not only about his work habits and the effect of such uncontrollable circumstances as illness and war on his composing process, but also about the chronological relationships among the late dramas. The striking similarities between *Iceman* and *Journey*, for example, are perhaps more understandable when we realize that the dramatist wrote the outlines for both during a single four-week period in the summer of 1939. In addition to being a useful record of writing planned and accomplished, the Work Diary sometimes includes brief critical observations about the play in progress. Fuller elaborations of O'Neill's thoughts about his work are captured in his letters, most importantly those to Kenneth Macgowan, his theatrical associate and friend; Barrett Clark, author of an early book about the playwright; Eugene O'Neill, Jr., his elder son; the Theatre Guild's Lawrence Langner; and the critic George Jean Nathan. The Macgowan correspondence has been published; all the other letters except those to Nathan (in the Cornell University Library) are in Yale University's Beinecke Rare Book and Manuscript Library—the single most important repository of O'Neill documents and home of the manuscript materials for *Iceman*, *Journey*, and *Moon*.[3]

When beginning a play O'Neill made initial notes of various kinds. None exist for *Moon* (although there were likely some that have not survived) but *Iceman* and *Journey* notes include lists of potential names for characters, comments about books read for background information, jottings on character relationships, even copies of song lyrics. O'Neill also wrote random notes after completing the next stage, the scenario, and sometimes drafted "notes for revision" at subsequent points in the composition process. These latter notes are valuable clues in interpreting the final text but must be used with care, for what he intended to include in a play occasionally does not square with what he actually included. O'Neill's minuscule handwriting presents another problem. His script was always small—particularly, as he himself remarked, when he was "absorbed in creative work" that demanded intense concentration—and in his later years he was forced to write even more minutely to compensate for the tremor in his hands caused by a debilitating neurological condition.[4] Moreover, the soft pencil with which he inevitably wrote blurs easily. Nevertheless, with patience, practice, and the occasional aid of a magnifying glass (which Carlotta, on the advice of her eye doctor, used when typing her husband's manuscripts), nearly all O'Neill's writing can be deciphered.[5]

The outline—also called by the playwright a "scenario"—was O'Neill's first complete run-through of a drama. He learned the technique of scenario-writing from George Pierce Baker, in whose English 47 Workshop at Harvard he enrolled in 1914, and used the method throughout his career. Baker was a firm believer in the necessity of scenarios and included an eighty-eight-page chapter on the subject in his book *Dramatic Technique*. According to Baker a good scenario indicates the story, the characters and their relationships, the setting, the act and scene divisions, and the "nature of the play" (comedy, tragedy, etc.) as well as clearly delineating the action. He also asks that a scenario include a list of *dramatis personae* and a "sketch of the desired arrangement of the stage." Baker insists that a scenario should be flexible—the dramatist need not feel bound to follow it exactly when writing the actual play—but it should clearly reveal to the writer and other readers the major components of the budding drama.[6]

O'Neill's scenarios fulfill many, though by no means all, of Baker's criteria. Those for the late plays all include lists of *dramatis personae* (the one for *Iceman* even more discursive than Baker specified), and all are accompanied by drawings of the set. In other ways the scenarios O'Neill composed early in his career follow Baker's prescription more closely than do those for *Iceman, Journey,* and *Moon*. Lawrence Langner, a founder of the Theatre Guild and longtime friend of O'Neill, writes of the early scenarios: "What struck me particularly at the time was the fact that each entrance of each character into a scene was marked with a symbol somewhat like an arrow, which indicated how carefully he had thought out the impact of each individual on each scene."[7] O'Neill's later scenarios lack such helpful notations; the entrance of a character is not always designated, and often the speaker of a particular line is not identified. Lacking the careful patterning of scenes—and frequently the major plot events—found in the finished texts, these outlines would be confusing to someone not familiar with the final play. Baker, who believed that scenarios could be submitted to actors or managers for consideration, would doubtless disapprove of these cryptic documents. Even the very tiny handwriting of the scenarios shows that O'Neill intended these pages for his eyes only; the writing on subsequent drafts is at least a little larger, presumably for the benefit of those unfortunate souls who would have to type them.

Exactly how much attention O'Neill paid to the completed scenarios is unclear. In 1925 he insisted that "having written a detailed scenario, I rarely ever look at it when writing the play or follow it at all except in the bare outline—and rarely in that!"[8] However, as Virginia Floyd points out, "entries in his Work Diary reveal that he did, at times, read over a scenario before beginning a first draft or when encountering a problem."[9] Because the scenarios are in some ways quite close to later drafts—lines of dialogue, for example, occasionally appear in almost identical form in the outline and in the published text—it is likely that O'Neill, at least in his later years, employed the scenarios more fully than his 1925 statement acknowledges.

The scenario of *Iceman* runs nearly thirteen thousand words, that for *Journey* almost eight thousand, and *Moon's* somewhat over four thousand. *Iceman*, the longest play of the three with the largest cast, warrants the lengthiest outline, but it is also probable that the scenarios shrank as O'Neill's progressive disease made the physical act of writing more difficult. *Iceman's* scenario is the most richly detailed; the *Moon* outline is so skeletal that one act is omitted altogether and another briefly sketched in a few lines. Divided into acts roughly corresponding to the divisions of the finished play, each scenario is composed primarily of character notes, stage directions and segments of dialogue, commonly strung together with dashes. Although each outline indicates general plot development, it is clear that at this stage O'Neill's primary concern is delineating character and establishing theme.

For *The Iceman Cometh* and *Long Day's Journey Into Night* O'Neill wrote only one complete manuscript, in pencil, and his method of revising them was similar. He evidently edited these manuscripts as he wrote, then went back and revised extensively after they were finished. In many cases pages with fractional numbers signal portions added later. There are also sheets uncharacteristically bare of revision and others that are only partially filled with dialogue, indicating that at times O'Neill removed whole pages and replaced them with new ones. *A Moon for the Misbegotten* gave the playwright more trouble, partly because of the intrusion of World War II. After completing the pencil draft of *Moon* in January 1942, O'Neill let it sit for a year while he turned to other work. He then edited the first act and the very beginning of the second in his usual manner, although the revisions were extremely extensive, but apparently decided that this play required more massive changes and subsequently began rewriting rather than revising. Thus O'Neill seems to have composed two handwritten drafts of most of the second act and all of the third and fourth acts. The first manuscript version of these portions of *Moon* has unfortunately not survived.

When O'Neill replaced original pages with new ones in the pencil drafts of *Iceman, Journey,* and *Moon,* we cannot recapture the substance of the removed pages. Problems also sometimes arise with minor deletions, where only a few words or sentences were canceled with a heavy line or erased, and with brief insertions following such deletions, which may be new additions or simply the canceled words rewritten. However, we can see which portions gave O'Neill the most trouble and which were substantial additions. Moreover, O'Neill frequently deleted material by drawing large **X** marks or narrow wavy lines through rejected passages. In these cases the original words as well as the revisions are legible.

After O'Neill finished editing the manuscript, the revised draft was typed to yield the first typescript. According to Donald Gallup, former curator of the Beinecke O'Neill Collection, the playwright did as much revision as he could on each draft in order to limit the number of times his wife Carlotta had to type and retype the work.[10] Carlotta prepared the first typescripts of *Iceman* and *Journey;* her daughter Cynthia prepared the *Moon* typescript, with understandable difficulty. Even Carlotta had trouble deciphering her husband's cramped writing, but she or O'Neill caught nearly all the errors while proofreading; only one fairly significant mistake (discussed in the *Journey* chapter) appears to have eluded them both. Although O'Neill corrected inaccuracies in the first two *Moon* typescripts, a few minor mistakes made in later typescripts survive in the published version.

The first typescripts of all three dramas received O'Neill's careful attention. Because some of the editing was in the form of cutting, each of the published plays is shorter than its respective typescript. At this stage the playwright was still making major alterations: frequently whole speeches were changed, added, deleted, or moved, and scarcely a page of first typescript is free of emendations. *Moon* once again was accorded extraordinary consideration. Displeased with the end of that work, O'Neill removed the last two pages of the third act and the entire fourth act and rewrote them by hand—a remarkable effort in light of his physical disability. The removed sheets are preserved in a folder at the Beinecke and can be compared with the new pages.

The story of the composition of *Journey* and *Moon* really ends with the first typescripts. Although O'Neill made minor changes in the second

typescripts, prepared from the revised first typescripts, none of these alterations was substantive. At the playwright's behest *Journey* remained
unproduced during his lifetime, and he was too ill to oversee properly the
premiere of *Moon*. When he published that drama in his last years, he
ignored the changes made for the first production, many of them made
reluctantly to appease overzealous censors. The saga of *Iceman* is a little
longer because O'Neill significantly revised the play for the 1946 production. The printed text varies considerably from the production scripts,
and these differences reveal the playwright's struggle to tailor his vision to
fit the limitations of the stage.

FEW CRITICS WILL DENY that *The Iceman Cometh, Long Day's Journey Into Night,* and *A Moon for the Misbegotten* are linked not only by
temporal proximity but by similar dramatic structures, characters, and
themes. Leaving behind the theatrical experimentation of earlier years,
O'Neill wrote these three plays in a style that can be called broadly "realistic." Mary Tyrone's morphine, the rotgut at Harry Hope's, and Jim
Tyrone's bonded bourbon all fill the same prescription for the alleviation
of kindred ills. Theodore Hickman, Don Parritt, and James Tyrone take
the stage to admit past transgressions against themselves and others while
James Tyrone, Jr., his expiation incomplete in *Journey,* survives long
enough to finish his tale in *Moon.* Even Larry Slade, Edmund Tyrone,
and Josie Hogan—three characters whose backgrounds, ages, and gen-
ders make them seem worlds apart from each other—form a triad of compassionate if disillusioned listeners to the others' confessions.

When we look at early drafts of these plays, we find still other connections: the revisions on all three follow similar patterns. The similarities are
not simply technical, the notes-scenario-manuscript-typescript routine
O'Neill favored, but are deeply rooted in the creative process and help
explain why these dramas are so much of a piece. When O'Neill gave his
wife Carlotta the original manuscript of *Journey* as an anniversary gift, he
composed the dedication that appears in the published text. Calling
Journey a "play of old sorrow, written in tears and blood," O'Neill added
that it was also written "with deep pity and understanding and forgiveness
for *all* the four haunted Tyrones." *Iceman, Journey,* and *Moon* are alike
compounded of tears and blood. As we shall see in the following pages,
the pity, understanding, and forgiveness extend to nearly all the inhabitants of O'Neill's late works and grew as the dramas themselves did.

CHAPTER ONE

The Iceman Cometh

"IT'S A COLD NIGHT—good night for a party! The iceman cometh!"[1] If Agnes Boulton's memory is accurate, Eugene O'Neill uttered these lines at a party in the autumn of 1917. More than twenty years later, the last three words became the title of one of O'Neill's most famous and controversial plays.

The very title *The Iceman Cometh* has itself fascinated scholars and theater-goers for years. The complexity of the play is foreshadowed in a title that combines a reference to bawdy jokes about amorous icemen and an ironic allusion to the biblical parable of the Ten Virgins. As Cyrus Day and others have pointed out, "The bridegroom cometh" announces the arrival of Christ in St. Matthew (25:6).[2] Indeed, when the curtain rises on O'Neill's play there are ten characters, not virgins but men now living an apparently celibate life in Hope's bar, awaiting the arrival of the overdue "bridegroom," Hickey. This savior, however, brings no salvation. O'Neill himself said in an interview that the iceman of the title is death.[3] Hickey's philosophy of honesty yields a disillusionment so painful that the only escape is the grave. Larry Slade, the wisest of the men, realizes that "Death was the Iceman Hickey called to his home!"[4] O'Neill was apparently fond of ringing changes on the biblical passage about the bridegroom, for he has Simon Harford allude to it in *More Stately Mansions*, written shortly before *Iceman*. Simon bitterly complains that life is "a daily appointment with peace and happiness in which we wait day after day, hoping against hope, and when finally the bride or the bridegroom cometh, we discover we are kissing Death."[5] On one level, if the bride and bridegroom are interpreted literally, this passage implies that marriage brings disappointment rather than fulfillment (witness the unions of Hickey and Evelyn, Hope and Bessie). On a deeper level, Simon's statement, like *The Iceman Cometh* as a whole, suggests that death is the individual's only hope for true peace.

Whether or not the title of *The Iceman Cometh* grew out of O'Neill's exclamation at that party in 1917, the characters and setting of the play clearly come from the playwright's own experiences. O'Neill wrote to George Jean Nathan that "the scene, Harry Hope's dump, is a composite of three places,"[6] and critics and biographers have carefully traced the models for the bar and its inhabitants.[7] O'Neill's notes provide numerous clues. The earliest notes and the scenario are labeled "Jimmy the P.— H.H. play," obviously referring to O'Neill's two favorite dives: Jimmy the Priest's and the Golden Swan, popularly known as the "Hell Hole."[8] The Garden Hotel, another O'Neill drinking spot, is the third place to which the playwright alludes.[9] In both notes and scenario O'Neill often called his characters by the names of their original models, and in one case even wrote "Major A.—same as life." The name Terry—signifying Terry Carlin, on whom Larry Slade is largely based—once crept into the manuscript.

An incomplete character list dated "June '39," probably drawn up immediately before O'Neill began work on the *Iceman* scenario, is especially helpful in identifying character sources. Eight of the names on the list clearly belong to people the playwright knew or about whom he had heard. "Tom W." (Harry Hope in *Iceman*) is the proprietor of the Hell Hole, Tom Wallace; "Jimmy B." (James Cameron) is O'Neill's friend James Findlater Byth, a press agent who provided him with information about the Boer War; "Joe S." (Joe Mott) is Joe Smith, a black gambler who frequented the Hell Hole; "Terry" (Larry Slade) is Terry Carlin, O'Neill's longtime friend and mentor; "Viljoen" (Piet Wetjoen) is a Boer War general about whom James Byth spoke; and "Major A." (Cecil Lewis) is one Major Adams, a British Boer War veteran who sometimes shared a drink with the playwright at Jimmy the Priest's.[10] The two bartenders are here named "Bull" and "Lefty," suggesting they are derived from John Bull and Lefty Louie, who served the drinks and kept the peace at the Hell Hole. O'Neill may also have had another "Lefty" in mind: "Lefty Louie" Rosenberg, a gunman he mentions in his 1912 poem "The Waterways Convention, A Study in Prophecy."[11] The character list identifies Lefty as a "Neapolitan . . . gangster"; Rosenberg was the latter but surely not the former. One character is called simply "Bella" and cryptically identified as a "jovial cynic." This may be one of the tarts, but his or her "real" identity is unknown.

Further notes and the scenario point to other character models. Willie Oban is at least partly based on the sons of Al Adams, a turn-of-the-century policy king and bucket shop owner who had his sons educated as lawyers to defend him. Hippolyte Havel (Hugo Kalmar), O'Neill's anarchist friend, is called by his actual name in the scenario. Although these documents are little help in identifying the originals for Ed Mosher and Pat McGloin, biographical evidence suggests that Mosher was derived from Jack Croak, a former carnival worker with whom O'Neill sometimes drank, and Bill Clarke, an ex-circus man the playwright knew.[12] It is unlikely (except perhaps for the unknown Bella) that O'Neill had specific tarts in mind when he created his three ladies of the pavement. Clearly, however, O'Neill was not only basing his characters on people he had known, the basis was substantial enough for him to use their names at the earliest stages of writing. The notes and scenario also contain biographical facts about the character models that do not appear in later drafts because they are inappropriate for the fictional figures that emerge from these roots. As O'Neill worked on *Iceman* he changed narrowly biographical characters into imaginative creations.

The characters whose origins have intrigued critics most are Don Parritt (and his offstage mother, Rosa) and Theodore Hickman. Following the Arthur and Barbara Gelb and Louis Sheaffer, Winifred L. Frazer argues at length in *E.G. and E.G.O.: Emma Goldman and "The Iceman Cometh"* that Donald Vose, the son of a friend of Emma Goldman's, was the model for Parritt. Frazer also contends that Parritt's unseen mother is patterned after Goldman herself. Frazer's research is impressive, and internal evidence in the notes and scenario supports both claims. In 1915 Donald Vose informed on two men who had been involved in the bombing of the *Los Angeles Times* building five years earlier. O'Neill was certainly familar with the Vose case, for his friend Terry Carlin knew Vose and was present when he met Matthew Schmidt, one of the people he betrayed. An early note for *Iceman* reads "1910 Times dynamited Oct 1st," a reference to the bombing over which Vose turned informant. In the scenario the young man boasts of having been an iron worker, thus implicitly linking him to the *Times* affair, for which members of the International Association of Bridge and Structural Workers were convicted.

What is curious is that the early character list gives the name Bob M. to the figure who becomes Potter in the scenario and Parritt in subsequent drafts. "Parritt" is obviously a fictional name that emphasizes the turncoat's status as a "pariah" who "parrots" Hickey, and "Potter" too is probably symbolic. As Cyrus Day argues, Parritt is a Judas-figure in *Iceman*.[13]

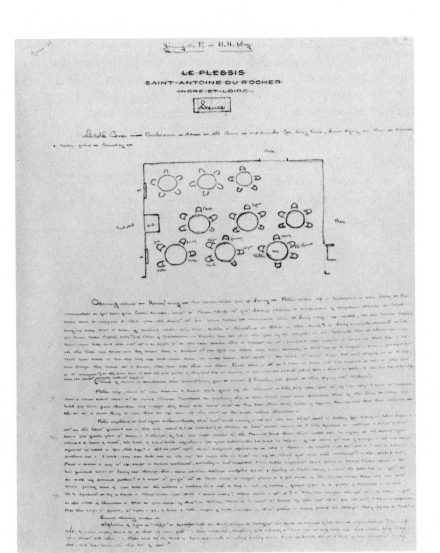

First page of the scenario of *The Iceman Cometh*. (Collection of American Literature, Beinecke Rare Book and Manuscript Library, Yale University.)

According to St. Matthew, the very same gospel from which O'Neill derived the title of his play, Judas eventually returned the thirty pieces of
silver he had earned for betraying Christ and the priests used the silver to
buy "the potter's field, to bury strangers in" (27:7). Unlike "Parritt" and
"Potter," however, "Bob M." is almost certainly the name of someone
O'Neill knew or knew about, since virtually all the other names on the
early character list fit actual individuals. The character list description of
Bob M. reads: "Anarchist—incorruptible fanatic—coldly pure, no wom-
en, no booze—passionate idealist—in hiding—suspicion wanted on
Coast for bombing activities with Wobblies—savagely intolerant weakness—about 30—." Little of this applies to the much younger Vose, although he may (like Parritt) have pretended to some of these attributes in
order to mislead his mother's radical friends and thus accomplish his mission of betrayal. It is possible that O'Neill had only a very hazy memory of
the Vose affair and either wrongly recalled the young man's name or had
heard of him under his alias "Meserve." More likely, O'Neill had another
man in addition to Vose in mind when he conceived Parritt; Bob M., in
fact, may have preceded Vose as the inspiration for the character. While
the evidence is at best tenuous, Bob M. could conceivably be Robert
(Bob) Minor, a radical who first gained prominence as a cartoonist and
later went on to edit the *Daily Worker* and run for mayor of New York on
the Communist Party ticket. Minor, who was twenty-eight in 1912, was
certainly a "passionate idealist" and considered by many a "fanatic." He
and O'Neill had friends in common, including Eleanor Fitzgerald, who
became an important member of the Provincetown Players, and John
Reed. Although he himself was not accused of bombing activities, Minor
was an outspoken defender of the labor leaders blamed for bombing San
Francisco's Preparedness Day parade in 1916. If O'Neill was thinking of
Minor, however, it seems strange that there is no mention of his being a
cartoonist, for Minor's drawings appeared on the cover of *Mother Earth*
and in numerous other publications. Moreover, although his political philosophy was not yet fully formed in 1912, Minor subsequently joined the
Communist Party and was for most of his life a Communist, not an anarchist. Bob Minor might have been one prototype for Parritt, and Donald
Vose almost certainly was another, yet the possibility of still other sources
remains.[14]

Parritt's mother is rarely mentioned in the scenario, and she is given no
first name there. The scenario does contain two references to Emma

Goldman: Parritt (Potter) says that in his early anarchist days he "heard Emma speak," and another character mentions "Emma G." in company with Kropotkin and Bakunin.[15] No direct references to Emma Goldman appear in later drafts, but in the *Iceman* manuscript Parritt's mother is called Emma (I, p. 9½). O'Neill apparently discarded the specific references to Emma Goldman, then developed Parritt's mother more fully, using Goldman as a rough model.[16]

O'Neill was himself often unclear, or deliberately evasive, about the degree of biographical reality in his *Iceman* characters. In a public interview he grandly announced, "All these people I have written about, I once knew,"[17] yet he was more restrained when addressing friends. The playwright informed Nathan:

> The story of Parritt has a background of fact, too. The suicide really happened pretty much as shown in the play. But it was not the man the character of Parritt is derived from who bumped himself off that way. It was another person and for another reason.[18]

Writing to his friend Kenneth Macgowan several months later, O'Neill was somewhat more vague about Parritt's background. His comments, however, could easily apply to Donald Vose:

> Parritt is . . . almost entirely imaginary. His betrayal of the Movement derives from a real incident, but I never knew the guy, or anything about his mother, so Parritt's personal history is my own fiction.[19]

The origins of the salesman, Hickey, are even more obscure than those of Don Parritt. Hickey is not mentioned in any early notes, and he appears in the scenario with the name he bears in the published play. O'Neill's letters concerning this character are almost contradictory. He told Nathan:

> The plot, if you can call it that, is my imaginative creation, of course, but it has a basis in reality. There was a periodical drunk salesman, who was a damned amusing likeable guy. And he did make that typical drummer crack about the iceman, and wept maudlinly over his wife's photograph, and in other moods, boozily harped on the slogan that honesty is the best policy.[20]

Eleven months later, when he wrote to Macgowan, O'Neill seems to have forgotten this particular drummer:

What you wonder about Hickey: No, I never knew him. He's the most imaginary character in the play. Of course, I knew many salesmen in my time who were periodical drunks, but Hickey is not any of them. He is all of them, you might say, and none of them.[21]

Louis Sheaffer believes that Hickey is partly based on Charles E. Chapin, a newspaper executive who shot his wife in her sleep in 1918. Sheaffer contends that O'Neill was familiar with the case, and he points out similarities between Chapin's statements and Hickey's.[22] The Gelbs cite a collector for a laundry chain named Happy as a possible prototype for Hickey, but they are perhaps closer to the truth when they mention the playwright's brother, James O'Neill, Jr., as an inspiration.[23] Jamie was actually a traveling salesman for a brief period, and he also spent two summers playing a traveling drummer (although not the title figure) in a road company of James Forbes's popular comedy *The Traveling Salesman*. Whether or not O'Neill saw Jamie in the role—the playwright was in Honduras during part of one season of the run—he did see his brother between seasons. If, as *Long Day's Journey Into Night* suggests, Jamie was given to histrionic outbursts, it is reasonable to assume that he regaled his brother with impromptu renderings of his role. In photographs of Jamie playing the part, he wears a sporty striped suit and smokes a cigar at a jaunty angle.

Even if O'Neill did not actually see a production, he very likely at least read Forbes's 1908 comic melodrama.[24] *The Traveling Salesman* tells the tale of a drummer with a heart of gold who rescues a pretty young woman's property from the hands of unscrupulous villains. As the curtain falls, the salesman and the young woman are about to be married. *The Traveling Salesman* is a far cry from *The Iceman Cometh* but Watts, the drummer played by Jamie, has a little in common with Hickey. A loyal friend to his buddy Blake, the salesman of the title, Watts enjoys drinking with his pals and travels with a well-stocked little red book of ladies' names. In addition, a few lines in the earlier play may have sparked O'Neill's imagination. Blake promises an offended neighbor, "All right, sister, we'll be good"; another drummer concludes that their alcoholic poker party is "no place for a minister's son"; and Watts, responding to Blake's fears that their dirty stories will reach the ears of his lady love, exhorts a companion to "lead us in prayer."[25] These casual religious references are not essential to the play, as Hickey's evangelical language is to *Iceman*, but they may have planted seeds in O'Neill's mind.

There is another way in which *The Traveling Salesman* may have obliquely inspired *Iceman*. O'Neill was always interested in what happens to an individual whose innermost drives toward one way of life are interfered with by love for a "good woman." Thus Robert Mayo in *Beyond the Horizon* marries and settles down on the farm with Ruth instead of following his propensity to wander. The result is disaster. Hickey marries the innocent Evelyn and the clash between his carefree nature and her desire for a respectable husband destroys them both. In Forbes's play, the hero characterizes being in love as "Simon-pure hell."[26] Perhaps in the neat working out of this conventional comedy O'Neill saw the seeds of the drama he was to write many years later. The marriage of the traveling drummer and the good woman that ends Forbes's play becomes in O'Neill's work "Simon-pure hell" indeed.

There are other and far better plays that resemble *The Iceman Cometh*. Maxim Gorky's *The Lower Depths* and Henrik Ibsen's *The Wild Duck* are often mentioned by critics as possible influences on *Iceman*. O'Neill was surely acquainted with *The Lower Depths*, for he admired Gorky greatly. In 1936 he wrote to Sinclair Lewis: "Yes, it's a damned shame Gorki never got the [Nobel] prize. When he died I wrote a tribute for the Soviet magazine in New York which exactly expressed my opinion that he had been the top of all living writers."[27] Helen Muchnic, who has done a careful comparison of *Iceman* and *The Lower Depths*, ultimately concludes that the implications and philosophical bases of the two plays are widely divergent.[28] The dramas are most similar in their cavelike settings, their large collection of down-and-out characters, and their use of the familiar motif of an outsider who disrupts the lives of an enclosed group. As Gerald Weales perceptively notes, however, "the characters in the two plays can only be compared by complicated cross-switching."[29] Luka, the intruder in Gorky's work, preaches a pity for human beings and a belief in the virtue of illusions that is almost diametrically opposite to the philosophy of Hickey, the intruder in O'Neill's play. Hickey's call for honesty more closely matches the attitude of Satin, the resident philosopher in *The Lower Depths*, while Luka's preachings resemble those of O'Neill's Larry Slade.

The Wild Duck, with its investigation of the lies by which people live and its portrait of the destructive realist, is in some ways quite close to *Iceman*. Robert Brustein has discussed the major parallels and differences between the two plays.[30] He points out that O'Neill's approach is more compassionate than Ibsen's: O'Neill sympathizes with both the misguided

truth-seeker and those whose lives he disrupts. Unlike his counterpart
Hickey, the arrogant Gregers Werle is a true fanatic who never renounces
his belief in the rightness of his dangerous quest for "truth." Similarly Dr.
Relling, Ibsen's defender of illusions, lacks Larry Slade's deep personal
involvement with the tragic events that transpire. Even the death of an
innocent child cannot give *The Wild Duck* the wrenching emotional impact of *Iceman*.

A few reviewers of the original *Iceman* production linked the play to
William Saroyan's *The Time of Your Life*.[31] *The Time of Your Life* opened
on stage after O'Neill began writing *Iceman*, but it is tempting to speculate that O'Neill may have seen the play in manuscript and been inspired
by it.[32] Saroyan claims to have written the first draft of *The Time of Your
Life* in six days in early May of 1939,[33] and he immediately sent the manuscript to George Jean Nathan. Although O'Neill does not mention
Saroyan's play before seeing it on stage in California several months later,
and Nathan was not in the habit of sending plays to O'Neill, the numerous
similarities between *Iceman* and *The Time of Your Life* make one wonder
whether Nathan might have passed Saroyan's manuscript on to his
friend.

The Time of Your Life is a more sentimental and optimistic work than
O'Neill's, yet there are remarkable correspondences of setting and character. Both plays include a large group of diverse individuals gathered
together in a run-down saloon. Saroyan's Arab, like O'Neill's Hugo, takes
little part in the action but keeps repeating the same few lines as a sort of
choral background. Tom and Kitty are roughly equivalent to Chuck and
Cora, although their planned marriage has a somewhat better chance than
does O'Neill's futile pairing of a bartender and tart. The policeman, Blick,
is a thorough villain with whom the audience has no sympathy, but in
other ways he resembles O'Neill's Hickey. Blick is a realist who, like
Hickey, causes "a strange fearfulness and disharmony in the atmosphere."[34] He believes, as Hickey does, in calling a whore a whore, and
Nick complains because Blick never drinks and continually harasses the
saloon patrons. Nick charges the policeman with wanting "to change the
world from something bad to something worse. Something like yourself."[35] Blick is, in short, an unwanted and disturbing intruder. Joe parallels Larry in his attempts to sustain people's dreams. A kind man who
refuses to be a useful member of society, Joe spends his days drinking and
talking. He agrees to call the whore by her "stage name" and pretends to

believe the wild tales of Kit Carson. Also like Larry, Joe is a philosopher who sees both sides of issues and claims, "Everything's right. Right and wrong."[36] When his attempt to shoot Blick fails, he approximates Larry after the death of Parritt, for he "sits down, dead to the world."[37] His dreams too have been shattered. Joe does not share the others' exuberant joy when Blick is killed, and his leave-taking suggests that he no longer finds Nick's place a comfortable refuge. Saroyan's world is far more promising than O'Neill's: long-awaited girlfriends do show up, would-be heroes sometimes achieve their fantasies, and pinball machines can be defeated. If *Iceman* was influenced by *The Time of Your Life*, and many surface similarities suggest it was, O'Neill turned a colorful honky-tonk into the "No Chance Saloon" and rather one-dimensional characters into complex figures.

Iceman clearly grows out of O'Neill's own earlier works as a whole, with *Lazarus Laughed* and *Chris Christophersen* (an early version of *Anna Christie*) most often cited by critics. While Leonard Chabrowe's claim that *Iceman* is "virtually" *Lazarus Laughed* rewritten "in minor key" seems an overstatement, he and Travis Bogard point out striking correspondences between the plays' messianic figures, Hickey and Lazarus.[38] The first acts of *Chris Christophersen* and *Anna Christie* take place in a bar called Johnny the Priest's which, like the *Iceman* setting, is modeled after Jimmy the Priest's. *Chris* even features a very drunk traveling salesman named Adams. Paralleling *Iceman*'s Hickey, the garrulous Adams is a good salesman who goes on periodical binges at Johnny's, a dive he favors "for old friendship's sake."[39] Largely because of his name, Virginia Floyd considers the *Chris* drunkard a predecessor of Willie Oban (called Adams in the *Iceman* scenario) rather than Hickey, but the links between the two traveling salesmen are stronger.[40] Another traveling drummer—younger than Hickey yet, like him, stout, breezy, and jocular—surfaces briefly in *Ah, Wilderness!* Minor *Iceman* characters also have counterparts in earlier O'Neill works. One example is Hartmann, a revolutionary in the 1915 drama *The Personal Equation* (originally entitled *The Second Engineer*). From his "flowing Windsor tie" to his skewed syntax, he is a rough draft of Hugo Kalmar.

There is one piece—O'Neill's 1917 short story "Tomorrow"—that is in many ways a compressed trial run for *The Iceman Cometh*.[41] In fact, "Tomorrow" was an early tentative title for the drama[42] and "Credit Tomorrow," another prospective title, appears on a scenario page. "Tomorrow" is the story of a man named Jimmy Anderson (largely based on James Find-later Byth) who rooms with the narrator of the tale, Art, in a run-down saloon called Tommy the Priest's. Jimmy, like "Jimmy Tomorrow" in *Iceman*, is an alcoholic former newsman who turned to drink when he found his wife in bed with another man.[43] His favorite word is "tomorrow," a reference to the day he will get his typewriter fixed and begin writing again. Jimmy is somewhat more successful than the men in *Iceman* for he does get a job, but both he and his employers realize he cannot handle the work and he is fired. Jimmy's new failure leaves him a broken man: "Life had jammed the clear, cruel mirror in front of his eyes and he had recognized himself—in that pitiful thing he saw."[44] In that respect he is like Harry Hope (and indeed most of the *Iceman* gang) who meets "himself" when he attempts to take his walk around the ward. The symbol of Jimmy's futile dreams is a sickly geranium he tends as carefully as the men in *Iceman* nurse their beloved fantasies. When the geranium is destroyed, a distraught Jimmy follows soon after, taking Parritt's suicide leap from the fire escape.

During Jimmy's brief period of sobriety, he resembles the reformed Hickey, to the annoyance of his roommate. The narrator complains to Jimmy: "The water wagon is fatal to your sense of humor. After a week's ride you've accumulated more cheap moralizing than any anchorite in all his years of fasting."[45] Like Larry Slade, the narrator has little patience with such reform movements because he recognizes that "some of the things he was saying were true; and truth—that kind of truth—should be seen and not heard."[46] Art's wisdom, however, cannot save his friend. As the numerous similarities suggest, the main characters, setting, plot, and themes of *Iceman* are present, in embryonic form, in "Tomorrow."

O'NEILL MAY HAVE BEEN CONSIDERING a dramatic version of the "Tomorrow" story as early as 1934. In February of that year Carlotta noted in her diary: "[Gene] tells me his idea for a new play—(Jimmie Blythe)."[47] "Jimmie Blythe" is surely Carlotta's misrendering of "Jimmy Byth" and, although O'Neill's Work Diary for the period makes no mention of such a drama, it is at least possible that O'Neill jotted down some notes at that time. More than five years later, on June 5, 1939, O'Neill recorded in his Work Diary that he was temporarily "fed up" with his efforts on the cycle "Tale of Possessors Self-Dispossessed." The following day he examined his collection of "notes on various ideas for single plays." The two that appealed to him most were "the Jimmy the P[riest].—H[ell]. H[ole].—Garden idea—and N[ew]. L[ondon]. family one." O'Neill chose to pursue the former idea first; the latter eventually became *Long Day's Journey Into Night.* After settling on "The Iceman Cometh" to replace the tentative title "Tomorrow," the playwright began working on "set plans, notes, etc." The "outline" (scenario) started on June 9 was, according to Diary entries, completed June 24.

The earliest extant *Iceman* material includes set sketches, six pages of notes, two character lists, and a scenario filed together at Yale's Beinecke Library. The scenario and character lists are dated June 1939. The undated notes were probably written on June 8, the day before O'Neill began the scenario, but they might conceivably be the earlier notes to which he refers in his Diary. Some notes have apparently not survived.[48] The carefully rendered set sketches, which the Work Diary states were drawn on July 6, closely match the description in the published text.

These pages testify to the background work O'Neill did even for a "memory play" like *Iceman.* The notes include dates and brief notations about Boer War events (background for Piet Wetjoen and Cecil Lewis); long lists of names, several of which are used in the play; an outline of the history of racketeer Al Adams (background for Willie and his unseen father); and some of the words to Hope's favorite song, "The Sunshine of Paradise Alley." The partial character list must have been written before the scenario. Although incomplete, this list contains important notations about the characters. Some of these comments accurately sketch the figures in the play. For example, the description of Tom W. (Hope) includes the statement that "he has never left place since wife's funeral—great sentimental respect for this myth which he has encouraged." Other character notes here differ significantly from the portraits that appear in the published *Iceman.* The later character list, probably written immediately after the scenario, is complete except for one curious omission: Hickey.[49] With minor exceptions, the names in this list match those in the final text.[50]

The *Iceman* scenario is composed of one set sketch, seven full and four half-filled pages of extremely small handwriting. Like O'Neill's other late scenarios, these sheets are covered mainly with bits of dialogue and stage directions, often separated by dashes. The scenario is divided into three acts, the last subdivided into two scenes (Act III, scene 2, would eventually become the play's Act IV). There is little of the careful patterning found in the published text, and some major plot elements are missing: while Harry's birthday occurs during the course of the scenario and is mentioned frequently by the characters, the meticulously choreographed birthday party does not appear. The action spans four days, rather than the less than two days covered by the final version. All the characters in the play are here, some still bearing the names of the people on whom they were based.

Not only was the scenario written very rapidly, the entire drama was composed in a much shorter time than O'Neill usually needed. At various points in his career O'Neill claimed that he would in the future spend more time on each play. In 1923 he told Macgowan, "I am reaching toward the artistic wisdom that in order to keep moving I've got to treat each play with more & more concentration of mind & effort over a longer period of time,"[51] but throughout his career the amount of time actually spent writing a play varied greatly. There is no indication that the longer a drama took to write the more successful it was: the unfortunate *Days Without End* went through at least seven drafts. The opposite may well be true, for his two later masterpieces, *Iceman* and *Journey*, occupied less writing time than many weaker works. Although it is impossible to know how long O'Neill brooded over a particular play before putting pencil to paper, it is likely that *Iceman* and *Journey*, because of their autobiographical nature, were more fully formed in his mind before he began writing. O'Neill confided to Nathan about *Iceman*, "If you recall various of my reminiscences, you will recognize in this play a lot of material I have talked about using ever since you've known me."[52] Years later the playwright told reporters that *Iceman* required less work than usual because he was dealing with people he remembered, and once he started writing it "flowed right along, page after page."[53]

From June 25, 1939, until July 3 O'Neill was working on the notes and scenario for *Long Day's Journey Into Night*. This done he returned to *Iceman*, completing the manuscript on October 12 and the manuscript revisions seven weeks later. As he finished revising each act, he gave it to the beleaguered Carlotta, who complained in her November 1 diary notation: "This is the most difficult 'script I have ever copied—his tremor is so bad!" The typescript she prepared was also carefully edited by O'Neill. On December 20 he wrote ecstatically in the Work Diary: "T[he]. I[ceman]. C[ometh]. (finish minor corrections, cuts, and will now call 'The Iceman Cometh' finished—one of best plays I've ever written!)." Subsequent Diary entries, however, show him "trimming" the play until January 3, 1940. A year later O'Neill, while rejecting Macgowan's suggestion of a "drastic condensation of the first part," told his friend that *Iceman* would get a "final going over" that would include "a general pruning."[54] This pruning was not done until 1945, when O'Neill was preparing the work for production and publication. Except for the minor 1945 changes, *The Iceman Cometh* was written in less than seven months.

O'Neill's revisions on the manuscript and the first typescript are copious. Manuscript pages with fractional numbers and others only half-filled with dialogue indicate places where O'Neill removed whole sheets and substituted new ones. More than one-third of the manuscript is composed of such replacement pages. Aside from substantive changes, O'Neill paid particular attention to language in the first typescript, making countless alterations in dialect. Roughly half these changes are corrections of Carlotta's typing errors, but the remainder are O'Neill's attempt to make the characters' language consistent and convincing.[55] While there was no massive reduction in the length of the play, O'Neill did moderate cutting on both the pencil and typescript drafts. Saxe Commins, O'Neill's Random House editor and personal friend, typed the revised typescript to produce the second typescript.[56] The drama remained in this form, untouched by the playwright, for nearly five years. The fact that O'Neill did not alter it at all during this time testifies to his satisfaction with *Iceman* in this draft.

The history of the *Iceman* text becomes rather complicated at this point.[57] From the second typescript the play developed in two directions: toward the printed version and toward the script of the first production. The evolution of the play toward publication is fairly easy to trace. One of three copies of the second typescript prepared by Commins was placed in the Random House vault.[58] O'Neill did no more than correct a few errors on the galleys when *Iceman* was later readied for publication; modifications were, however, made in the plate proof, necessitating revised pages. Even the plate proof revisions are relatively minor, although about half the pages have some alterations and many had to be completely reset. Approximately thirteen hundred words were altered or removed. The last act, from which over six hundred words of dialogue were deleted, shows the heaviest editing. Someone—O'Neill or, more likely, Commins—was evidently worried about the amount of blasphemous and racy language in *Iceman*. Words like *hell, bastard, damned,* and *whore* frequently fell under the editorial pencil, and Harry Hope's favorite epithet was changed from *bejeeses* to the somewhat less obviously blasphemous *bejees*. While O'Neill himself made these changes, he may well have done so at his publisher's urging.[59] It is difficult to ascertain the exact dates O'Neill worked on this material, but a note in an unknown hand on the plate proofs suggests the proofs were ready by August 1946.

Another copy of the second typescript contains a dedication to Carlotta dated 1941, yet it was not revised until four years later. The typescript is labeled, in Carlotta's hand, "Property of Eugene O'Neill / Nov. 1945 / 2nd draft with cuts made before rehearsal." This particular typescript has been fairly heavily revised, more than four thousand words having been deleted. As Lawrence Langner comments, O'Neill "did a great deal of cutting prior to going into rehearsal."[60] This altered second typescript[61] was typed by the Hart Stenographic Bureau to yield a third typescript.

The Theatre Guild Collection at Yale University contains three scripts from the first production of *Iceman*, the Yale O'Neill Collection contains three, and the New York Public Library at Lincoln Center has three more. One Yale script bears Lawrence Langner's name and his suggestions for cuts; the playwright rejected most of them.[62] A second script is labeled "Mr. O'Neill" and contains blue-pencil revisions in the playwright's hand. A third is heavily revised and shows production information such as cues and working property plots. This unbound promptbook in Yale's Theatre Guild Collection[63] reflects most of the changes O'Neill made in his own script (and some additional ones), including slightly revised endings for Act II and Act III and an altered last act. In her dissertation on Theatre Guild productions of O'Neill's plays, Mary Arbenz considers this script the one used by the stage manager for the *Iceman* production.[64] It is labeled "Rehearsal record Sept 3rd 1946," the date of the first rehearsal, and was obviously used as a prompt script.

Newer scripts—which have most directions for actor movement typed in and which omit material marked for deletion in the stage manager's promptbook—also exist. Most of these have still another slightly modified ending for the play, although one, containing the most detailed production information, has the earlier promptbook ending inserted. The difficulties in ascertaining which last page was followed will be discussed later, but all these scripts are substantially alike and may collectively be considered the final production script. This version of *Iceman* is roughly 2500 words shorter than the second typescript was *after* that typescript had been revised for production, and these deletions presumably were made during rehearsals. More than a third of the cuts occur in the last act. In total, the final production script for the 1946 Theatre Guild premiere is nearly six thousand words shorter than the published text.

The problem arises as to which may be considered O'Neill's final intention: the published *Iceman* or the production script. O'Neill had previously published dramas at the same time they first appeared on stage—*Ah, Wilderness!* and *Days Without End* are two examples[65]—but like most playwrights he usually waited until after production to put his work into print. Saxe Commins asserts, for instance, that the printed version of *Mourning Becomes Electra* was edited "to conform absolutely with the acted version of the play."[66] Why O'Neill chose to have publication of *Iceman* simultaneous with the premiere is unclear. Financial considerations may have been a factor; he had released no new play for more than a decade, and book revenues would be welcome. O'Neill's longtime distrust of critics is another possible explanation, for advance copies of the text were sent to many New York reviewers prior to the opening.[67] Finally, O'Neill's health was fragile, and he frequently voiced fears about his physical ability to withstand the rigors of rehearsals. This, along with his reluctance to return to New York from California and his suspicion that wartime audiences would reject *Iceman* as too pessimistic, had led him to withhold the play for several years.[68] By late 1945 the war was over and O'Neill had moved back East, but his physical condition remained precarious. Perhaps he worried that he would be unable to oversee the publication after enduring the ordeal of production.

Whatever O'Neill's reasons for publishing *Iceman* when he did, it seems safe to assume that changes made for the acting script, both before and during rehearsals, were motivated more by the limitations under which he worked than because he changed his mind about the play itself. Although O'Neill's comments must be taken with a grain of salt—he was very much a man of the theater—his letters are filled with distrust of productions and anger over the way his plays were handled on stage. About *Iceman* he rather confusingly insisted "that it takes place for me in life not in a theatre." His reservations about stage production are made clearer in his additional remarks: "the fact it is a play which can be produced with actors is secondary and incidental to me and even, quite unimportant—and so it would be a loss to me to sacrifice anything of the complete life for the sake of stage and audience."[69] Shortly after finishing the play O'Neill even told his agent, Richard Madden, "If no one has the guts to do it as is, I'll simply let Cerf go ahead and publish and let it go at that."[70] While O'Neill ultimately could not resist the urge to have *Iceman* performed, the implication of these letters is that he felt changes made for production tend to harm rather than improve the drama. More important, O'Neill had ample time to make further revisions in the published version, had he so wished. The second typescript was cut for production in November 1945; O'Neill's changes in the plate proof were certainly made much later. The fact that most of the alterations made in the second typescript were *not* made in the proof indicates that O'Neill wished the text to stand as it was published.[71] Although the production script will be considered in the following discussion of *Iceman*, references to the "final play" are to the published text.

THE ICEMAN COMETH never underwent the drastic rewritings that such other O'Neill works as *Days Without End* and *Anna Christie* did, yet there are definite changes in character, theme, and tone as the play develops from the scenario to the published version. Some of the revision on all drafts consisted of cutting, a job many critics think O'Neill never finished, but he also made alterations that affect the impact and meaning of the drama. The most important modifications O'Neill made in *Iceman* concern character portrayal. The difficult task of precisely defining a large and varied cast of characters, of giving each figure necessary emphasis, was largely accomplished in revision. Even in minor details O'Neill's sharp eye and ear are impressive. Seemingly insignificant changes of just a few words add ironies that were missing in early drafts and subtly alter the tone. These lesser revisions are proof of the care O'Neill took with his work.

Iceman is very carefully structured, both visually and verbally.[72] Seating arrangements on stage reveal much about relationships among the characters at various points, and repeated phrases are clues to important themes. One aspect of this meticulous verbal patterning is that each of the first three acts ends with the word *happy*. In the manuscript, the second act alone concludes with this word. Act III was edited in the typescript to end on *happy*, and the first act was cut in plate proof to close on this adjective. By the simple repetition of a single word, O'Neill set up a sequence of multiplying ironies. *Happy* is far too strong a term to apply to the bums at Hope's: at best they are contented or at peace. Further, only

Hickey utters the word *happy* and it is, of course, the very opposite of happiness he brings. By focusing on the same word with each curtain, O'Neill encourages the audience (and especially the reader) to note the context in which the word arises. In the first and third act *happy* refers to how Hickey wants and expects the men to feel after following his advice. At the end of Act II happy is what Evelyn always wanted Hickey to be. The happiness Evelyn's futile expectations brought Hickey is precisely the kind of happiness he brings to Hope's crew when he destroys their pipe dreams. The ultimate irony is that the men approach happiness only at the play's final curtain—after Hickey and his inappropriate terminology have departed.

Unfortunately, the repetition of the word *happy* was not carried through into the production, in which only the first act ended this way. Hickey's final speech in the second act was heavily cut, and the speeches concluding Act III were edited and reversed so that the curtain fell on Hugo's pitiful ravings. This change may have resulted in more theatrical act endings, but O'Neill's carefully planned irony was lost.

Tone and atmosphere were also of particular interest to the playwright. *Iceman, Journey,* and *Moon* all begin on light notes with varying degrees of humor; the developing tragedy is emphasized by contrast. O'Neill was especially concerned in *Iceman* with the jokes, bantering, and kidding insults that initially mark the back room society. However, he made one small change that brings the joking to a slightly earlier halt. In the manuscript and typescript the first act, like the last, ends in laughter. Hope tells Hugo, "Begeeses, you half-pint Hunky bomb-thrower, if you ever seen a willow tree it must have been in a beer garden!" and all chuckle with appreciation as the curtain falls (TS, I, p. 49).[73] Such a conclusion emphasizes the circularity of the play (it is circular as far as Hope and the gang are concerned) but it fails to show the gloom that the arrival of Hickey has already brought. O'Neill revised the first act by giving the curtain lines to Hickey and leaving the boys "puzzled, resentful and uneasy" rather than laughing. He thus foreshadows the trouble to come.

A related modification in atmosphere as well as characterization is O'Neill's increasing emphasis on the isolation of the back room's inhabitants and their essential harmlessness. By stressing their distance from the world outside the dirty windows, and their peaceful passivity, he again highlights the disastrous effects of Hickey's intervention. In the scenario O'Neill briefly considered showing the upstairs rooms in the second act: "Scene shows bar, beginning of backroom—and if necessary rooms above—"(II, p. 5). He rejected this expansion of the set (just as in revising *A Touch of the Poet* he omitted scenes in Simon Harford's bedroom and confined that play's action to the Melody Tavern dining room). By retaining only the back room set in this act, O'Neill emphasizes the claustrophobic nature of the men's hideaway and the contrast between the somnolent back room of the first two acts and the brighter barroom of Act III.

More important, O'Neill removed references to previous outside excursions by the men. The scenario reveals that both Hope and Jimmy have already tried to take the walks Hickey is urging. At that time "Hope got half way across street . . . Jimmy got his job back—fired in three days" (II, p. 7). In the manuscript, when Parritt inquires what the boys do for a living, Larry replies: "Odd jobs of a few days now and then are all they can hold or want to hold" (I, p. 17). This line was cut, leaving only the vague comment, "Once in a while one of them makes a successful touch somewhere" (p. 35). In both the pencil draft and the first typescript, O'Neill excised references to Cecil's visiting the British Consulate and spending the money he received at various bars around town. The sole recent excursion the published text mentions is Willie's trip to the pawnshop for a change of clothes. The journeys Hickey forces the men to take are traumatic precisely because the world outside Hope's is an alien one.

Death pervades *The Iceman Cometh* but violence, like work, is anathema to most of the characters. Although some of the men become pugnacious under Hickey's nagging, their aggressiveness is clearly not ingrained. Several characters, particularly Rocky, Chuck, and Joe, are much more potentially dangerous in preliminary drafts. The earliest character list describes Rocky (there named Lefty) as a "Neapolitan immoralist—gangster—jovial, humorous and yet hard as nails—." Bull (the scenario character who becomes Chuck) is a tough former professional pugilist, a background Chuck retains through the manuscript. When Larry suggests that a drunken Hickey could be forced to reveal his "secret," Chuck offers to hold the salesman and force liquor into him (MS, II, p. 9). The scenario finds the bartenders and Joe briefly plotting to murder the offending Hickey, although they make no effort to carry out their plans. Cut from the first typescript description of Joe is the note that "one feels that it would not be wise to look for trouble with him unless one really wished a whole lot of trouble" (I, p. 2). In the published play Rocky says Joe returned from his walk with a gun and a threat to kill Hickey, but "den he dropped it and begun to cry" (p. 216). The bartender's story is more ominous in the scenario: he claims he had to give the gun-toting Joe "drops" to prevent his taking revenge on the salesman, and he believes Joe "pulled a stick-up" while he was gone from the bar (III, 2, p. 10). The production script cuts back the implied violence even further. Rocky's promise to take revenge on Joe and Joe's threat to "stick up some white man" (text, p. 171) disappear, as does Hugo's harmless promise to hang Hickey "to a lamppost the first one!" when the revolution comes (text, p. 201).

The change in the tone of the play is subtle yet clearly motivated. As O'Neill informed Macgowan, the first part of *Iceman* is designed to reveal "the atmosphere of the place, the humour and friendship and human warmth and *deep inner contentment* of the bottom."[74] The fact that these are normally gentle and harmless individuals makes Hickey's treatment of them all the more terrible. The diminution of acts and threats of violence highlights Hickey's own act of violence—the murder of Evelyn—as well as Parritt's death. Finally, by de-emphasizing physical violence, O'Neill points up the much graver danger Hickey's philosophy represents: the death of hopes, of spirit, of the will to live.

As *Iceman* developed from notes to finished drama, O'Neill made other significant changes in the subsidiary characters. In terms of revisions, Bull (Chuck) is the most curious and fascinating of the secondary figures. The longest notes in the early character list pertain to him:

> Bartender—periodical drunk—who is never going to again—who is in love with the whore, Cora—who is determined to reform and marry her—live in country (where he has never been, except on Boys Club outing as kid, and on political club rackets later [)]—has ideals of this as vague, sentimental Promised Land—he gets her to believe in this in spite of herself, just out of love—she was raised on farm—she doesn't believe he'll never drink again—nor believe a man can be happy married to whore, or ever really forget and forgive past—the real wish of her love [?] is to have him for pimp and work for him, give him all money so he needn't work—
>
> It is Bull who encourages Jimmy in "tomorrow" and Tom to get out of house
>
> At end, he becomes pimp—goes on his drunk.

There are several things to note about this description. The first is that the bartender was apparently to play a much larger role in *Iceman* than he eventually does. The Chuck-Cora relationship is potentially very important: it is the only relationship between a man and a woman that is actually shown on stage. In the scenario Bull and Cora's aborted marriage attempt (they apparently never get out the door in this version) takes place in the second act, thus separating it from the others' forays and giving it special attention. Further, some early drafts suggest that Chuck and Cora's wedding venture is not primarily catalyzed by Hickey. Although the published *Iceman* contains references to Chuck's unusually long period of sobriety, the pencil draft and first typescript show the characters more obviously worried—even before Hickey arrives—that the two will try to tie the knot. In a speech deleted from the typescript, for example, Rocky notes: "I wouldn't worry, I'd know it was all de same old junk dey's been pulling for years, if it wasn' for Chuck stayin' on de wagon so long. Hell, he'd ought to gone on his periodical months ago. Jees, sometimes I gets scared he means it" (I, p. 38). This was replaced by merely another speech about the foolishness of their farm fantasies and the comment, "Dey been dreamin' it for years, every time Chuck goes on de wagon" (text, p. 68). Through these changes, O'Neill implies that Chuck's present sober state is not unique but rather a recurrent situation always accompanied by visions of wedded bliss. The couple's dreams of being married are thus drawn more into line with the other characters' pipe dreams: repeated intentions never to be taken seriously. It is Hickey's taunts, not some unusual inner urgings, that actually send them in the direction of the altar. The Chuck-Cora wedding is simply one of a number of pipe dreams that can't be realized, and Chuck, stripped of his past as a promising prize fighter ruined by drink, becomes a minor character. While in the production script the roles of the would-be newlyweds were further reduced, even without these cuts Chuck and Cora do not approach the significance O'Neill at one time envisioned for them.

There is another tantalizing possibility about the bartender originally called Bull. Hickey's name does not appear on either early character list, and Bull may actually have taken Hickey's place in O'Neill's initial conception of *Iceman*. Bull is the one, according to the first list, who encourages Jimmy to believe in tomorrow and Tom (Harry) to leave the house. Terry (Larry) "has growing irritation & hostility to Bull," echoing Larry's attitude toward Hickey. The relationship between Bull and Cora is an ironic reversal of the Hickey-Evelyn situation—the man rather than the woman wishes to settle down—but it is a more equal relationship because both have weaknesses and past transgressions to overcome. *Iceman* with Bull rather than Hickey as the pivotal figure would have been a far less dramatic work, for at the end of the cast-list note Bull merely "becomes pimp—goes on his drunk"; he does not kill Cora in his anguish. It would also be a less complex play: the bartender-tart relationship is on stage for all to see, not filtered to the audience gradually through the mind of one of the parties. But if Bull was O'Neill's original for Hickey, then the central tensions in the drama—between dreams and reality, between the demands of the loved one and the individual's own needs—preceded his conception of Hickey as a character. It is, of course, also possible that O'Neill had Hickey in mind as a fully developed character when he wrote the notes on Bull and envisioned Bull as a supportive and parallel figure to the salesman. He may well have cut back the bartender's role in order to focus more completely on the major figures: Hickey, Larry, and Parritt.[75]

Another character who would have been a potentially parallel figure to Hickey vanishes from *Iceman* altogether. This is a dope addict and pusher named Buzy who appears in the first two acts of the scenario.[76] Buzy is apparently a resident at Hope's and his pipe dream is that he will one day take the cure. It is very possible there is a personal, psychological reason for the disappearance of Buzy. O'Neill wrote the scenario for *Long Day's Journey Into Night* between the scenario and first draft of *Iceman*. He may have felt unable to deal with drug addiction as just one "failure" among many others when his mother's addiction was so painfully in his thoughts. Further, an addict is on a different level from the mere drunkards in the "no-chance saloon," for drugs and the world of the pusher have far more sinister connotations than do alcohol and taverns. (One of the most repulsive characters in the O'Neill canon is a drug-user, the vicious murderer Steve in his early one-acter *The Web*.) Buzy, in fact, is a hot-tempered individual who carries a gun. Most important, Buzy is a pusher as well as an addict and hence, like Hickey, a threat to the others. Hickey and Buzy are linked in the scenario when Hickey's unusual actions lead Rocky to ask Buzy if he has sold dope to the salesman. Like Hickey, Buzy attempts to impose his own way of life (addiction) on the others, in his case by selling drugs rather than "honesty." The addict complains that Hickey accuses him of wanting "everyone else be like myself." While Buzy protests that his drug-dealing is "only business," the tarts insist "you try make addicts just the same, and that makes you a lousy skunk, don't it?" (II, p. 5). Except for Rocky's half-hearted attempt to recruit fellow pimps, in the published play it is Hickey alone who tries to impose his

personal brand of salvation on the others. Thus Buzy's presence diminishes the salience of Hickey without adding any significant dimension to
the play. Although a drug pusher would be an appropriate touch for a
drama about "pipe dreams," O'Neill wisely chose to delete this character.

REMOVING THE SUGGESTION that Hickey has allies in Hope's camp
was only one step in O'Neill's development of the traveling salesman. The
playwright expended great effort in clarifying the nature of Hickey's mission, the extent of his self-delusion, and the effect of his actions on the
men in the bar. O'Neill's ultimate intention seems twofold: to make clear
the devastating effect of Hickey's preaching while at the same time showing the basic sincerity of the salesman himself. O'Neill's revisions finally
reveal a Hickey who is essentially neither mad nor misanthropic but
rather the purveyor of a philosophy with which most people, himself included, cannot live.

Mosher's story of the snake oil doctor, recounted at the end of Act I, is a
picture in miniature of Hickey. Like a preacher, the doctor "practised on
street corners." The doctor dies because he fails to get drunk one night;
Hickey, Mosher tells us, is suffering from "almost fatal teetotalism." As
Hickey comes bearing a cure for the bums' mental suffering, so the doctor
pretends to be offering a cure for humanity's physical ills: "rattlesnake oil,
rubbed on the prat" (text, p. 88). Only a few minutes before Mosher tells
his tale, Hickey compares his peace to that a doctor provides when he
"gives you a shot in the arm, and the pain goes, and you drift off" (p. 86).
Ultimately, the doctor too is peddling death, for he laments, "I'd hoped
I'd live to see the day when, thanks to my miraculous cure, there wouldn't
be a single vacant cemetery lot left in this glorious country." The final
irony comes when Hickey, who has slept through Mosher's narrative, raises his head and agrees, "That's the spirit—" (p. 90).

Mosher's story, which does not appear in the scenario, was substantially
expanded during O'Neill's revisions. More than two hundred words were
added to the tale in the first typescript, and a few lines deleted from the
second typescript were reinstated in the final production script. Since
O'Neill's general tendency was to cut as he edited, this expansion testifies
to his belief in the significance of the story. It is unlikely that the playwright extended the tale solely because of its humor, since he also deliberately changed the ending of the first act to prevent the curtain's coming
down on laughter. Mosher's anecdote neatly foreshadows the trouble to

come in *Iceman*. However, Mosher's doctor is in fact closer to the Hickey of the scenario than to the Hickey who emerges in the published play. The doctor is a charlatan who is fully conscious of his cure's lethal nature; it is only in early versions of *Iceman* that Hickey seems aware he is bringing "death" to his friends. As the play moves through the various drafts, the magnitude of Hickey's self-deception is increased. The salesman, unlike the doctor, does not fully know the effects of the remedy he peddles.

Although the scenario is not completely legible at this point, it is evident that Hickey's long last-act confession and his exit here are far different from those in later versions of *Iceman*. The salesman, who has begun drinking again, prefaces his account by including the others in it: "I suppose Hope & Jimmy having once been married men will understand me best—but we've all loved someone or something and lived with it—if it wasn't a wife, it may have been a mother, or a sister, or a Cause—or oneself, eh, Larry?" The scenario continues:

> He tells story of himself & Evelyn—as he tells it, he draws out the stories of the others and they join in with them, interrupting him—until at the end he puts it up to them. "Well, you can see, can't you, that the time had to come when something, some very little thing, like her kissing you goodnight and saying 'I know you'll never drink again' would show you you had to do now, at once, what you'd wanted to do for so long"—(pause)—Hope bursts out "I know. Kill the God damn bitch"—(Then all, all join in one by one with a fierce revengefulness) Hickey says "Yes, that's exactly what I did. I murdered Evelyn—knife—in her sleep—she felt no pain—just stared at me— . . ."
>
> (III, 2, p. 10)

Hickey is unmoved by Hope's characterization of Evelyn. Despite his earlier protestations of love, he has known all along that he hates her, and he tells his story so the boys can voice their agreement with his viewpoint. Although McGloin briefly attempts to play the policeman and arrest Hickey, he decides that he sympathizes with the salesman, as do the others. Only Larry realizes that Hickey does not wish to escape, for death is what those without dreams desire. Hickey is taken away still proclaiming the philosophy of honesty he has espoused throughout the scenario. The tarts return just before Hickey departs, and the bartenders tell them they have "given up jobs, pimps now." The women are "delighted" by this decision, as is the salesman. "Hickey points out [the bartenders] to others, congratulating Rocky & Chuck, 'you've got to face what you are & be it. You've got to face what you want to do and do it'" (III, 2, p. 10).

This scene presents a harder, thicker-skinned character than the Hickey of the final play. His speech, more a recitation than a confession, reveals to him no painful new insights. While he insists that Evelyn's death was for her benefit—he claims she died looking "grateful and relieved because she didn't have to hope any more"—Hickey tacitly agrees with Hope's calling her a bitch. He seems little concerned with whether the murder was an act of hatred or of love; it was merely an act of necessity. Moreover, Hickey, like Mosher's doctor, deliberately tries to instill in the other men the desire for death he recognizes in himself. The Hickey of the scenario is scarcely self-deluded: he came to the saloon knowing the reasons for and the consequences of his actions. He need not, and does not, plead insanity.

In the scenario and early drafts of *Iceman*, Hickey's love for Evelyn and the sincerity of his belief that love motivated the murder are questionable. The manuscript has Hope insisting, "Never was nothing to Hickey's bull (about the Iceman). Only a joke, and he wouldn't give a damn if it was true anyway. No one dame'll ever bother Hickey much. He's got too many substitutes, begeeses!" (I, p. 28).[77] The implication is not merely that Hickey spends time with whores (which we know in the published play) but that he speaks about them frequently and appreciatively. There is a further suggestion that he has never told the gang he cares very much for his wife.

Hickey's delusion that the murder was for Evelyn's benefit is far shallower in the scenario. The printed text has him announcing his wife's death by explaining: "You see, I don't feel any grief. . . . I've got to feel glad, for her sake. Because she's at peace. She's rid of me at last" (p. 151). In the scenario he says:

> Her death was good riddance—I mean, for her, to be rid of me—I feel no grief—I mean, for her sake—it was inevitable—she was much too good for this world—too good for me—and now she's dead, thank God—I mean, thank God for her sake. (He breaks off hastily)   (II, p. 7)

Hickey's hatred of Evelyn is so blatant in this scenario passage it is scarcely credible that he himself is not aware of the true meaning of his claims. His feelings are further evidenced in his remarks to Hope about Hope's late wife Bessie. Cut from the first typescript was Hickey's suggestion to the tavern owner, "You must have been calling her every bitch in the world under your breath, weren't you?" (III, p. 23). A few moments later in this typescript, when Hope shows signs of depression after his walk, Hickey encourages him with the assurance, "You're really rid of the past and Bessie now" (III, p. 28). Hickey is obviously ascribing to Hope his own hatred of his dead spouse.

Gerald Weales correctly comments: "From the moment that Hickey steps on stage, it is clear that he is being driven by a desperate need of his own, that his desire to save his friends is a great deal more than misguided charity. O'Neill indicates this in the way he flaws Hickey's smooth hard-sell speeches with hesitation, hints that are leading toward the final revelation."[78] However, these hints are far more numerous in the early drafts, so numerous that Hickey often seems less a driven man than a calculating one. The final text makes it apparent something is driving Hickey while showing that the salesman himself is not fully conscious of this. A large part of him truly believes he has found peace and is doing his friends a favor by sharing his new insights.

To emphasize the sincerity of Hickey's mission, O'Neill made several revisions that change the focus of Hickey's speeches from what he did to Evelyn to what he is doing for the men. In the first typescript Hickey blatantly exclaims: "You've got to listen! You damned fools, can't you see you're all mixed up in it now, because that's what made me want to help you?" (IV, p. 13). This was deleted and the statement that remains—"It makes me think, if I got balled up about you, how do I know I wasn't balled up about myself" (text, p. 231)—is more equivocal, implying that his uncertainty about himself came only after his failure to make the others happy. Similarly, in a long passage cut from the second act of the first typescript, Hickey tells Larry:

> On the level, you can save your old bean a lot of wear and tear by just being a little patient. Because I'm going to tell [you] all when the right time comes. That's a promise. But I've got to get all of you in a proper state of grace first, so to speak. It wouldn't work to tell the truth to a lot of pipe-dreamers. . . . You wouldn't be able to believe it. You've got to be honest with yourselves first, the same as I had to be or you'd think my honesty was a lie.
>
> (II, p. 12)[79]

This speech implies that Hickey visits the bar for the sole purpose of telling his story, and the actions that he forces the boys to perform are intended simply to prepare them to accept his interpretation of Evelyn's murder.

More minor wording changes also move the focus away from Evelyn's death. In the first typescript, for example, Hickey's long speech near the end of Act II culminates with his promise: "You'll know, what I know, that

the best thing for the happiness of all concerned is to do what you really
want to do, and no faking about it! And you'll do it—Just as I did!" (II, p.
32). This was deleted, so that Hickey's argument concludes with the assertion "you can all see that I don't give a damn about anything now. And I
promise you, by the time this day is over, I'll have every one of you feeling
the same way!" (text, p. 148). The point is not that Hickey never refers to
his own deed in the published *Iceman;* he does so fairly often. But his
references are significantly less frequent and less obvious than in early
drafts, for O'Neill wishes to show that, however misguided Hickey is and
however much his actions in the bar are tied to his guilt over the murder,
he genuinely believes in the path to peace he recommends to the others.
One final cut neatly illustrates this. In his long speech near the end of Act
II, Hickey likens his present mission to convincing "some dame . . . her
house wouldn't be properly furnished unless she bought another wash
boiler" (text, p. 147). The first typescript line reads: "her house wouldn't
be properly furnished unless she bought another wash-boiler that wasn't
half as good as the old one she had" (II, p. 32).[80]

The question of Hickey's sanity, even more than that of his sincerity, has
troubled critics since *Iceman* first appeared. While Eric Bentley's characterization of Hickey as a "maniac" is probably the best-known erroneous
judgment of the salesman, many reviewers of the first production, including Stark Young and Mary McCarthy, assume that Hickey is insane.[81] As
we shall see, those who base their conclusions on the production alone
may have some reason for being confused, but O'Neill carefully altered
the play as he revised to show that Hickey's murder of Evelyn and his
actions in the bar are the deeds of a sane man. He becomes unbalanced
only in his last moments on stage, when forced to confront his true
motives.

The complex reiteration of words and phrases in *Iceman* often builds up
a texture of meaning that is not traceable to one particular speech. As he
revised, O'Neill reduced the number of times one character calls another
character, particularly Hickey, "mad," "bughouse," "crazy," or the like.
Although a few such terms were added, significantly more were removed,
most from the first typescript. The fact that O'Neill often canceled only
the particular word or phrase, rather than the whole speech in which it
occurs, suggests that these terms were not inadvertently cut during general trimming. Typescript deletions include Parritt's remark about Hickey,
"I think he's gone batty"; Larry's agreement that the salesman is "batty"

(II, pp. 18–19); and Margie's claim that "Stayin' sober's drove him coocoo" (II, p. 27). The longest canceled passage is one in which Margie exclaims: "What a sweet party! Jees, I gotta notion . . . to phone the asylum and tell 'em to send round de net! Dey could grab everybody here and not make no mistake!" (II, p. 25).[82] The published *Iceman* still includes numerous speeches where the word *crazy* or a synonym appears, but there are fewer than in early drafts. These deletions help undermine both the notion that Hickey was insane throughout his visit and the gang's claim that they immediately spotted his mania.

Robert Brustein points out that Hickey's last-act claim to insanity is challenged by Parritt, who during his own confession declares: "And I'm not putting up any bluff, either, that I was crazy afterwards when I laughed to myself and thought, 'You know what you can do with your freedom pipe dream now, don't you, you damned old bitch!' " (text, p. 247).[83] Earlier, Hickey himself had told Larry, "As for my being bughouse, you can't crawl out of it that way. Hell, I'm too damned sane" (p. 117). Hickey does, nevertheless, try to "crawl out of it that way" after his confession, and O'Neill had more trouble with Hickey's exit than with almost any other scene. If we include the production script, there are five different variations of this scene (not counting the scenario version discussed previously). Trying to reconstruct the intentions behind O'Neill's changes is extremely tricky.

In what appears to be O'Neill's first manuscript attempt at Hickey's departure, Parritt's remarks, paralleling the salesman's, do not appear at all.[84] The scene runs:

> HICKEY ⟨(in a strange, low tone)⟩ So I killed her. And as soon as the first
> shock was over, like another flash of light, I saw I'd always known that was
> the only way to set her free—what I'd always wanted to do but I'd never
> had the courage to face myself and kill my ⟨lying⟩ pipe dream. And sud-
> denly, standing there beside the bed, I felt free at last, and I know she felt
> free, without love to torture me any more—without a single damned hope
> or dream left—at peace on the bottom of life! Why, I suddenly knew I
> didn't ever have to get drunk any more! I—I remember now I laughed. I
> shouldn't have but I know Evelyn forgave me. She always forgave me. I
> remember I heard myself talking out loud, speaking to her, saying some-
> thing I'd always wanted to say: "Well, you know what you can do with your
> pipe dream now, don't you, you damned bitch!" (He starts in terror—then
> bursts into frantic, sobbing protest) No! Oh God, no! I never said that!

Good God, I couldn't! If I did, I was insane! I must have been stark, raving
crazy. Why, I loved Evelyn ever since I was a kid better than anything in
life! She was the sweetest woman that ever lived! (Appealing piteously to
the crowd) Boys, you're all my old pals, you've known old Hickey for
years, a poor good-natured sap with no harm in him, who was his own
worst enemy! You know I must have been crazy as hell, or I never could
have—God, I'd have torn my tongue out before I'd—I'd have killed myself first—if I hadn't been crazy! (Hope is staring at him. There is an
extraordinary expression beginning to creep into his face—a thought coming into his mind at which he is grasping—a hope of escape. And all the
others, except Parritt, seem to become dimly aware of this same idea.
They stir and become less like wax figures and light appears in their eyes.
Meanwhile the two detectives close in on Hickey from behind)
HOPE (at first mechanically repeats his defensive jeering) Who the hell cares?
(Then with an uncertain, groping eagerness) Crazy? Begeeses, didn't I say
all along you must be crazy to—
MORAN (taps Hickey on the shoulder) I arrest you for the murder of your
wife. (The other detective handcuffs Hickey, who offers no resistance,
doesn't even seem aware of what is happening)
HICKEY (continues his protest) I couldn't have said it! I couldn't have
laughed! You know me, Boys. Not unless I was insane.   (III, 2, p. 16)

Moran then advises the salesman to "tell it to the jury" and warns the
gang not to believe Hickey's lies. Hope responds with a lengthy speech
about how the men knew all along that Hickey was crazy, and Hickey, still
protesting his insanity, is led out. Moran's and Hope's speeches are similar to those in the published play.

There are several points to note about this version of the scene. First,
Hickey's protestations of insanity are allowed to run on longer than in the
published *Iceman*. Second, Hickey's ravings are essentially independent
of the other people present; he appeals to his friends to confirm his
claims, but not nearly as directly as he does in the final rendering of the
scene. He has virtually lost touch with his surroundings, for he "doesn't
even seem aware of what is happening." His blank bewilderment suggests
that whether or not he was insane when he killed Evelyn, he becomes
unbalanced at the moment he recognizes his hatred.

Perhaps most important, Hickey does not, as he does in the final play,
briefly attempt to deny Hope's assertions that he was crazy when he came
to the bar. In the published *Iceman* Hickey obviously realizes that Hope
is using his insanity as an excuse, and this recognition militates against the

assumption of the salesman's madness. Hickey there tells Hope, "I see what you're driving at, but I can't let you get away with—" (text, p. 243). Such a statement qualifies Hickey's subsequent capitulation to Hope: it implies that in exchange for Hope's agreeing Hickey was mad when he called Evelyn a bitch, the salesman will "admit" he has been insane during his visit to the saloon. They fall into the pattern that marks all the *Iceman* characters: if you support my pipe dream, I'll support yours. In this initial manuscript version, by contrast, Hickey is oblivious to Hope's bargain, suggesting that the salesman really is insane at this point and raising the possibility that his actions throughout the play were the work of a madman.

Finally, Hope's response to Hickey's claim that he is crazy varies significantly from the printed version. In the published play, Hope's reaction is more tentative and questioning. "Insane? You mean—you went really insane?" he asks. "And you've been crazy ever since? Everything you've said and done here—" (pp. 242–43). In this early draft he is more sure of himself, and answers almost immediately, "Crazy? Begeeses, didn't I say all along you must be crazy to—." Since Hope and the others have in the manuscript referred to madness so frequently, Hope's confident reply is appropriate. This version of Hickey's confession and exit suggests that Hickey may well be insane when he leaves, and Hope's claim that he sensed madness all along is not clearly a lie, as it is in the published *Iceman.*

In another pencil draft rendering of Hickey's exit, the salesman does recognize the bar owner's game. When Hope asks whether he has been crazy all along, Hickey answers: "Now, now, Harry! Up to your old tricks, eh? I see what you're driving at, but I can't let ⟨you⟩ backslide like that. I—" (III, 2, p. 17½). This line, almost identical to that in the printed text, shows that Hickey is at least rational enough to understand Hope's motive. But he needs a sharp prod to make him realize he must capitulate in order to gain his friends' support. Larry applies the prod:

(glares at Hickey with hatred—horribly and meaningly) So you're ⟨denying now you were⟩ crazy, eh? You stood by your Evelyn's body after you'd murdered her and you said in cold blood "You know what you can do with your pipe dream now, you damned bitch!" (III, 2, p. 17½)

Hickey of course must surrender under this onslaught, for Larry has clearly demonstrated the connection between Hickey's claim that he was in-

sane when he cursed Evelyn and Hope's desire to believe that the salesman has been mad ever since.

There is still a third version of this scene in the pencil draft, the one
which survives into the first typescript and is there altered to produce the
scene as it finally stands. At this time Parritt's comments about the hatred
he bears his mother, paralleling Hickey's confession, were added. Parritt's
remarks not only tell the audience what they have long suspected about
the young man's feelings, but may also serve as a cue to Hickey. Parritt's
admission that he hated his mother precedes and perhaps unconsciously
spurs Hickey's acknowledgment that he hated his wife.

In this third rendering, O'Neill once again revised the dynamics of the
pact struck between Hickey and Hope:

> HOPE (eagerly) And you've been insane ever since, ⟨you mean⟩? All the
> things you've done here—? (Almost with enthusiasm) Begeeses, I knew it,
> Hickey! I could tell the first minute you came in the door, you were out of
> your mind! I said to myself, I won't hold him responsible, I won't expect
> anything he says or does to make any sense, I'll just humor him and do any
> crazy thing he wants, even if it doesn't mean anything.
>
> HICKEY (staring at him—for a moment he forgets his own preoccupation and
> his face takes on its familiar expression of affectionate amusement and he
> chuckles—admonishingly) Now, now, Governor! Up to your old tricks,
> eh? I see what you're driving at, but I can't let you backslide like that!
>
> HOPE (his face falls—dully resentful) Then who the hell cares—(But he
> throws this off and drives on again, ⟨looking pleadingly at Hickey⟩) I know
> you couldn't have said a lousy thing like that to her, Hickey! I know
> damned well you must have been insane!
>
> HICKEY (stares back into his eyes. It is as if a crazy bargain were being con-
> cluded between them. He blurts out) Yes, Harry, and I've been insane
> ever since. I don't remember coming here. I don't remember anything
> except some crazy joke I wanted to play on you and the gang by kidding
> you and pretending I was a temperance crank or something coming to save
> your souls. So you just forget anything I did because I was just as insane
> and irresponsible as when I told that crazy lie to Evelyn—.
>
> (MS, III, 2, p. 17)[85]

This time it is Hope, rather than Larry, who forces Hickey to capitulate.
More clearly than in earlier drafts, Hope is well aware of the pact he is
striking with the salesman. Further, Hickey's claim—"I don't remember
anything"—is so patently untrue, so obviously a story concocted on the

spur of the moment, that both Hickey's claim to insanity and Hope's contention he recognized that madness are undercut.

O'Neill's great difficulties with the scene reflect the fact that there are several questions which must be answered at this point. Was Hickey insane when he killed Evelyn? Was Hickey mad when he preached to the boys in the saloon? Did the gang believe he was crazy? Is he insane now when he claims to be? Can the gang accept his insanity plea and thus regain their peace and pipe dreams? The initial version of the scene implies that the answer to all these questions is "yes." O'Neill obviously could not leave Hickey's final moments this way, for such a conclusion undermines the entire drama. If his preaching has been simply the ravings of a lunatic, then the tensions between Hickey's urgings and the gang's desires are meaningless. In the second and especially the third versions, Hickey is more rational. Hope is less sure of himself, and the whole tone of the scene suggests that both Hope and Hickey are grasping at insanity as an escape from realities they cannot face.

The published version of the scene differs once again from preceding variations. The bargain between Hickey and Hope is here made silently: Hickey reads his choices in Hope's face. Through this change, O'Neill shows that Hickey's claim to have been mad for days is fallacious, while at the same time making plausible the men's ability to use this excuse to return to their former state. The audience sees the speciousness of the insanity claim, but they must also accept the alacrity with which the gang grasps at this explanation for their suffering. When in the immediately preceding version Hope verbally and blatantly forces Hickey into the bargain, it is difficult to accept how readily Hope convinces himself that no bargain has been made. The new, subtler pact makes the men's transition from misery to celebration more dramatically credible.

O'Neill, however, was still unhappy with his portrait of Hickey. The published *Iceman* indicates that Hickey is well aware he is purchasing his own peace of mind by giving the gang theirs: he briefly resists Hope's blandishments and recognizes that the saloon keeper is "up to . . . [his] old tricks" (p. 243). But O'Neill inserted in the first typescript a passage that works against this evidence of rationality:

HICKEY (*With a strange mad earnestness*) Oh, I want to go, Officer. I can hardly wait now. I should have phoned you from the house right afterwards. It was a waste of time coming here. I've got to explain to Evelyn. But I know she's forgiven me. She knows I was insane.   (text, p. 245)

The stage direction is not the only hint that Hickey has gone mad. The lines, reminiscent of Orin's suicidal ravings about apologizing to his dead mother in *Mourning Becomes Electra,* seem the exclamations of a maniac. The implication is not merely that insanity is the last pipe dream to which Hickey clings, but that suddenly facing the truth about his feelings for Evelyn has driven him over the brink. This does not mean that he was insane when he shot her or when he came to the bar. Without destroying the validity of what Hickey has done during his visit to the saloon, O'Neill suggests that looking too hard at unbearable truth may actually drive one mad.

When we turn to the production script we find even more complications. The last act was heavily cut for production, altering Hickey's exit once again. Deleted from the script were Hickey's verbal recognition of Hope's motives for calling him mad ("Now, Governor! . . . I see what you're driving at"); Hope's argument with the detective, in which he insists they all knew of Hickey's insanity; Hope's and the gang's promise to testify for the salesman; and the men's noisily expectant drink after Hickey's departure. Removing Hickey's acknowledgment of the bargain struck with Hope makes the salesman seem far less rational. Moreover, as Mary Arbenz comments in her discussion of the production script, Hope's deleted speeches show clearly that the tavern owner "is deliberately lying, seizing on the excuse Hickey has given them" when he claims they knew all along that the salesman was demented.[86] The production cuts could lead one to miss Hope's calculated lying and misunderstand Hickey's insanity plea.[87] Whether or not Hickey is on the verge of madness, or beyond it, as he exits, the published play shows that his claim to having *been* insane when he killed Evelyn is as specious as Hope's contention that he immediately spotted the traveling drummer's lunacy. The production omissions greatly confused Hickey's final moments and left the opportunity for some reviewers to erroneously conclude, as they indeed did, that Hickey is a maniac.

CLARIFYING HICKEY'S SINCERITY and sanity was only one major challenge O'Neill faced as he developed *Iceman.* An even more complex case is Larry Slade, a character for whom O'Neill had a great deal of affection. Although the traveling salesman is the protagonist of *Iceman,* Larry (the main antagonist) is in many ways the moral and ideological center of the drama, at times nearly a *raisonneur.* A study of the drafts reveals that Larry and his relationship with Parritt seem to have given the playwright the most difficulty. In the manuscript and first typescript, the scenes between Larry and Parritt are generally edited at least as heavily as Hickey's scenes, and O'Neill was still tinkering with these figures in plate proof. Similarly, the very end of the production script was revised several times, apparently because O'Neill was dissatisfied with his handling of the "old Foolosopher." He was concerned both with the exact characterization of Larry and with preventing his being overshadowed by the others on the stage.

Perhaps the best way to approach Larry is through his young friend and tormentor, Don Parritt. O'Neill apparently began with only a hazy conception of this character, emphasizing his participation in revolutionary movements. The earlier cast list identifies Bob M., Parritt's precursor, as an anarchist and a member of the radical International Workers of the World. In the scenario Parritt (called Potter) rarely mentions his mother; only at the very end is it revealed that she was one of those arrested when he sold out his comrades, and the play's anguished mother-son relationship is barely foreshadowed there. It is in the manuscript that O'Neill clearly delineates the mutual betrayals of Parritt and Rosa (called Emma) for the first time, thus placing Parritt in O'Neill's parade of male characters whose love-hate bonds with their mothers ultimately destroy them. As Michael Manheim comments, this relationship has strong echoes of that between O'Neill's mother and his brother Jamie, and even between their mother and the playwright himself.[88]

Don Parritt's secondary function in *Iceman* lies in his connection to Hickey: the young man also has betrayed a woman, and he "parrots" Hickey at several points, particularly in the final act. The "parroting" of Hickey's confession was partly added by O'Neill as the play progressed. In the earliest manuscript version Parritt says nothing between his admission that he burnt his mother's picture and the salesman's exit. O'Neill added lines for Parritt first in an overly schematic way (Hickey's "Because I loved her so much" is immediately followed by Parritt's "Because I hated her, Larry") and then in the slightly more subtle form in which they finally appear. Hickey, as noted, may be responding subconsciously to Parritt's professions of hatred for his mother when he admits he hated his wife, although there is no indication in the text that the salesman is listening to the young man. The two confessions are parallel yet essentially separate. Parritt's long speech immediately following Hickey's departure was slightly altered to emphasize the parallel. This speech originally ended with Parritt calling his mother a "damned—"; in the first typescript this was altered to "damned old whore" (IV, p. 22). But in plate proof this was changed once again, to "damned old bitch" (p. 247), thus verbally aligning Parritt with Hickey and Hope, who each applied the epithet *bitch* to the woman in his life.

Finally, the Parritt plot is a clue to the Hickey plot, for it proceeds much faster. In early drafts, in fact, it moved too quickly: Parritt's guilt, his desire for death, and even the mode of his suicide were all presaged in the opening minutes of the drama. O'Neill resorted to deletions to create at least a little suspense. For example, he cut Rocky's prophetic description of Parritt's chamber, "best room in de dump in summer—top floor back with a window and a fire escape you can camp on when it's too hot" (MS, I, p. 10). The playwright also removed Parritt's claim that Larry's "Long Sleep" (death) appeals to him except that he doesn't "want to wait" (TS, I, p. 15), and the young man's incriminating remark, near the beginning of the typescript, that his mother is probably the only one of those arrested who knows the identity of the traitor. Even with these revisions, however, we are already suspicious of Parritt in the first act when he overreacts to Hugo's favorite insult, "Gottammed stool pigeon" (text, p. 33), and our suspicions are confirmed in Act II when Parritt tells Larry "I want you to guess now!" (text, p. 127). We know that the young anarchist is an informer long before we learn that the salesman is a murderer. The question of motive rather than deed becomes central to the Parritt story early in the play, and this subplot indicates the direction in which the main plot will develop.

There is only one way in which the Hickey-Parritt parallel is slightly weakened in successive drafts. Evelyn's crucial failing was that she loved Hickey not for what he was but in spite of what he was. Perhaps, as Egil Törnqvist argues, her pity and forgiveness make her a Christ-like figure,[89] yet such feelings imply something lacking in the one pitied and forgiven. Like Bessie, who tried to nag the indolent Hope into action, Evelyn made demands her husband could never fulfill. There is a suggestion of a similar situation in early versions of the Parritt story, where it appears that Rosa had great expectations she attempted to impose on her son just as Evelyn tried to impose her ideals of respectability on Hickey. In the manuscript, Larry notes that Rosa hoped Parritt "would ⟨grow up to⟩ be a great leader" (I, p. 15). Parritt himself scornfully recalls: "Sometimes I think she thought she was the Movement, or it was her. And she'd brought me up to be a Robespierre or Danton or some other pipe-dreaming faker. She hated not to get what she wanted. She hated to fail in anything. She'd hate me for making her fail" (TS, III, p. 4). These passages disappear, although the more important similarities between Hickey and Parritt remain.

Despite these numerous parallels, the Hickey plot would have almost all its implications even if Parritt were not in the play. Hickey's story does not depend upon Parritt, but the young ex-anarchist is essential to the presentation of Larry Slade's transformation. While Hickey is wrong about many things, he is prescient when he tells Larry that Parritt will "do as good a job as I could at making you give up that old grandstand bluff" (text, p. 197). Actually, Parritt succeeds with Larry where Hickey ultimately fails with the others, and Parritt affects Larry in a way that Hickey never could.

John Henry Raleigh claims that Parritt is "a moral leper," and Robert C. Lee agrees that he is "the most repugnant character ever created by O'Neill."[90] Certainly Parritt has many unappealing traits, but these critics ignore the very genuine pathos in Parritt's situation, a pathos emphasized by his being so much younger than anyone else in *Iceman*. Bob M., the forerunner of Parritt, is described in the early character list as "Anarchist—incorruptible fanatic—coldly pure, no women, no booze—passionate idealist . . . savagely intolerant weakness—about 30—." This is a far cry from the desperate young boy of the published play. Just as Hickey in the scenario seems to feel little guilt over his murder of Evelyn, so too Parritt in this draft exhibits scant remorse over his betrayal of Rosa. He goes to his death insisting, "It isn't on her account. I'm glad, as far's she's concerned—it's thinking of those other guys—I never thought of them" (III, 2, p. 11). Although in these notes and the scenario Parritt does seem to be the completely reprehensible individual Raleigh and Lee condemn, he emerges in the final play as much a victim as a villain, no longer a thirty-year-old political turncoat but a confused youth taking revenge on an unloving mother. Rosa Parritt, Evelyn Hickman, and Bessie Hope form a sort of unholy trinity of unseen women whose power reaches from beyond the jail cell or the grave to torment the men unfortunate enough to love them. O'Neill's late dramas, like so many of his earlier plays, explore women's destruction of their husbands, lovers, and children. But *A Moon for the Misbegotten* and even *Long Day's Journey Into Night* show the feminine force to be redemptive as well as destructive; *Iceman* centers on the latter, negative quality. Whether the woman loves too much (Evelyn) or too little (Rosa), the results are devastating to herself and her men.[91]

Don Parritt is overwhelmed by the mixture of love and hatred that has led him to strike back at his mother. Unlike most of the other characters in *Iceman*, he cannot rationalize his actions, hide his pain behind fabricated excuses. O'Neill's revisions emphasize his predicament. In early drafts, the fourth act finds Parritt still insisting he double-crossed the anarchists for money. In the published *Iceman*, even this pitiful pretext has disappeared by the last act. Twice in the first typescript and once in plate proof O'Neill deleted Parritt's Judas-like claim that he betrayed his comrades for cash, for "a lousy wad of dough" (plate proof, p. 219). By the final act of the published text Parritt, stripped of all his rationalizations, can do little but beg Larry to put him out of his misery.

Estranged from his mother, Parritt is deeply dependent on Larry, and this relationship was gradually strengthened as O'Neill developed the drama. Specifically, the playwright minimized direct confrontations between Parritt and the other characters except Larry. The scenario shows some of the bar's residents introducing themselves to Parritt (Potter) rather than being introduced by Larry. Hugo's (Hip.'s) cries of "stool pigeon" have apparently upset the young man in the scenario even more than they do in the final play, for he goes to confront Hugo in his room. Hugo later comes downstairs "furious" because Parritt "came in woke him up" (III, 1, p. 8). Most significantly, Hugo apparently participates in Parritt's condemnation in this version. The scenario reads: "Pause after Hickey goes—then scene Potter, Larry—and Hip starting to life for second to stare at Potter condemningly—'Pig of a stool pigeon! Traitor! To the guillotine!'" (III, 2, p. 11). The young man then makes his final speech and exits. Exactly what was to occur in the "scene Potter, Larry" is unknown. Hugo may be the sole person passing judgment on Parritt, but it is more likely that he is echoing a sentence Larry has already pronounced. In either case, Hugo assumes a role in Parritt's suicide that he does not play in later drafts. Although there is already little interaction between Parritt and the saloon's inmates in the published text, two more connections were excised from the second typescript for production: Parritt's exit line to the drunken Hugo, and Willie's offer to be Parritt's lawyer (text, pp. 249, 179–81).

Parritt's dealings with Hickey, more important than those with the other men save Larry, were also diminished. In a long passage cut from the manuscript's last act, Parritt claims that the salesman will force Larry to come to his aid. "But wait till Hickey comes back!" Parritt warns. "He'll make him make up his mind [to help me], before he's through with him!" (III, 2, p. 5). Shortly thereafter Parritt reiterates: "I wish Hickey'd come back and help me" (III, 2, p. 6). When the drummer returns, Parritt begs him to "come on over here and make this yellow old bastard [Larry] do what he ought to do for me!" (III, 2, p. 8). This too was cut, as was a comparable speech in the first typescript. The published play shows no interaction between Hickey and the young man at this point. Similarly, in the drafts Hickey reacts angrily to Parritt's first outburst during his confession; in the final text Hickey is "too absorbed in his story now to notice this" interruption (p. 232). Moreover, the deleted retort contains surprisingly concrete advice about Parritt. Hickey admonishes Larry, "He's nothing to me but if I was you I'd tell him to go up and take a jump off your fire escape! If only out of pity for him!" (TS, IV, p. 13). Nowhere in the final play does Hickey so explicitly spell out what kind of "help" Larry should give his unhappy young friend. Larry, urged on by the desperate Parritt, must make this decision himself.

SOON AFTER O'NEILL FINISHED *Iceman*, rumors about the play began. In an attempt to forestall misleading gossip, O'Neill asked George Jean Nathan to mention the drama in an article he was writing and enumerated several points he wished Nathan to make. One of the points was "that a travelling salesman is the character around which the play develops, but there is no 'lead' in the usual sense."[92] With this comment O'Neill touches on what may be the greatest difficulty with the play: while *Iceman* does indeed "develop" around Hickey, Larry Slade is an equally if not more important character. O'Neill's problems in balancing Hickey and Larry are myriad, and of greater magnitude on stage than on paper, but even critics of the printed drama often underestimate or overlook Larry's unique position. Travis Bogard, for example, lumps Larry with Parritt and Hickey as "betrayers," and gives most attention to Larry's abandonment of Rosa.[93] Robert Heilman treats *Iceman* in the context of a general discussion of American tragedy, yet he fails to distinguish Larry from the other saloon residents and to notice that he alone is a tragic figure.[94] In fact, O'Neill made a deliberate effort as he revised the play to show that Larry's condemnation of Parritt is primarily the result of his feelings about the young man rather than about Rosa, and to emphasize how Larry ultimately differs from all the other characters.

Shortly after *Iceman* begins, we learn that Larry has four pipe dreams: that he is through with the Movement; that he no longer cares about his former mistress, Rosa Parritt; that he is eagerly awaiting and unafraid of death; and that he is "in the grandstand," unconcerned about his fellow men. The first two are the least important in the final play. As he wrote the various drafts, O'Neill de-emphasized Larry's allegiance to anarchism, and his lingering attachment to Rosa was also gradually relegated to secondary status, even though the whole Larry-Rosa relationship was conceived during rather than at the beginning of the composition process. The fourth is the most crucial, and the playwright focused on it as he sharpened the characterization of the "old Foolosopher." It is this pipe dream of noninvolvement that Parritt forces Larry to renounce.

In the scenario, Larry's reaction to Parritt—like Parritt's actions—seem largely politically motivated. Hugo and Larry are both involved in Parritt's suicide, and the link between them is their past in the Movement. The published *Iceman* does at one point show Larry threatening Parritt with "justice," the justice accorded a traitor, but the notion that he primarily views Parritt as a turncoat who must be punished for his crime against the Cause is far stronger in the scenario. When the denizens of the bar inquire about the noise Parritt's body makes as it hits the ground, Larry unconcernedly replies, "It's Justice falling off of the roof. Don't interfere with it," and proposes a toast to Harry's health (III, 2, p. 11). Moreover, Larry's attachment to the Movement in the scenario is shown by the fact that he introduces the subject of his anarchist activities where such a reference is not absolutely called for. When Joe and the bartenders caution Larry not to reveal their plot to murder Hickey, Larry scoffs: "Squeal? If I'd wanted to squeal I've known things I could have sold to Burns that would have made me rich. When I was in Movement, if I'd wanted sell out the Revolution" (III, 1, p. 8). This scenario outburst suggests Larry's continuing pride in his political past and serves as an indirect attack on his young "squealer" pal. In the published text Larry only mentions the Movement when someone else raises the topic first or when, as in explaining how he knows Parritt, a reference to it is essential.

Larry's attachment to anarchism was subtly muted in the manuscript and typescript. Excised from the manuscript was Larry's reference to

Hickey as a "⟨stinking⟩ capitalist lackey" (II, p. 12), and a deleted stage direction in the same draft apparently alludes to Larry's political feelings: "As his eyes fix on Parritt, his expression hardens ⟨automatically⟩ for a second into an implacable, almost cruelly fanatical detestation" (II, p. 15½). Cut from the typescript are several instances in which Parritt directly accuses Larry of still being interested in the Movement, including one in which he charges: "You lousy old faker, you'll be on a soapbox again spouting with the other bunco-steerers, wait and see!" (III, p. 5). Parritt, of course, makes several similar although milder claims in the final *Iceman*, but the number of these has been considerably reduced in order to show that political allegiances play only a small part in Larry's "sentencing" of the young man. A reference by Parritt to the Movement was even included in the cuts from the plate proof, and a few more were excised from the production second typescript.

Equally telling is the fact that O'Neill substantially expanded and edited Larry's long first-act explanation to Parritt about why he abandoned his political activity. The embryo of this speech appears in the scenario, where Larry reveals that he defected when he "came to realize men & women didn't want to be saved through Anarchism or anything else" (I, p. 1). In pages added to the manuscript as O'Neill rewrote the scene between the two former revolutionaries, he has Larry detail more fully the reasons for his loss of faith: his inability to continue viewing life through one ideology, and his disillusionment with his comrades as well as society at large. O'Neill himself felt a lifelong affection for the anarchists he had known in his younger days and some sympathy for their views. His interest led him to commence work on "The Visit of Malatesta," a comedy about anarchists that Virginia Floyd considers "an outgrowth of *The Iceman Cometh*."[95] Yet for all his evident interest in and sympathy with anarchism, O'Neill's plays—including *The Personal Equation*, with its band of futile revolutionaries, and *The Hairy Ape*, whose suspicious radicals spurn the confused Yank—betray his reservations about such movements. Whether or not Larry's thinking reflects the playwright's own, O'Neill put into the character's mouth a cogent exegesis of his motives for abandoning the "Great Cause." Larry Slade is surely not the cynic he pretends to be, but his soapbox and bomb days are over.

Don Parritt's mother, the link between Parritt and Larry and between both men and anarchism, is a very minor factor in the scenario; we are told that she and Larry were acquainted, but there is no indication in this draft that they were lovers. Except for Parritt's indefinite "I've always liked you Larry" (II, p. 6), we never learn why the young man particularly sought out Slade. A speech early in the manuscript is similarly vague. While noting that Larry was his mother's friend, Parritt recalls: "I didn't see much of you when you used to be in the Movement" (I, p. 12). O'Neill subsequently canceled these lines and introduced the bygone love affair, thus explaining why Parritt has chosen this particular confessor and also providing yet one more male-female relationship that has turned sour. Without Rosa, Larry would be the only major character in *Iceman* who did not have a troubled alliance with a woman sometime in the past. Once he had introduced the Larry-Rosa affair, however, O'Neill was careful to avoid according it undue weight, and the anarchist woman plays a slightly smaller role in the final play than she does in the manuscript and type-script. Most of O'Neill's changes with respect to Rosa are of two kinds, both of which have the same effect: to decrease emphasis on Larry's *present* attachment to her.[96] The one major alteration in the Larry-Rosa relationship that cannot be classified as a minimizing of his feelings is a clarification of what happened when they parted many years before. In a long passage deleted from the first typescript, Parritt tells Larry, "But I'll bet she wasn't faithful to you, either. That's why you finally walked out on her, isn't it? . . . [Her promiscuity] made home a lousy place. Hell, some-times I'd get to thinking it was like living in a whorehouse—only worse, because she wasn't making her living—" (II, p. 19). This was revised to include a final argument Parritt claims to have witnessed. The new pas-sage, which appears in the published text, reads:

> I remember that last fight you had with her. I was listening. I was on your side, even if she was my mother, because I liked you so much; you'd been so good to me—like a father. I remember her putting on her high-and-mighty free-woman stuff, saying you were still a slave to bourgeois morality and jealousy and you thought a woman you loved was a piece of private property you owned. I remember that you got mad and told her, "I don't like living with a whore, if that's what you mean!"   (p. 125)

Parritt is obviously projecting his own hostility toward his mother onto Larry: it is now the lover, not the son, who calls the woman a whore. Like Jim Tyrone in *Moon*, Parritt cannot bear to associate his mother with sexu-ality. But Larry's furious denial hints that Parritt remembers the incident accurately. Although this speech and Larry's response fail to clarify Larry's current attitude toward Rosa (he may still be angry over her infidelity, ashamed of his conventional reaction, or simply appalled at the young man's lack of respect for his mother), it does ally him in his younger days with the many O'Neill men who cannot tolerate anything less than complete loyalty—including sexual loyalty—in the women they love.

Most of the revisions involving Rosa concern Larry's present feelings. O'Neill deleted two passages in which Larry praises his former mistress. Curiously, most of one passage was added to and then cut from the first typescript.[97] In that speech Larry, recalling how he played games with and told stories to Parritt, says that he did not blame Rosa for neglecting her son because "she couldn't do her work and be a fond parent, too. She's a fine brave woman. I may have no use for the Movement, but I still respect the ones in it who've given it their lives and would die for it" (I, p. 11). Whatever O'Neill's reasons for wanting to include this speech—perhaps his own admiration for the anarchist friends of his youth—he apparently realized such a paean by Larry was out of character. Deleted from the typescript later in this same act was Larry's declaration that Rosa is "the one person in the Movement who's not dead to me—except poor Hugo, here. . . . (Moved) Your Mother's a grand, sincere, brave woman" (I, p. 16). In the final play Larry never admits to this kind of lingering fondness for his erstwhile mistress.

O'Neill also removed some instances in which Parritt bases his appeals for help on Larry's feelings about Rosa. For example, in a long manuscript passage Parritt taunts the older man and concludes: "Christ, imagine me hoping a guy like that would help me have the guts, for my mother's sake—." When Larry angrily threatens to sentence Parritt to living with his guilt, the terrified Parritt begs, "No, Larry! Jesus, no! You can't do that to me—and Mother! Not when you used to love her! Christ, haven't you any pity? I can't keep on!" (III, 2, p. 5). His plea is that a death sentence would not only relieve him but appease Rosa as well. This interchange was cut and the speech that replaces it was further altered in plate proof, where Parritt's charge that Larry would "like to forget Mother's in jail and might as well be dead" and his cry, "won't you help me for Mother's sake?" (p. 219) were deleted. Parritt still mentions his mother in this speech, noting that Larry "used to love her, too" (text, p. 219), but the emphasis is on the past rather than the present. In the published *Iceman*, especially as the play moves toward its climax, Parritt's appeals are usually based directly on his *own* need for help. Larry must ultimately respond to

Parritt's anguish, not to remembered loves, betrayals, or political allegiances.

Larry Slade's treatment of Don Parritt, which marks his permanent exodus from the "grandstand" of noninvolvement, is only the most salient evidence of his compassion for all the people around him. As the apostle of pity and forgiveness in the drama, he finds himself in opposition to the truth-seeking Hickey, yet it is interesting to note that both these characters undergo similar transformations as O'Neill develops *Iceman*. Just as Hickey becomes a more appealing character as he grows through the various drafts, so too Larry is shorn of certain negative (and sometimes bewildering) traits.

It is difficult to see exactly what O'Neill had in mind in his original conception of Larry, for stage directions in the early drafts attribute a menacing "diabolical" aspect to the aging philosopher. In the manuscript and typescript descriptions, his eyes possess "a contrasting gleam of sharp mockingly-diabolical irony in them" (TS, I, p. 1) rather than the "gleam of sharp sardonic humor" mentioned in the published text (p. 4). Similarly, numerous stage directions ask the actor playing Larry to show "mockingly diabolical irony" or a "strange diabolical grin" or to speak with a "comic diabolical whispered intensity." It is dangerous, of course, to take O'Neill's stage directions too literally. The "diabolical whisper" is sometimes modified to a "comically intense, crazy whisper," hardly a reflection on Larry's sanity. Presumably, O'Neill in early versions meant to suggest a less gentle Larry than finally appears. Defending Hope against Hickey in the typescript, Larry threatens the salesman: "Be God, for a plugged nickel I'd choke the stinking life out of you!" (III, p. 22). His actions and attitude, however, can scarcely be construed as diabolical. O'Neill had previously attributed "diabolical," "sinister," and "Mephistophelian" qualities to characters, notably to the masked Dion Anthony in *The Great God Brown* and Loving in *Days Without End*, and he would soon write *Long Day's Journey Into Night*, in which Jamie Tyrone's face has a "Mephistophelian cast."[98] What Larry shares with these figures is his cynicism, his professed disbelief that human beings are more than "a mixture of mud and manure" (text, p. 30). Yet Larry's cynicism, despite his more advanced age and experience, is far shallower than that of the villainous Loving or even that of Dion and Jamie. Larry uses his "sardonic laugh" to break up fights, not to start them, and his cynicism is only a façade over his genuine concern for the other inmates: he can apply it to people in general, but his pity shows through when he deals with individuals. As Jimmy notes, Larry is "the kindest man among us" (text, p. 44). The attribution of diabolical characteristics to Larry accordingly disappears completely in the first typescript.

Parritt in fact comes to Larry because the ex-anarchist was kind to him when he was a child. Travis Bogard notes that "Larry has stood in loco parentis to Parritt. Whether or not he is actually Parritt's father is deliberately left ambiguous. Slade denies it when Parritt suggests that he is, but with such vehemence as to raise the possibility."[99] Parritt himself admits that his mother said she did not meet Larry until after her son's birth. However, even this statement must be viewed skeptically, for Parritt may be agreeing with Larry's protestations simply to placate him. More important, before changes were made in plate proof it was clear that Larry is *not* Parritt's father, who died long ago. Added to the typescript and subsequently removed from the plate proof was Larry's explanation that Parritt's "father was dead, and his mother's time was taken up by her work for the Movement" (plate proof, p. 19).[100] Likewise, the speech in which Parritt concedes that Larry is not his father was longer in early versions. O'Neill canceled Parritt's admission, "Oh, I guess I knew, anyway, it was just a pipe dream about your being my father. I guess I just wanted to have one who was alive, and I liked you" (plate proof, p. 160). By doing so, he increased the pathos of Larry's predicament, for it might be his own son he is condemning. By removing the information that Parritt's real father is dead, O'Neill also hints that Larry is not simply the only person to whom Parritt could turn. Rather, he is the only person who has shown the young man attention and consideration.

Larry's dilemma and his essential selflessness are highlighted by many of O'Neill's revisions. One important change subtly affects Larry's characterization in several ways. Toward the end of Act III of the published text, Larry and Hickey have a confrontation in which the salesman urges Larry to face the truth about himself. "With increasing bitter intensity" Larry exclaims, "I'm afraid to live, am I?—and even more afraid to die!" He then proceeds to analyze his fears quite accurately, paradoxically concluding that Hickey cannot force him to acknowledge these terrors. He finishes by challenging Hickey: "You think you'll make me admit that to myself?" (pp. 196–97). The playwright told Lawrence Langner that this was one of his "favourite" speeches. After listening to a recording of himself reading the passage, O'Neill declared, "It wasn't Larry, it was my ghost talking to me, or I to my ghost,"[101] suggesting an identification between the playwright and his character that several critics have detected. This identification is reinforced by the fact that in some early versions of the speech Larry refers to the mythical Gorgons, also mentioned by Edmund in *Long Day's Journey*. Both characters share with their creator a simultaneous longing for and fear of the peaceful oblivion of death.

A rough version of Larry's speech appears in the second act of the scenario, during a general airing of grievances against Hickey, so O'Neill evidently had it in mind when he began writing *Iceman*. What puzzled O'Neill was where exactly to place this revelation. The manuscript first locates the passage in Act III, in a scene including Rocky, Parritt, and a few others but not Hickey. Although the speech is longer, more elaborate, and more caustic in this early rendering—replete with references to a "skull full of worms" and "eyes of maggots"—it is substantively similar to the final version. Rocky assumes that Larry is confessing his own feelings, while Larry insists that the views are Hickey's, not his (III, 1, pp. 7–7½). O'Neill then moved the speech to a spot very near the end of the act, after Harry Hope has returned from his abortive walk. Hickey is now, as he should be, both instigator and auditor of Larry's revelations. The salesman can chide Larry about his death fears: "but you just did admit it, didn't you?" (III, 1, p. 23). However, O'Neill was still displeased with the placement of this vital speech, and in the first typescript he moved it to its final resting place, the few minutes when Hope is outside trying to gather the nerve to cross the street.

Moving this confrontation between Larry and Hickey was partly motivated by structural demands. When it appears after Hope's walk, there is some confusion of issues, for Hickey must carry on his debate with Larry at the same time he is trying to assess the results of his "experiment" with the saloon owner. Moreover, by having the discussion take place while Hope is outside, O'Neill fills a dramatic gap on stage. A stage direction added to the typescript indicates that Rockey watches Hope's walk "as if it were a race he had a bet on" (text, p. 196), but this race-track atmosphere is more prominent in the scene as it was originally written. At one point Rocky even urges on his fading favorite, yelling: "Hey, yuh crazy old sap, keep movin'!" (MS, III, 1, p. 20). Because nothing is happening on stage at this time, attention is focused on Rocky's account of an action the audience cannot see.

Most important, by moving Larry's speech away from the end of the act, Larry's role as protector of Hope and the other men is emphasized. At the end of Act III Larry verbally attacks the salesman, demanding to know what has changed him: "What was it happened?" (text, p. 203). When Larry's question almost immediately follows Hickey's taunting of him, as it initially does in the typescript, it seems merely motivated by personal revenge. Shifting Hickey's unmasking of Larry to a point slightly earlier in the act makes the attack on Hickey seem less motivated by Larry's personal discomfort than by a wish to help Harry and the others. Larry is, in the published play, the only one who genuinely attempts to protect his fellow inmates from Hickey. In the typescript Rocky orders Hickey, "Aw, lay off Harry, you bastard!" when the salesman badgers Hope to go out (III, p. 21), but this was deleted and in the final *Iceman* it is Larry alone who comes to Hope's defense. Larry's antagonism to Hickey is, of course, partly a reaction to Hickey's attempts to make him face the painful facts about himself; he would like to give the salesman a dose of his own truth serum. Nevertheless, O'Neill's revisions show that Larry is also very disturbed by the misery Hickey's crusade is causing his friends.

The ending of *Iceman*, both in the published text and in the production, caused O'Neill even more trouble than Act III did. O'Neill's major problem was contrasting Hope and his gang's return to pipe dreams with the death of Parritt and the change in Larry. Giving sufficient attention to the old ex-anarchist apparently occupied the playwright most, for he rearranged events, pared speeches, and added revealing stage directions in an effort to distinguish Larry from the remaining characters. O'Neill succeeded in his aim in the published play, but he found possibly insuperable problems when he attempted to put Larry on the stage.

O'Neill's revisions of Hickey's exit scene begin the isolation of Larry. In the manuscript's second rendering of this scene, it is Larry who forces the salesman to concede that he was insane during his visit to the saloon. Larry "glares at Hickey with hatred" and taunts him into telling Hope and the other men what they want to hear (III, 2, p. 17½). In the light of his earlier actions, Larry is the logical defender of the gang, the final antagonist to Hickey. However, O'Neill took this speech away from Larry, thus underscoring the old man's growing alienation from the group as a whole and his increasing preoccupation with Parritt. The men can now take care of themselves; Parritt cannot. In the typescript, as he awaits Parritt's fall, Larry responds to Hugo's query about his mumbling by demanding: "Can't I say my prayers in peace without you disturbing me, you suspicious little anarchist?" (IV, p. 24). This was deleted, so that in the published *Iceman* Larry speaks to no one except Parritt once Hickey becomes absorbed in his confession (text, p. 227). After Parritt leaves, Larry never speaks to anyone at all: he does not answer the men's gibes and they are tipsily oblivious to his suffering. His final speeches are soliloquies, not intended for listeners and unheard by the others.

O'Neill as he wrote shortened the time between Parritt's departure and his suicide, and between the suicide and the final curtain. In the manuscript and typescript, Parritt's exit is followed by numerous speeches in which the characters recount their previous day's adventures and proclaim their instant recognition of Hickey's insanity. Some of this banter was trimmed from the first typescript; considerably more was excised from the plate proof. By far the largest change in the plate proof was O'Neill's canceling here more than forty lines of dialogue belonging to Hope, Mosher, Jimmy, Wetjoen, and others. O'Neill was not merely telescoping the time between Parritt's exit and the sound of his fall; he was minimizing the attention given to the gang as a whole in order to focus on the anguish with which Larry awaits Parritt's suicide. The production scripts show still more severe cutting as O'Neill chipped away irrelevant business that distracts the audience from Larry.

The playwright was even more concerned that Parritt's death and Larry's benediction come as close as possible to the end of *Iceman*. In the manuscript, Parritt dies a few minutes earlier than he does in the published text. The heavily edited manuscript version places Margie and Pearl in the doorway before Parritt's fall, but they do not actually come on stage until *after* his suicide and Larry's blessing. Thus attention is turned sharply away from Larry while the tarts negotiate their reconciliation with Rocky. To prevent this, O'Neill moved Parritt's jump until just after the whores' entrance. The production scripts do not mention the whores' reappearance at all, although Tom Pedi, who originated the role of Rocky, recalls that "the tarts [did] return and resume their career."[102]

Larry's response to Parritt's fatal leap was also carefully delineated. The scenario shows Larry virtually unaffected by the young man's death: he resumes drinking with his pals and repeats his claim that death holds no terror for philosophers like himself. At the conclusion of the scenario

Larry is "out," asleep in an alcoholic stupor. In the manuscript Larry reacts by rising slowly from his seat. "His hands clutch the edge of the table. His eyes are wide open and staring with pity and horror." As he whispers "Poor bastard!" the stage directions note that "a long-forgotten faith of his boyhood grips him and he raises his hand automatically and makes the sign of the cross." Then he mumbles, "God rest his soul in peace!" (III, 2, p. 24). However appropriate the gesture—Larry is Irish and presumably Catholic, as were both O'Neill and Terry Carlin—the playwright subsequently decided to delete it, thus making Larry's blessing a generalized religious expression of compassion by one human being for another.

O'Neill took such pains to highlight Larry's benediction because it contrasts sharply with the ironic religious allusions that fill the play. Some—like Harry's birthday party, with its echoes of the Last Supper—were added as O'Neill developed *Iceman*. Others, including Hugo's references to the biblical willow trees and the association of Parritt with Judas, were present as early as the scenario. Most notably, Hickey is the heir of his evangelical father. While Hickey's religious background is not mentioned in the scenario, the characters there frequently comment on his messianic style. Rocky complains that Hickey is "like a damned minister, preaching religion" (II, p. 5), and Parritt reports that the salesman exhorted him: "Brother, I can save you" (III, 1, p. 8). In the manuscript Hickey says he was raised by a minister uncle, but the uncle was changed to a father, making his relationship to the minister closer. The revivalist aspect of Hickey is slightly less prominent in the published *Iceman* than in the manuscript and typescript; one change was the removal of a hymn Hickey claims to have sung on his trek to the saloon. The hymn promises:

> On the other side of Jordan,
> Where the tree of Life is blooming
> In the green fields of Eden
> There is rest for the weary
> There is rest for the weary
> There is rest for you.
>
> (MS, I, p. 39)

This is surely a suitable song for one who feels he has finally found peace. "The other side of Jordan" also connotes a paradise of the dead, equally apposite for this literal and figurative murderer. Moreover, Eden is an illusory goal for people in this fallen world, a utopia of the past projected into the future, just like dreams of the aptly named Hope and his friends. Possibly O'Neill suppressed this hymn and a few other of Hickey's religious references because he felt they were redundant, or perhaps he feared offending his audience.[103] Whatever his reasons for these deletions, the revivalist aspect of Hickey still remains strong in the published text. And this aspect is important. Hickey does not have simply a preacher's language and mannerisms: he has the "saved" individual's fervent belief and desire to convert the unenlightened. When O'Neill cut the play for the first production, he removed Hickey's account of his father and his childhood as a preacher's son (text, p. 81). Some of the reviewers' confusion over the character of Hickey may be attributable to the absence of these important clues. This material was reinstated in the 1956 revival of *Iceman.* Reviewing the revival, Brooks Atkinson commented that "Jason Robards, Jr. plays Hickey, the catalyst in the narrative, like an evangelist. His unction, condescension and piety introduce an element of moral affectation that clarifies the perspective of the drama as a whole. His heartiness, his aura of good fellowship give the character of Hickey a feeling of evil mischief it did not have before."[104] Insofar as Robards portrayed a consciously and deliberately evil Hickey, he was going against the basic sincerity of the character that O'Neill tried to convey. Yet insofar as he enacted Hickey as a well-meaning but misguided preacher of a dangerous faith, he brought out an aspect that James Barton (the original Hickey) would have had difficulty realizing because of script changes made for the first production. Part of Hickey has the salesman's—and the evangelist's—sheer love of selling. Part of him genuinely believes in the salvation he preaches.

Two religious references by Hugo, one implicitly linking the Revolution and the Day of Judgment, were removed from the plate proof. But O'Neill left the more subtle connection between political revolution and religious salvation in Hugo's "The days grow hot, O Babylon! / 'Tis cool beneath thy willow trees."[105] These lines from Ferdinand Freiligrath's poem "Revolution" allude to Psalm 137. This psalm is a fitting epigraph to the play in its reference to the Jews' Babylonian captivity, for its subject is the memory of better times and the anticipation of a return to those happier days. In the mouth of the sodden and defeated Hugo, that religious belief becomes, like the hope of a true political revolution, merely another unrealizable pipe dream.

Set in the context of religious allusion, language, and symbolism, the blessing by Larry (whose face has "the quality of a pitying but weary old priest's") takes on added meaning. "God rest his soul in peace" (text, p. 258), which echoes Larry's rather profane benediction for Hickey, "May the Chair bring him peace at last, the poor tortured bastard!" (p. 247), is not an abstract promise of salvation but instead a simple expression of pity and the hope that one tormented individual will find release in death.

Larry's words and actions are the only ones in the play with religious connotations that do not turn out to be either ironic or specious. Cyrus Day is among those who see Hickey as a false Christ, and he is surely right.[106] Day partly bases his argument on his claim that Act II is a deliberate visual imitation of Leonardo Da Vinci's "Last Supper." Day did not know when he wrote his seminal essay that shortly after completing *Iceman*, O'Neill worked on a religious drama he never finished—"The Last Conquest"—which was to contain a reenactment of the Last Supper.[107] This fact lends credence to Day's theory that O'Neill had this event in mind when he composed Hope's birthday feast. Travis Bogard disputes Day's interpretation of Act II, insisting that O'Neill could not be copying Da Vinci's painting of the "Last Supper" because neither Hickey nor Hope is placed in the position given by the artist to Christ. Harry Hope, Bogard suggests, is an equally likely Christ-figure, because it is his party and he is the one "who rises from the death they suffer to bring life again to the bums."[108] What Day overlooks and Bogard mentions but does not pursue is that O'Neill specifically places Larry Slade "Near the middle of the row of chairs behind the table" (p. 94).[109] It is Larry who occupies the central place in O'Neill's Last Supper, the position Da Vinci assigned to Christ. It is also Larry who makes the Christ-like sacrifice of his own security to help another human being: his "Judas," Parritt.

Ironically, Larry's prayer follows the death of a young man whom he has himself condemned. Rolf Scheibler argues that Larry's sentencing of Parritt is an act of both "pity" and "revenge."[110] Robert C. Lee believes "Larry was impelled by hate, but it led to a compassionate act, and transformed even him, at least momentarily."[111] Scheibler is closer to the truth. Clearly something very different from "hate" is at work, for Larry has at least as much to lose by Parritt's death as the boy himself does. O'Neill continued trimming Parritt's dialogue even as late as the plate proof, perhaps to prevent the audience's thinking that Larry gets rid of the young man simply to escape his taunting. Parritt's remaining fourth-act speeches consist primarily of his begging to be sentenced to death. Added to the typescript was Parritt's plea, "I'd be glad of the Chair! It'd wipe it out! It'd square me with myself!" (text, p. 227). The manuscript, interestingly, has Larry suggesting suicide to Parritt near the *beginning* of Act III, scene 2 (the play's Act IV). When Parritt complains "I can't keep on!" an angry Larry retorts: "God damn you! If you go up to my room— it's the fourth floor back on this side above this window—and there's a fire escape—." Parritt rejects his hint, protesting: "No, you can't leave it all up to me—as if you didn't give a damn! Christ, can't you help me? I'm scared! ⟨I'm all shot!⟩ I can't make up my mind!" (III, 2, pp. 5–6). Apparently Parritt dismisses Larry's advice because it is a suggestion rather than a command. O'Neill might well have canceled this incident because it makes Parritt's later suicide anticlimactic, but there is another problem here as well. This confusing interchange could imply that Parritt really does not want to die. O'Neill's revisions, including the deletion of this conversation, underscore the young man's desire for a swift and final end to his suffering.

Larry is not only a father-figure for Parritt; he must be a stand-in for Rosa as well. In his final supplication, Parritt says he is incapable of making the decision himself because his mother has "always decided what . . . [he] must do" (p. 247). His reaction to the merciful sentence is to thank Larry twice, and his second expression of gratitude links the older man with the Christian savior: "Jesus, Larry, thanks" (p. 248). Larry, on the other hand, does not want to make such decisions. Lazarus in *Lazarus Laughed* regretfully allows his wife Miriam to eat the poisoned peach she covets, yet his anguish is lessened because he himself has no fear of death. In *Mourning Becomes Electra*, Lavinia lets her brother shoot himself at least partly because she hopes Orin's death will set her free from the family guilt. Larry does fear death, and he has little to gain from Parritt's suicide. His most prized pipe dream is that he is "in the grandstand," unconcerned with other people, and he fully realizes that his commitment to Parritt will destroy forever this sustaining belief. Lee is wrong when he asserts that Larry was compelled by hate and transformed afterward. The old philosopher knows full well that the price of his sending Parritt to the fire escape is the loss of his cherished illusion of neutrality. As he condemns Parritt, Larry's face is "convulsed with detestation" (text, p. 248). What Larry detests most is not the young man but the necessity of giving up his seat in the grandstand. Compassion rather than hatred is his guiding motive.[112] Had he truly hated Parritt, Larry would have sentenced him to the ultimate O'Neill punishment: a life of guilt without hope of parole.

O'Neill's final problem was how to convey the sincerity of Larry's conversion while also showing the others' return to their pipe dreams. Larry's last speech in the manuscript and typescript is ambiguous. In the typescript his speech concludes:

> Be God, there's no hope for me! I'll never be a success at life! I'll be looking double at the two sides of everything till the day I die! And may that day come soon! (*He pauses almost startledly—then with a sardonic wry grin*) Be God, I'm the only real convert Hickey made here. From the bottom of my coward's heart I mean that now!   (IV, p. 29)

Although Larry does now admit he is a failure, it is not clear what he means by "life." Moreover, there is little to separate Larry's wish to die from, for example, the "sincerity" of McGloin's renewed claim that he didn't go to the police chief simply because "it ain't the right time" for reinstatement (text, p. 253). Throughout the play Larry has been insisting that he craves death.

In the published text the end of Larry's concluding speech has been altered:

> Be God, there's no hope! I'll never be a success in the grandstand—or anywhere else! Life is too much for me! I'll be a weak fool looking with pity at the two sides of everything till the day I die! (*With an intense bitter sincerity*) May that day come soon! (*He pauses startledly, surprised at himself—then with a sardonic grin*) Be God, I'm the only real convert to death Hickey made here. From the bottom of my coward's heart I mean that now!
>   (p. 258)

Nearly all the alteration was done in the first typescript; "to death" was added in plate proof. Changing "life" to the more specific "grandstand" and adding "pity" emphasize Larry's realization that he can no longer feign indifference to others. The insertion of "to death" and the crucial stage direction "With an intense bitter sincerity" prove that Larry has indeed been converted to a longing for oblivion. Without his pipe dream of neutrality, death really does hold all the appeal he once only pretended it did. In *Long Day's Journey Into Night*, Edmund Tyrone quotes Nietzsche: "God is dead: of His pity for man hath God died." While the symbolically named Slade ("slayed") is still alive, pity for man has destroyed his will to live, although not his fear of death.

At the end of *Iceman*, Larry sits by himself staring straight ahead. His separation from the others is both visual and aural: he sits alone at a different table; he is quiet while the others talk, sing, and drink. The silence itself is a potent clue to Larry's change. O'Neill's characters, especially in his late plays, are constant (often compulsive) talkers; stillness is usually a sign that something is amiss. Yet silence is also much less dramatically striking than noise, and there is the danger that Larry will be overlooked by the audience. Further, the important stage direction, "With an intense bitter sincerity," is a fine hint to the reader but extraordinarily difficult for an actor to convey in the midst of all the false sincerity being exuded around him.

O'Neill was well aware of the difficulty he faced in staging the conclusion of *Iceman*. When Kenneth Macgowan apparently questioned the necessity of having the gang repeat their pipe dreams at the end, O'Neill replied:

> Each character tells his face-saving version of his experience when he went out to confront his pipe dream. *I* don't write this as a piece of playwrighting. *They do it. They have to.* Each of them! In just that way! It is tragically, pitifully important to them to do this! They *must* tell these lies as a first step in taking up life again. Moreover, their going through with this pathetic formula heightens by contrast the tension of Larry's waiting for the sound of Parritt hurtling down to the backyard, and the agony he goes through. If our American acting and directing cannot hold this scene up without skimping it, then to hell with our theatre! You know as well as I that the direction and acting of the old Moscow Art Theatre, or Kamerny, could sustain the horrible contrast and tension of this episode and make it one of the most terrible scenes in the play, as it is to me now.[113]

Evidently by the time O'Neill was ready to permit a production he was convinced that an American cast could not succeed with this ending, for he modified it considerably. The characters' face-saving speeches were, as already noted, drastically cut—and most of these deletions were made before rehearsals began.

Exactly how *The Iceman Cometh* ended in the original production is unclear, although the conclusion obviously differed from the conclusion in the printed text. Several of the scripts from the first production have the following business after Larry's last speech:

> HOPE Hey, there, Larry. Have a drink. Come and get paralyzed. (Then as
>   LARRY doesn't reply, HOPE immediately forgets him and turns to the party.
>   They are all very drunk now, just a few drinks ahead of the passing-out
>   stage and hilariously happy about it) Bejesus, I'm oary-eyed. I want to

sing! (There are loud shouts of approbation, back-slapping, gay laughter in the crowd, as WILLIE OBAN starts his Sailor Lad ditty, they all join in)

[two stanzas of Willie's song follow as the curtain comes down] (IV, p. 31)

This is potentially a somewhat quieter ending than that in the printed text, where each character drunkenly shouts a different song before joining in a jeering chorus of Hugo's "willow trees" chant, but it is still boisterous. Larry would very likely be drowned in the yells and laughter. Moreover, Willie's Sailor Lad ditty is a less fitting epigraph than Hugo's " 'Tis cool beneath thy willow trees" line, with its political and religious implications.

The final promptbook in the New York Public Library is identical to these scripts except for the last page. This page, clearly an addition, reinstates the ending found in the stage manager's prompt script at Yale. Here O'Neill has rearranged a few lines and interpolated two additional ones into the dialogue just before the conclusion. Instead of ignoring Hope's invitation to imbibe, as he does in the published text, Larry replies: "To hell with your drink. I couldn't get drunk now." Apparently afraid that the audience would not realize how Larry differs from the other characters, the playwright added a clue. Drink and dreams have been linked throughout the play; when the men were forced to face the truth about themselves, they couldn't get drunk. O'Neill now calls upon this association to show that Larry has indeed been converted to Hickey's brand of "honesty." While the others tipple happily, Larry states what his actions already show: he alone can no longer hide in a bottle.

The very end of this version is almost the same as the conclusion of the printed version except that, along with the shouts and laughter, only "The Sunshine of Paradise Alley" and Willie's song compete with "La Carmagnole." The singing and yelling, however, were either very subdued or omitted altogether. In his opening night review, George Jean Nathan complained: "The play's ending, which presently goes a little flat, might also, as Dowling wished, have been inspirited if, as counterpoint to Slade's final 'Be God, I'm the only real convert to death Hickey made here; from the bottom of my coward's heart I mean that now!,' the drunken singing and wild pounding on the table by the assembled, happily unredeemed bibuli had not been cut by the author and had been moved a bit forward from its place in the original script."[114] Barrett Clark claims that O'Neill told him "how he had had to change the business at the end of the play because few if any of the cast could sing," but this explanation seems specious: vocal harmony is scarcely needed here.[115] O'Neill more likely omitted the boys' drunken crooning in an attempt to further spotlight Larry's speech. Unfortunately, as Nathan noted, this destroyed the crucial contrast between Larry's silence and the others' raucous celebration.

Although there is no such indication in the available scripts, the reviews suggest that O'Neill went even a step further in his attempts to focus on Larry. Several critics contended that Larry, like Parritt, is converted to suicide. This would seem to be merely a misunderstanding, yet more than a few reviewers also claimed that Larry left the stage at the end, presumably to follow his young friend. Arthur Pollock of the *Brooklyn Eagle* reported that Larry, "deciding finally that life is too much for him, goes out to kill himself."[116] Joseph T. Shipley of the *New Leader* was more specific: "While in the book, 'in his chair by the window, Larry stares in front of him, oblivious to their racket,' on the stage Larry turns from the relieved drinkers, and begins the suicide's march through the door toward the waiting window."[117] Afraid that simple aural and visual separation would not illustrate Larry's metamorphosis, O'Neill presumably tried to convey this by having Larry walk, or start to walk, off stage. (It is unlikely that the director, Eddie Dowling, would have made such a change on his own, for O'Neill was deeply involved in rehearsals and Nathan's comments indicate that the playwright had his way when he differed with the director.) Obviously this did not solve his problem but instead muddied a vital point: Larry must *live* with the pain of his pity for humanity.

Judging by the reviews, O'Neill's revisions did not succeed in gaining Larry Slade the attention he merits. Many critics failed to single out Larry, and many more misunderstood the points O'Neill was desperately trying to make. The difficulty does not lie solely in the final moments of the drama.[118] O'Neill considered Larry an important, perhaps the most important, character in *Iceman*. He made changes in dialogue and stage directions to emphasize the nature of the aging philosopher's situation and the implications of his commitment to Parritt. But on the stage it is difficult for the actor playing Larry to compete for audience attention with the far more flamboyant Hickey, and even with Hope. Larry is the only genuinely tragic figure in this complex dramatic work, yet he is also less histrionic than many of the others. Compassion and understanding, Larry's primary attributes, are not always theatrically arresting qualities—a dilemma O'Neill would face again with Edmund Tyrone in *Long Day's Journey Into Night*.

CHAPTER TWO

Long Day's Journey Into Night

IN THE FINAL ACT of the scenario of *Long Day's Journey Into Night*, Mary Tyrone tells her younger son that it is futile to remind her of his illness. "You can't make me remember," she says, "except from outside, like a stranger—audience at a play."[1] Morphine is the anodyne Mary Tyrone uses to remove herself from her painful memories. Eugene O'Neill's drug was time: it distanced him from the events of his past and thus enabled him to present them in dramatic form.

Commenting on a biographical sketch Barrett Clark had written about him in 1926, O'Neill noted that it "is legend. It isn't really true." He added that the truth would emerge only if he told his own story. "If," the playwright added, "I ever can muster the requisite interest—and nerve—simultaneously!"[2] He began to muster the interest only a few years later, but the nerve to complete the portrait was a long time in coming. Whether the resulting play is more truth than legend remains a moot point.

On March 8, 1927, O'Neill wrote in his Work Diary: "Worked doping out preliminary outline for 'The Sea-Mother's Son'—series of plays based on autobiographical material." While many of his earlier dramas had been obliquely autobiographical, he was now contemplating a more direct theatrical rendering of his life. The following year he informed Kenneth Macgowan:

> The grand opus of my life—the autobiographical "Sea-Mother's Son"—has been much in my dreams of late. If I can write that up to what the dreams call for it will make a work that I flatter myself will be one of those timeless Big Things. It has got me all "het up." It should be a piece of writing not like any that has ever been done before the way I plan it. My subtitle is to be "The Story of the Birth of a Soul"—and it will be just that![3]

The Work Diary "memoranda," summaries of time spent on each play, indicate that O'Neill worked three days in 1927 and two in 1928 on "Sea-Mother." Although O'Neill told various correspondents that "The Sea-Mother's Son" might encompass as many as nine or ten plays, he apparently did not get far with his ambitious scheme. The very brief outline he composed for the projected work concerns a forty-year-old man who surveys his life as he lies near death in a hospital. His survival "depends now on whether he wants to live or not." The "important episodes" of his life, "the influences that moulded him, are enacted before him—he is participator and spectator—interpreter." After witnessing these scenes, the man ultimately accepts his past, says "yes to his life," and renounces his "death wish."[4]

A letter to George Jean Nathan in November 1929 may well refer to this drama. Discussing the possibilities that the "talkies" open up for the stage, O'Neill added, "At any rate, my inspirations on this subject have had one practical result that I see the next play after the trilogy (an idea I set aside because I couldn't see how to do it) as a stage play combined with a screen talky background to make alive visually and vocally the memories, etc. in the minds of the characters."[5] O'Neill eventually abandoned "Sea-Mother's Son,"[6] yet the idea of writing a work centered on his life continued to intrigue him. Carlotta noted in her diary on August 11, 1936: "Gene tells me that when the Cycle is finished—he would like to write an *autobiography* in the form of *short stories*—." When O'Neill began *Long Day's Journey Into Night* a few years later, he chose the dramatic mode, and the technique he adopted was much simpler than the one proposed to Nathan. But the characters' memories did form the texture of the autobiographical *Journey;* the "sea" and "mother"—as both separate and related entities—remained major factors. Moreover, the later play included a man with a potentially fatal illness, a character who serves as "participator and spectator" and even "interpreter": Edmund Tyrone.

The principal source of *Journey* is, of course, O'Neill's personal experience. The major characters are given the first names of his immediate family members, O'Neill's own switched with that of his dead baby brother. Even the names of the minor characters seem deliberately chosen, for the second girl is dubbed "Cathleen," recalling O'Neill's first wife, Kathleen Jenkins, and the unseen cook Bridget bears the name of the playwright's maternal grandmother, who died before he was born but of whom he had surely heard.[7] The influence of at least one other figure

Notes for *Long Day's Journey Into Night*. (Collection of American Literature, Beinecke Rare Book and Manuscript Library, Yale University.)

from O'Neill's life may also be detected in *Journey*. Florence Eldridge, who originated Mary Tyrone on the American stage, recalls:

> José Quintero was particularly anxious for me to meet Carlotta O'Neill as he felt that O'Neill had woven a bit of her into the character of his mother. The director arranged for us to have lunch, and I could find such echoes of Mary Tyrone's speeches in Carlotta's love-hate anecdotes. She would start to reminisce so sweetly and suddenly repressed resentment would burst through into bitter complaints or self pity just as Mary Tyrone does repeatedly when she is reviewing the past with James Tyrone.[8]

Carlotta's diary reveals the same mixture of loving appreciation and angry reproach that Eldridge perceived in her meeting with the playwright's widow. Interestingly, Carlotta's diary also records that O'Neill wanted her to return to acting to play Deborah Harford in *A Touch of the Poet*.[9] Deborah is only a minor role in *Poet*, but in *More Stately Mansions* she becomes a central character who, alternating between maternal overprotectiveness and withdrawal into a private fantasy world, strikingly resembles Mary Tyrone.

Specific themes and ideas, as well as characters and events, came out of O'Neill's own life. To give merely one example, James Tyrone's moving speech in the fourth act, in which he tells how he ruined his chances to be a great actor, echoes exactly sentiments O'Neill attributed to his own father in a letter written in 1920. When the producer George Tyler asked the younger O'Neill to write an adaptation of his father's famous *Monte Cristo*, the playwright seriously considered the plan yet finally informed Tyler:

> My direst grudge against Monte Cristo is that, in my opinion, it wrecked my father's chance to become one of our greatest actors. Since he did not mince this matter himself but confessed it to me during our very close "palship" last winter, I feel free to state it. Monte Cristo, he often said with great bitterness as he lived over his past out loud to me, had been his curse. He had fallen for the lure of easy popularity and easy money— . . . How keenly he felt this in the last years, I think I am the only one who knows, the only one he confided in.[10]

O'Neill never made the adaptation.

It is probably to *Journey*'s disadvantage that its biographical roots are so well known. Critics have tended to spend too much time discussing how

Act One

Act I, page 24 of the manuscript of *Long Day's Journey Into Night*.
(Collection of American Literature, Beinecke Rare Book and
Manuscript Library, Yale University.)

the drama does (or does not) square with the facts of O'Neill's life and condemning historical inaccuracies. In his influential book *Contour in Time*, Travis Bogard is willing to grant O'Neill poetic license in the various "self-portraits" he finds in the playwright's earlier plays, but even so fine a critic as Bogard balks at allowing O'Neill this kind of freedom in *Journey*. Bogard argues that "Edmund is more than an imaginary figure. He is a figure from history and one upon whose truth-to-life an audience has a right to insist."[11] This is patently unjust. Few complain because Shakespeare's kings are compounded of the author's imagination and historical fact. Matthew W. Black notes in his introduction to *Richard II* that "as usual, . . . [Shakespeare] altered history for dramatic effect."[12] *Journey* is as much a work of art as *Richard II* or *Strange Interlude*, and O'Neill is free to manipulate characters and events to achieve his thematic and aesthetic aims. While it is certainly a valid question whether Edmund is a fully developed, dramatically convincing character, O'Neill is not obligated to make him a biographically exact copy of anyone. Bogard himself, in an essay written a few years after *Contour in Time*, warns against demanding biographical precision from a dramatic work: "It is not accurate to assume as some do that *Ah, Wilderness!* is a comic treatment of that reality which *Long Day's Journey Into Night* faithfully depicts. Both plays stem from reality, but neither presents it faithfully. Art never holds a mirror up to nature. It edits, distorts, shapes so that the dramatist's sense of what the experience meant or could have meant can be discerned."[13] Bogard's admonition echoes comments that O'Neill made about manipulating history in the interest of artistic truth. Writing to Kenneth Macgowan about his work on *The Fountain*, O'Neill averred that his Juan Ponce de Leon would be a composite figure based on several different Spanish explorers. He added: "And I am afraid too many facts might obstruct what vision I have and narrow me into an historical play of spotless integrity but no spiritual significance. Facts are facts, but the truth is beyond and outside them."[14]

Actually, O'Neill was surprisingly faithful to many historical details in *Journey*, and his work on this drama does not always show a direct progression from biographical accuracy to artistic fiction. His choice of names provides one example. He did not, as with *Iceman*, begin by using "real" names and then move to fictional ones. The earliest notes and the scenario refer simply to Mother, Father, Elder Son, and Younger Son.[15] O'Neill tried various different first names for the characters, even giving the first names eventually used in the play to different figures. In a few

places he named the father and older son Edmund,[16] he considered calling the mother Stella, and at one point he designated the younger son
Hugh. Further, O'Neill once dubbed the *younger* son Jamie. While none
of this name-changing is significant in terms of the play itself, those who
(justifiably) see a death wish in O'Neill's choice of his dead brother's name
for the autobiographical character[17] might well ponder the psychological
implications of his contemplating that name for the characters based on
his father and surviving brother. Equally provocative is his identifying
with his brother Jamie to the point of considering his name for the character modeled not on Jamie but on himself.

More important to *Journey* is the fact that O'Neill seems to have felt
compelled to keep the play accurate in terms of specific chronology. He
had no qualms about placing Edmund's bout of tuberculosis in the summer rather than the fall of 1912 (when his own occurred), keeping Mary
Tyrone's father alive longer than Ella Quinlan O'Neill's father survived, or
postponing the first meeting between the matinee idol and the convent
girl, but he consistently changed dates and ages mentioned in the play to
accord with biographical facts.[18] In the *Journey* typescript O'Neill altered
the age at which James Tyrone received Booth's praise from "just turned
thirty" (IV, p. 18) to "only twenty-seven years old," the age at which his
father received such praise.[19] He also removed from the typescript the
claim that this accolade was conferred the "year after" Tyrone was married
and substituted the date 1874—the actual date, three years before his
marriage, on which James O'Neill was complimented by Booth.

Similarly, while in the scenario Jamie says he was not yet "four [?] years
old at the time" he gave his baby brother measles (IV, p. 4), this was
changed in succeeding versions to make Jamie seven, approximately the
age at which Jamie O'Neill infected his sibling.[20] In this case the age
change does have an effect on the drama, for a seven-year-old is more
likely to understand the danger of exposure than is a child two or three
years younger. The alteration in age makes Jamie Tyrone seem more
culpable. However, other revisions make him appear *less* guilty of his
brother's death. In the manuscript, Jamie's fourth-act confession includes
the admission that he deliberately infected his infant brother out of jealousy, an admission that never appears in the published play. Although
Jamie Tyrone's responsibility for his brother's death remains ambiguous,
the conflicting changes suggest that O'Neill, in altering Jamie's age, ad-
hered to biographical accuracy at the expense of his thematic aims.

Like *Iceman, Journey* has its roots in O'Neill's earlier work as well as in his life. While there is no direct antecedent, as the short story "Tomorrow" was for *Iceman,* nearly all the plays contain themes or characters related to those in *Journey.* So many critical comparisons between *Journey* and the rest of the O'Neill canon already exist that further general discussions would be repetitive,[21] but a few connections may be noted. Edmund's sea speech, although prose, is linguistically and thematically akin to the poetry O'Neill composed in his early years. The sea appears in more than a dozen of these poems, including a free verse piece that exults: "I am one with the great restless spirit of sea and sun and / sky and wind. I am part of the Great Purpose. I am Life— / triumphant, unafraid, moving ever onward."[22] Another poem finds the speaker lamenting, "I am only a seagull / Dolefully squawking / When it would sing"[23]—a combination of Edmund's yearning to be a sea creature ("I would have been much more successful as a sea gull or a fish") and his fears about his artistic powers. If O'Neill's intention in Edmund's sea speech was to duplicate his own youthful work, the intention was fulfilled.

The fog that returns to enshroud the Tyrone family is central in several of the short sea plays as well as in later works like *Anna Christie.* Baby Eugene is just one in a line of dead infants that figure in such diverse dramas as *Before Breakfast, The First Man, All God's Chillun Got Wings,* and *Desire Under the Elms.* Even so minor a play as *Warnings,* completed in 1914, bears seeds of the tragedy to come. Here Mary Knapp (wife to James) shares Mary Tyrone's dislike for the medical profession. Both Marys refuse to believe a doctor's diagnosis of a serious illness and claim that physicians exaggerate patients' problems in order to keep them coming back. Nina's reverie in the much later *Strange Interlude*—"we can talk together of the old days . . . when I was a girl . . . when I was happy . . . before I fell in love with Gordon Shaw and all this tangled mess of love and hate and pain and birth began!"—could, with a change of names, have come from Mary Tyrone.[24] Mary's desire to pray and to be reconciled with the Church also have antecedents in O'Neill's previous work. One inspiration may have been Coleridge's "The Rime of the Ancient Mariner," which O'Neill adapted for the stage in 1923. "If I could only find the faith I lost, so I could pray again!" Mary yearns, but her plea is cut short by the demon of self-loathing: "You expect the Blessed Virgin to be fooled by a lying dope fiend reciting words!" (p. 107). Her dilemma strikingly recalls that of the distraught Mariner:

> I look'd to Heaven, and tried to pray;
> But or ever a prayer had gusht,
> A wicked whisper came, and made
> My heart as dry as dust

Nora Melody in *A Touch of the Poet* also longs to confess her sins. The typescript of *More Stately Mansions*, *Poet's* sequel, reveals that Nora eventually finds peace in a convent—a boon denied Mary Tyrone.[25]

All God's Chillun Got Wings, the tale of another mismatched couple, and *Ah, Wilderness!*, sunny mirror-image to the bleak *Journey*, are most commonly linked to the autobiographical drama. *Wilderness* and *Journey* share both setting and characters, the naive Richard Miller aged into the less innocent Edmund Tyrone. Bogard persuasively argues that the comedy partly gains its lightness from the splitting of characters.[26] By making the parents in *Ah, Wilderness!* overwhelmingly positive and assigning less appealing traits to an aunt and uncle, O'Neill avoids the complex relationships and concentrated tension that breed *Journey's* tragedy. Still another connection between the two plays are the notes O'Neill wrote for a sequel to *Wilderness* that would have been, in tone if not in plot, far closer to *Journey* than to the nostalgic comedy. These notes describe a family ravaged by World War One and changing times, the mother dead and the "bewildered" father alienated from his children. Young Richard was to return from battle "maimed, embittered, [his] idealism murdered."[27]

On June 6, 1939, O'Neill reviewed his "notes on various ideas for single plays." According to the Work Diary, he was attracted to the "N[ew]. L[ondon]. family one." He turned first, however, to composing a scenario for *Iceman*, which occupied the following few weeks. The next mention of *Journey* appears in Carlotta's diary on June 21:

> Gene talks to me for hours about a play (in his mind) of his Mother, his Father, his brother and himself (in his early 20's) in New London—! (Autobiography)
>
> A hot, close, sleepless night—
>
> An ache in our hearts for things we can't escape![28]

O'Neill's Work Diary shows that he began notes for the play on June 25, started the scenario the next day, and completed this roughly six-page outline on an appropriately foggy July 3.[29]

In early October O'Neill informed Nathan that after *Iceman* was finished he would either resume work on the "Tale of Possessors Self-Dispossessed" cycle or go on to "a second separate play." He continued, "I have a fine idea for one that is much on my mind. But it's no good prophecying now. It all depends how the spirit moves then."[30] The "fine idea" was almost certainly *Journey*. On January 5, 1940, two days after completing *Iceman*, O'Neill wrote in his Diary: "The Long Days Journey (read outline—want to do this soon—will have to be written in blood—but will be a great play, if done right.)." O'Neill was apparently reluctant to begin the bloodletting; he tinkered with the cycle for several weeks. Late February and early March found him working intermittently on *Journey* notes and on notes for his never-completed comedy "The Visit of Malatesta" while struggling with low blood pressure attacks. He began dialogue for the manuscript on March 21 and finished the first draft of Act I on April 30. In mid-June he told Nathan: "Haven't been able to write a line for the past couple of months." He gave a brief account of *Journey* and added, "I finished the first draft of Act One (five acts in it) and then got physically washed up."[31] Diary entries bear this out and also show he was very troubled by the war. Late in June he looked over the first act and was "deeply held by it."[32] July found him back at work; with more aptness than taste, he wrote Lawrence Langner that "I'm working again on something—not the Cycle—after a lapse of several months spent with an ear glued to the radio for war news. You can't keep a hop head off his dope for long!"[33] O'Neill briefly interrupted work on *Journey* to toy with ideas for a few other plays but completed the manuscript on September 20. Nearly four weeks were spent revising this draft. Contrary to his usual practice, he made substantial additions during revision: the first act grew from twenty-two pages to twenty-eight.[34]

O'Neill occupied the next months laboring on the "Possessors" cycle, on outlines for a series of short plays entitled "By Way of Obit," and on random notes for other works, including "Blind Alley Guy," "Time Grandfather Was Dead," the "Malatesta" comedy, and "The 13th Apostle" (later renamed "The Last Conquest").[35] It was not until March 17 that he returned to the *Journey* typescript Carlotta had prepared from the revised manuscript. Typescript editing went swiftly, a pleased O'Neill noting in his Diary on March 30: "like this play better than any I have ever written—does most with the least—a quiet play!—and a great one, I believe." After "checking dates, quotes in play, etc.," O'Neill completed *Long Day's Journey Into Night* on April 1, 1941.[36] Although he did considerable cutting and revising on the typescript, the amount of editing is slightly less than that done on comparable drafts of *Iceman* and *A Moon for the Misbegotten*. O'Neill's revisions at this stage were the last substantive changes he made in the play.[37] Only a few minor corrections, mostly of typographical errors, appear on the second typescript, which Carlotta finished in mid-May.

According to the Gelbs, Carlotta stated, "I typed this play twice, because he went over it a lot. I wept most of the time, it upset me so."[38] Perhaps because she was so disturbed by *Journey,* Carlotta's typing is even less accurate on these scripts than on the first typescript of *Iceman*. Most of the inadvertent mistakes were caught later by Carlotta or O'Neill, but there is one fairly significant error that was never corrected. At the end of the second act Edmund and Mary have a painful confrontation in which he realizes that his mother will neither fight her addiction nor admit the gravity of his illness. At the conclusion of their discussion the other Tyrone men come down the stairs and summon Edmund to leave with them. Tyrone and Jamie each call a goodbye to Mary from the hall, but Edmund, in the published play, does not say goodbye and exits silently. His wordless departure is noticeable and suggests that he is too disappointed in his mother even to wish her farewell. However, in the first typescript there are lines for Edmund:

> EDMUND (jumps up from his chair, calling) I'm coming. (He stops beside her—without looking at her) Goodbye, Mother. (II, 2, p. 16)[39]

This speech is *not* marked for deletion. It disappeared between the first and second typescripts, perhaps because Carlotta was confused by the proliferation of "goodbyes." Whether the usually careful O'Neill missed this omission when he proofread the script, or whether he noticed it but chose to leave out the lines, the passage does not appear in the printed text.

O'Neill presented the manuscript of *Journey,* with its inscription, to Carlotta on July 22, 1941. Early the following year Saxe Commins, while visiting the O'Neills at their home in California, typed four fresh copies of the play. In outline at least, the rest of the *Journey* story is well known: O'Neill placed the play with Random House in 1945 with instructions that it remain sealed until twenty-five years after his death, at which point it could be published. According to some accounts,[40] the playwright stipulated that *Journey* should never be produced. Carlotta removed the script from Random House in 1956 and permitted it to be published by Yale University and performed by Stockholm's Royal Dramatic Theatre.

Shortly thereafter she allowed José Quintero, whose revival of *Iceman* had been a stunning success, to direct the American premiere.[41] When Carlotta released *Journey*, she maintained that her husband had suppressed the play at the request of his son Eugene O'Neill, Jr.[42] Her claim is obliquely supported by the fact that one page of *Journey* notes includes calculations for the running times of each act and of the play as a whole. Perhaps O'Neill worried that directors of posthumous productions would abridge the drama if it ran too long, but the calculations more likely suggest that he initially contemplated being involved in a production. O'Neill might have changed his plans at his son's behest.

On the other hand, O'Neill himself expressed reticence about *Journey* in letters to his friends. As early as January 1941 he wrote Nathan: "There are good reasons in the play itself why I'm keeping this one very much to myself, as you will appreciate when you read it. It isn't a case of secrecy about a new play merely for this or that practical reason, as with 'The Iceman Cometh.'"[43] The following month he informed Nathan, "I'm not even having it copyrighted so it won't be on record anywhere."[44] Although Eugene, Jr., had probably heard about the play before this time,[45] he had not yet read a full draft. It was nearly seven months later, September 4, that O'Neill noted in the Work Diary: "E[ugene]. reads 'L[ong]. D[ay's]. J[ourney]. I[nto]. N[ight].'—greatly moved, which pleases me a lot." Saxe Commins insists that Eugene, Jr., never mentioned to him any reservations about a *Journey* production, and Louis Sheaffer points out that "In 1951, nearly a year after his elder son's suicide," O'Neill renewed his request that Random House keep *Journey* sealed until twenty-five years after his death.[46] While O'Neill may well, as Carlotta insisted, have considered publishing the play in his last years, it is doubtful that his earlier decision to withhold it was solely (if at all) motivated by a promise to his son. The dramatist had his own reasons for suppressing the deeply personal *Journey*.

DESPITE *JOURNEY'S* AUTOBIOGRAPHICAL NATURE, which virtually precluded the need for historical research, the extant notes for this drama are more numerous and varied than those for *Iceman*. Some preceded the scenario, some were written between the scenario and the first draft, and some undated "notes for revision" were jotted down later.[47] These notes include possible surnames for the characters (several of them Irish place names), drawings of the set, quotations used in the play, lists of important themes, scraps of dialogue, and calculations of characters' ages.

One interesting note, entitled "shifting alliances in battle," shows the various "sides" the characters take at different times: "Father, two sons versus Mother," "Father, younger son vs. Mother, older son," etc. O'Neill carried through this military motif, the family as battleground, in two of his proposed titles: "The Long Day's Insurrection" and "The Long Day's Retreat." Other potential titles scribbled on note and scenario pages include "What's Long Forgotten" and "What's [?] Long Unforgotten" which emphasize the salience of the past in the play as well as O'Neill's personal relationship to the material, and "Diary of A Day's Journey."[48] The last two words of the title do not appear until the manuscript. The scenario is entitled "A Long Day's Journey" with *The* written in above the article; O'Neill solved that dilemma by dropping the article altogether. The earliest Work Diary entries refer simply to the "N. L. play," the initials standing for New London, where O'Neill's family had their summer home.

One note, a description of a wedding gown, is in Carlotta's handwriting. It is entirely possible that Carlotta knew more about such things than did her husband and provided the account which he adapted as Mary Tyrone's description of her gown. In the manuscript the description is written in unusually tiny letters, as if a too-small space had been left for the passage, which was inserted later. Curiously, Carlotta's note is written in the first person, in dialogue form. It ends with the query, "I wonder did you even notice any of this?" Several phrases from the note were transferred directly to the play, and even where Mary Tyrone's wedding-gown speech is worded differently from the note, the details of the gown are identical. Carlotta may merely have been writing from O'Neill's dictation, but it is conceivable that she was trying her own hand at dialogue, and that the playwright used a few of her lines. Another note, dated February 22, 1940, is entitled "Weather Progression" and charts the gradual appearance of the fog, which O'Neill almost completely neglected in the scenario he had written eight months earlier. While this note outlines Mary's growing acceptance of the fog (by the last act she "exults in it—it is in her"), it does not mention that Edmund too prizes the fog's protectiveness. O'Neill considered having Mary take a late-night stroll—"she has taken walk, coat over nightdress?"—but in the published text Edmund is the one who wanders through the nocturnal haze beyond the windows. Wrapped in her morphine fog and trapped in the family home, Mary lacks her younger son's freedom to roam.

The scenario includes all the themes and characters that appear in the published *Journey*. The scenario's five acts correspond roughly to the final play's four acts; O'Neill merely combined the second and third into one act of two scenes. The crucial last act received most attention: while Act I is skimpily rendered on half a page, the last act almost completely covers two sheets. Moreover, the scenario tends to have the stage directions or the characters baldly state points that are more subtly, and more powerfully, conveyed indirectly in later drafts. Near the end of the scenario, for example, Mary laments, "if I could have foreseen I would have cut my heart out rather than loved—love is so horrible" (V, p. 6). Certainly this idea is conveyed in the play—their situation is so painful because they are bound together by affection, and when they betray each other they are betraying loved ones—yet without the melodrama of such a declaration. At times a character's words seem less like dialogue than like commentary on the play itself, as when Mary muses: "And it comes to this, we four together here now—all that we are—from love—we are so alone—we are everything to each other—even hate" (IV, p. 4).[49] The word *love* is more common in the scenario than in the published text not because the characters display more love in this version but because the final drama shows how very difficult it is for the Tyrones to express their deepest feelings. Similarly, the word *morphine* appears more often in the scenario (and the manuscript and typescript) than in the printed text, where it is uttered only three times. The Tyrones' reluctance to name the drug that has enslaved Mary is mute testimony to their horror and disappointment.[50] O'Neill is often (sometimes justifiably) accused of hitting his audiences over the head with his themes, but his revisions show that he knew which statements belonged in a character's mouth and which were more effectively conveyed through the cumulative effect of the drama as a whole. Most important, the *Journey* scenario—like the *Iceman* scenario—lacks dramatic focus; there is little of the building tension that makes the finished play so powerful. This lack of tension has a twofold cause: the grimness of the scenario's opening act and the weakness of its final act, which is largely spent in repetition of recriminations made earlier.

  Iceman, Journey, and *A Moon for the Misbegotten* all begin in a state of relative calm and move into tragedy. The dramas' power partly arises from the contrast between the opening humor and the later gloom. This contrast is absent from the *Journey* scenario, its first act lacking much of the joking and affectionate teasing that leaven the first minutes of the published text. One way O'Neill lightened the opening scene was by inserting the Shaughnessy story at this point. The only scenario reference to the story is in the third act, when James says he has business uptown. The scenario reads: "complaint Harkness about Dolan—pigs in his ice pond" (III, p. 3).[51] The Younger Son makes a reference to "dirty Standard Oil money," but there is no indication that anyone tells the tale in full, or that its humorous aspects are appreciated. The Shaughnessy story is suspiciously clean in the manuscript, suggesting that it was added during revision. Support for this assumption lies in lines deleted from the manuscript's fourth act. Returning from his walk, Edmund tells Tyrone that he has met the "tenant on that farm of yours where the principal crops are weeds and rocks" (IV, p. 7). Shaughnessy, he adds, has bought a drink—an unprecedented occurrence. The rest of Edmund's story is missing (apparently a page was removed) but on the top of the next extant sheet Tyrone complains, "A fine son you are to help that scoundrel get me into trouble!" (IV, p. 8). Evidently O'Neill placed the Shaughnessy story here when he first wrote the manuscript and then moved it during revisions. The tale, if told humorously, would certainly be inappropriate in the tragic final act. Moreover, by moving the story to Act I O'Neill can show how all the family members react to it. Despite Tyrone's grumbling, he shares his sons' delight in this small Irish victory over the English, as does Mary.

There are just two events in *Journey*: Mary's return to drugs and the identification of Edmund's consumption. Everything else of consequence has happened in the past. The scenario lacks shape and dramatic tension largely because these events have occurred before the curtain rises. Mary has taken drugs the previous night, and the doctor has already told Tyrone the nature of his younger son's illness. While the timing of the doctor's diagnosis is a relatively minor issue, the question of when Mary first returns to the needle is central not only to the themes of *Journey* but to the very structure of the work.

On an undated note page labeled "N.L. play," probably written before the scenario, a brief outline of the drama's early moments indicates that the three men, rather than the father and mother, are present in the opening scene. All but Edmund have already heard the doctor's report, and "The strain of knowing has been too much for M[other].—has started her off again." The scenario, although less blatant than the note, also suggests that Mary succumbed to her craving the preceding night. The beginning of the scenario is very sketchy, yet the Mother's manner is described as "a bit strained" and she is "talking all the time" (I, p. 1), characteristics of the drugged Mary. Her behavior makes her Younger Son wary.

Later the Elder Son chastises his brother for leaving the Mother alone for her nap and concludes, "Anyway it's too late now, I'm afraid. God damn it! . . . Didn't you notice her eyes last night?" (II, p. 2).

Although the manuscript is ambiguous, it was apparently while revising this draft that O'Neill decided to postpone Mary's first injection until after Act I. Deleted stage directions portray an ominously defensive Mary. Further, in a passage excised from the manuscript, Tyrone condemns Jamie for reminding his mother of Edmund's illness. Tyrone insists, "Well, I made her forget it. She's all right again," but Jamie responds with "a probing look of questioning cynicism." Evidently Jamie believes his mother has returned to drugs. Tyrone too is suspicious, despite his verbal bluff. He is "disturbed by" his son's probing look, and stage directions for Jamie state that "there is the feeling he is evading something they *both* have in mind" (I, p. 13, my emphasis).

Finally, on a page of notes "For revision," O'Neill outlined the situation as it appears in the published *Journey*: "More hopeful belief, even on Jamie's part, that she is cured—uneasiness only because of fear effect of Edmund's sickness—denial of suspicions of happenings previous night— it is she who arouses their suspicions by suspecting they have them, accusing them & denying." But, the note continues, Mary had not taken drugs during the night, she had "conquered craving." Rolf Scheibler's contention that "O'Neill opens the action only after she has spent a night under the influence of drugs"[52] is contradicted by Jamie in the final text. The important scene occurs in Act I when the elder son, having told Tyrone that he was worried about Mary's nocturnal wanderings, admits he "was all wrong" in his suspicions (text, p. 38). Jamie is an acute judge of Mary's condition; as she enters in the second act, "Jamie knows after one probing look at her that his suspicions are justified. . . . his face sets in an expression of embittered, defensive cynicism" (p. 58). His earlier admission that he was wrong can only mean that he sincerely believes she did not take drugs during the night, and we must trust his claim. It is not in Jamie's nature to lie about this issue to spare anyone's feelings.

There are numerous ramifications of O'Neill's decision to delay the initial injection, and one effect is to gain audience sympathy for and understanding of Mary's readdiction. The first act of the scenario merely concludes with the Mother's exit; the Younger Son is left alone on stage. In the finished play, by contrast, we witness Mary fighting "a desperate battle with herself" (p. 49), a silent and ultimately futile struggle against her craving. We see that she has, in her way, genuinely fought against the overwhelming impulse to return to the solace of morphine. Her return to drugs is a betrayal of her own wishes as well as a betrayal of her family.

Postponing Mary's first shot also clarifies her reason for resuming the habit. In early notes O'Neill states that it is "the strain of knowing" about Edmund's illness that started Mary on drugs the previous night. In the final *Journey* Edmund's illness is not alone the cause of her return to drugs, as his birth was not alone the cause of her original addiction. A more powerful stimulus for Mary's relapse is the suspicions of the others. The notes "For revision" assert:

> What really happened—she had been frantic—given in—gone to bathroom, spareroom—then, thinking of Edmund, for his sake had conquered craving which was brought on by continual worry about him—at end, she tells Edmund this—he wants believe but can't help suspecting—it is this lack of faith in him, combined with growing fear, which makes her give in—

Mary never puts the burden of trust so directly on Edmund in the published text, and he is certainly not the only male Tyrone whose apprehensions disturb her. But O'Neill does, as the note indicates, focus upon the men's mistrust as a very direct cause of Mary's backsliding.

A comparison of the early notes and the notes for revision suggests that O'Neill changed the impetus for Mary's readdiction from Edmund's consumption to the family's suspicion. In fact, however, he used both as motivations even at the scenario stage. Although concern for her son's health seems to dominate Mary's mind in that draft, she does complain: "It isn't fair for you all to be so suspicious without any reason—it makes it so hard" (I, p. 1). O'Neill retains both causes in the published play; he simply places more weight on the men's apprehensions than he had previously. This new emphasis complements his decision to delay Mary's initial injection. If Mary has taken drugs before the curtain rises, then any misgivings on the part of the men are fully justified. Mary might claim that their suspicions caused her return to morphine, but we would have only her word to go by, and we know her interpretation of past events is suspect. By keeping her drug-free during the first act, O'Neill can show that there is a basis for her complaints: we actually see the men scrutinizing and doubting an as yet innocent Mary.

Egil Törnqvist accurately asserts that focusing on the men's apprehensions stresses "the inescapability of the past . . . it is because they cannot

forget all the earlier dope periods that the men cannot help being suspicious. We end up with an inextricable web of guilt."[53] If it is only fear for
Edmund's health that has set Mary off, presumably she could at some
future date, when he is well again, overcome her addiction. Mary says as
much herself, looking forward to the day when she will see Edmund
"healthy and happy and successful" and she will not "have to feel guilty
any more" (text, pp. 93–94). But there can never be a day when the
Tyrone men will not recall how often she has tried and failed to give up
drugs. While time can cure Edmund's illness, it cannot erase the past and
the men's fears that the past will be repeated. By emphasizing the importance of her family's lack of faith in her, O'Neill virtually destroys the hope
that Mary can ever be free of her habit.

Not only does O'Neill make Mary's addiction seem inescapable, he also
implies that this particular bout with drugs is worse than previous ones.
Mary Adrian Tinsley correctly recognizes that typescript changes make
Mary's actions in the last scene seem unique and final, rather than mere
repetitions of past actions.[54] Examining the manuscript and scenario confirms that O'Neill gradually worked toward making the play's closing minutes climactic. The concluding act in the early drafts suggests that this is a
familiar pattern to the Tyrones: they have seen Mary like this before and
they will see her like this again. The published text's last act, in contrast,
implies that this is a final and tragic situation, a moment beyond which no
future can be seen.

In the scenario Act V, the father tells his Younger Son that the Mother
is "up in her room—you remember—same old game . . . only been
down once—looking for something or someone, God knows what—you
know way" (V, p. 6). His comments emphasize the similarity between
Mary's actions tonight and her conduct on other drugged nights. O'Neill
cut from the manuscript Edmund's statement that Mary is going back into
the past "the way she always goes back" (IV, p. 8). The most significant
deletion is part of a speech by Tyrone in the typescript: "We've seen her
like this before. It's the damned poison. She'll be sane again tomorrow if
she gets a good sleep. It isn't often she drowns herself in it like this. She'll
be more careful from now on" (IV, p. 35). All except the second line of this
was excised, and the published text reads: "It's the damned poison. But
I've never known her to drown herself in it as deep as this" (p. 174).
Tonight is different, and Tyrone can no longer predict how she will be in
the morning. This sense of finality is emphasized by alterations O'Neill

made in the early scenes. Making Mary drug-free at the opening allows the audience to see how she acts when she does not have her morphine support. However, this means that the audience has never seen her "sane again" although drugged, and thus we have no reference point that allows us to gauge how she will appear after this shattering night. Törnqvist argues that "depending on whether we include the preceding night or not, we may speak either of a linear development from light to darkness or of a circular progression from foggy night through sunny daylight back into foggy night. I believe O'Neill had both movements in mind when he composed his play."[55] This is largely true, but O'Neill de-emphasized the circularity as he worked on *Journey*. Although Mary's readdiction begins as part of a repetitive cycle, the stress is on the uniqueness and even finality of this day. It is a journey "into night," as the words O'Neill added to the title underscore.

O'Neill further increased the bleakness of *Journey's* last act through revisions that make Mary less aware of what is transpiring around her.[56] Early draft stage directions that cite Mary's emotional distress were consistently changed to directions that mention her obliviousness. Comments on her surroundings were deleted, and her ability to distinguish present reality from the idealized convent world of her past was minimized. For example, in the manuscript Mary tells her husband: "I was so lonesome I kept Cathleen with me just to have someone to talk to—or rather, to have an excuse to dream aloud to myself" (III, p. 11). This speech shows Mary recognizing that her reveries about her childhood are merely wishful dreams. O'Neill deleted everything after the dash, as well as several other instances where Mary uses the word *dream*. In so doing, he muted her perceptiveness.

More striking are the changes made in the last act. Where early drafts present a Mary who is at least intermittently alert and rational, the published *Journey* presents a woman so sunk in her morphine fog that she neither hears nor recognizes her loved ones. In the scenario's final act Mary, although confused, worries aloud about Tyrone's health when she learns that he is sitting on the porch in the chill night air, and she recognizes the two young men in the living room as her sons. Only at the very end does she become "entirely unaware of them" (V, p. 6). By the final moments of the manuscript and typescript she has lost most of her rationality: she speaks "vaguely," as if "from a great distance." Yet in these drafts she does respond to the recitation of Swinburne's "A Leave-taking," adding such comments as "That is true, but it's very sad," or "It is too bad it has to be so sorrowful" after each stanza. This was canceled and by the last act of the published *Journey* she is almost completely unconscious of who the men are and what they are saying. She fails to recognize Tyrone when he takes the wedding gown, and responds only with a curt "No!" to Edmund's plea that she acknowledge his consumption.

Mary's obliviousness is, however, subject to one ironic twist. The most crucial circularity in *Journey* occurs in Mary's mind. Just before the curtain falls, she returns to the point when all the troubles unveiled in the drama began, when she "fell in love with James Tyrone and was so happy for a time." O'Neill had a different ending for the scenario. There Mary's last speech concerns her hopes for the Virgin Mary's forgiveness, and the scenario's last line is from the Lord's Prayer: "Forgive us our trespasses as we forgive those who trespass against us" (V, p. 6).[57] While this is a fitting epigraph to this tale of betrayals, it is just that: an epigraph rather than a dramatic conclusion. O'Neill ends succeeding drafts with Mary's memory of her first meeting with James, the first step in the Tyrone family's journey. Yet the last irony is that Mary has not quite, in her mind, made a complete escape into the past. Törnqvist argues, "The Dancer in *Thirst* and Mary Tyrone in her curtain speech reveal that they have completely recreated their past, seeking protection there from the unbearable present."[58] Törnqvist, like many other critics, fails to see that Mary is not as successful as the Dancer. When Mary enters in Act IV of the published play she speaks in the present and future tenses—"I play so badly now. I'm all out of practice. Sister Theresa will give me a dreadful scolding" (p. 171)—as if she really believed she were back in the convent. By the conclusion of the drama she is talking in the *past* tense: "Then in the spring something happened to me. Yes, I remember. I fell in love with James Tyrone and was so happy for a time." Even in her deepest drugged stupor she cannot quite escape from the present, cannot wholly return to the past. It is, indeed, past.

Heightening Mary's obliviousness makes the end of the play more terrible and final. However, the change also makes Mary a more sympathetic character: she is less aware than in previous drafts of the grief she is causing others, less responsible for her words and deeds. At the same time O'Neill was increasing the tragic nature of *Journey*, he was also lightening the burden of guilt each Tyrone bears. Sheaffer identifies the paradox O'Neill faced:

He was writing at once an indictment and a defense of his family. The need to justify himself drove him to picture his parents and brother in all their frailties and offenses, but at the same time he was saying that he had at last made his peace with them; he was projecting both his original view of the family, as he remembered it, and his deeper insight, his more compassionate attitude afterward.[59]

It is in the preliminary drafts that O'Neill most vividly outlines "all their frailties and offenses"; the playwright is gentler to his characters in the published text, and they show more understanding toward each other. While fervent exclamations of devotion and absolution are sometimes found in the scenario, these ring hollowly amid the torrent of abuse the Tyrones hurl throughout every act. Love and anger are the warp and woof of *Journey* from O'Neill's first conception of the play, yet the fabric is more darkly colored in early versions. The final drama makes clear that the Tyrones' bitterness and even hatred grow out of the very bonds of need and love that hold the family together. When O'Neill inscribed the original *Journey* script to his wife Carlotta, he called it a "play of old sorrow" but added that it was written "with deep pity and understanding and forgiveness for *all* the four haunted Tyrones."[60] As O'Neill worked on both *Iceman* and *Journey*, he seems to have gained new insight into the characters' situations, a deeper comprehension of their motives. The act of composition apparently was, for the playwright, a lesson in compassion. One striking aspect of the development of *Journey* is the way in which the pity, understanding, and forgiveness O'Neill mentions in his dedication led him to modify his initially harsher portraits of James and Jamie, and especially Mary, just as he had softened the portrayals of Hickey and others in *Iceman*. This newfound compassion was further projected into the plays through Larry Slade and Edmund Tyrone, who learn sympathy for their tormented friends and kin.

LONG DAY'S JOURNEY INTO NIGHT, like *Iceman*, is set in 1912. Interestingly, calculations on an early note page suggest that O'Neill considered setting *Journey* in 1907. This was the year of his own parents' thirtieth anniversary, and he at first envisioned placing the play on the Tyrones' thirtieth anniversary. One early jotting reads:

It is 30th Wedding Anniversary?—F[ather]., reproaching M[other]., acts hurt & sentimental about it—she reminds him how often he has forgotten—

or remembering, pretended to forget, hoping I had forgotten—so there
need be no present—

The scenario, although set in 1912, also places the action on the Tyrones'
anniversary, and a scribbled marginal note suggests that O'Neill may even
have contemplated using the word *anniversary* in the play's title. The few
scenario references to the event again evoke only bitterness. The mother
proposes that the cook drink to the occasion and adds that her husband
"doesn't like anniversaries—cost money—and remind him getting old"
(IV, p. 4).

It is not surprising that O'Neill considered using the Tyrones' anniversary. Several of his later works are set in whole or in part on "special days":
Ah, Wilderness! on the Fourth of July, *Iceman* on Harry Hope's birthday,
and *A Touch of the Poet* on the anniversary of the battle of Talavera, in
which Con Melody fought. The wedding anniversary would be an appropriate touch for *Journey* because it recalls the time when much of the
trouble began. The anniversary is not really necessary, however; Mary's
appearance in the final scene, dragging her yellowed bridal gown, is a
vividly dramatic reminder of the wedding day. Further, the anniversary
concerns the two elder Tyrones more directly than the two younger ones;
omitting this event broadens the focus to encompass all four family members. More important, the inclusion of the anniversary would intensify
the play's bitterness. Mary's escape into drugs and the men's abandonment of her would appear all the more cruel if they occurred during what
should be a celebration of familial unity. By removing the anniversary,
O'Neill mutes all the Tyrones' culpability.

Each character was also individually the recipient of O'Neill's "gentling" revisions. Changes made in descriptions of Mary both at the beginning of the drama and at the opening of the third act signal revisions made
in her speeches and actions. In *Journey* the initial description of Mary
includes the remark, "Her most appealing quality is the simple, unaffected charm of a shy convent-girl youthfulness she has never lost—an
innate unworldly innocence" (text, p. 13). A rough version of the line was
added during revision of the manuscript and polished into its final form in
the first typescript. It softens the portrait of Mary and shows that her
naïveté is an intrinsic quality, not simply the result of the drugs. The
third-act revision is even more revealing. Expanding on his description of
Mary in the scenario, O'Neill writes in the manuscript:

She is calm and quiet, her nerves are steady and yet she is continually moving, her body seems charged with an artificial vitality, as an automaton might
be charged into life-like movement by an electric current. There is apparent
now in her a peculiar duality of character. At moments, she is like the Mary
of the opening of the first act, but a much younger Mary who possesses the
incongruous quality of simple, naive, happy, chattering girlishness which
must have belonged to her in the past before her marriage, in her convent
school days. In contrast to this, there is another opposite self that suddenly
breaks through, a hard, bitter, cynical, aging ⟨woman⟩ who reminds one of
her elder son, a woman who can taunt with a biting [??] cruelty, as if suddenly possessed by an alien demon of revenge.   (III, p. 1)

Part of this account, including the phrases after "elder son," were canceled
in the manuscript.[61] The demonic quality—which O'Neill frequently attributed to his characters and which links Mary to Jamie, with his "Mephistophelian" appearance (text, p. 19)—disappears. Just as O'Neill eliminated *Mephistophelian* from his descriptions of Larry Slade in *Iceman*
when he realized that the old philosopher's cynicism was scarcely as sinister as this adjective suggests, so too he removed the implication of a
malignant demonism underlying Mary's darker moods. The remainder of
this manuscript portrait of Mary was canceled in the typescript, where it
was replaced by the final version:

She has hidden deeper within herself and found refuge and release in a
dream where present reality is but an appearance to be accepted and dis-
missed unfeelingly—even with a hard cynicism—or entirely ignored. There
is at times an uncanny gay, free youthfulness in her manner, as if in spirit she
were released to become again, simply and without self-consciousness, the
naive, happy, chattering schoolgirl of her convent days.   (text, p. 97)

O'Neill firmly believed in the duality of human nature. In a 1937 letter
to his older son, he contended the "events, like revolutions, are but outer
symbols of the eternal struggle of the duality in the soul of the individual."[62] As several critics have pointed out, this conviction is reflected
throughout the dramatist's canon, whether in paired characters (often
brothers) who seem like two sides of the same individual, or in single
characters whose conflicting actions betoken divided feelings and desires.[63] The hero of the 1914 play *Abortion* laments his impregnating a
lower-class woman and insists: "Do you suppose it was the same man who
loves Evelyn [his proper fiancée] who did this other thing? No, a thou-

sand time no, such an idea is abhorrent."[64] This concept reaches its peak in *Days Without End*, where the protagonist is dogged by a cynical alterego who appears on stage yet is not seen by any character except the hero himself. There are in fact similarities between John Loving of *Days Without End* and Mary Tyrone. The John side of his personality is searching for a lost faith and begs, in almost the same words Mary uses, "If I could only pray! If I could only believe again!"[65] His skeptical Loving side mocks his attempts, as Mary mocks herself. With Mary, however, O'Neill presented this duality more subtly—and more convincingly—than he had with such characters as John Loving or *The Great God Brown*'s Dion Anthony. By removing the implication of two discrete selves within her, he eschewed the simplistic notion of two wholly separate personalities inhabiting one body—just as, after *Days Without End*, he rejected the crude theatrical technique of two actors representing one character. Mary is not "possessed by an alien demon." She is a complex individual, not a split personality. Her alternating feelings of love and anger grow from a common root: concern for, and disappointment in, her family; regret over dreams that have been shattered by time. Further, although the final version mentions Mary's occasional "hard cynicism," nothing is said about cruelty or vengefulness. Mary does indeed manifest these traits in the published *Journey*, but they are not the dominant aspects of her nature, as early stage directions imply. O'Neill has moderated his original portrait of a viciously spiteful woman.

O'Neill changed Mary's words and deeds to accord with the new, more appealing descriptions he composed.[66] Two important changes have already been mentioned: postponing Mary's first injection so the audience better comprehends her motives, and blunting her awareness of the pain she is causing her family. O'Neill also removed the suggestion, occasionally present in early drafts, that Mary enjoys tormenting others with the idea that her addiction could prove fatal. Mary is alone in the published play when she muses aloud about her desire to accidentally "take an overdose" (p. 121). In a deleted typescript passage, she tells Cathleen of the drug's deadliness: "You have to be very careful. It will kill you if you take too much" (III, p. 5). The scenario, however, presents a nastier Mary. There she boasts to her worried husband and sons, "Why, Doctor said I was taking enough daily to kill herd of elephants" and then "smiles with a perverse childish pride" before shuddering at her own words (V, p. 6). It is no wonder that the men's fear of suicide is stronger in early drafts than in the final play.

In addition to these revisions, O'Neill decreased both the quantity and variety of charges Mary makes against her kin. Any accusations made in *Journey* reflect on the accusers as well as the accused, for the former appear unforgiving and self-righteous when they attempt to blame others for their own failings. Mary makes the most indictments, charging her husband with insensitivity and cheapness, her elder son with debauchery, and so on. Nevertheless, Mary's denuciations are far more numerous and acerbic in early versions. Through deletions, O'Neill tempered the portrait of Mary and of the family members against whom she levels her attacks.

Although James Tyrone is the most difficult family member to fit into a clear pattern of development, he too ultimately emerges in the final play as a more sympathetic—and more believable—character than in the early drafts.[67] This occurs despite O'Neill's alteration and even deletion of what could be considered "points" in Tyrone's favor. Like his sons and wife, Tyrone in the scenario is better able to verbalize his feelings than he is in later versions. Moreover, the scenario has him making an uncharacteristically generous offer when Edmund protests being sent to the state farm for treatment. A "crushed" Tyrone first "excuses" his action, then declares: "go anywhere you like—I don't care what it costs if it makes you well & you'll get hold of yourself & be a man. . . . Don't you know you're my son and I love you?" (V, p. 5). On the basis of these lines, Virginia Floyd argues that "O'Neill presents a far more compassionate picture of the Father here than in the final draft, where the early softness in his nature and tremendous vulnerability are muted."[68]

This passage does reveal a "softness" often difficult to discern in the Tyrone of the published text, yet it also introduces serious difficulties. It is possible, of course, that O'Neill modified Tyrone's lines because they deviated too far from biographical fact: O'Neill himself was initially consigned to a state institution. The moderately priced sanitorium Tyrone ultimately selects in *Journey* resembles the place to which O'Neill was later sent. More significantly, the scenario lines are simply out of character. It is very hard to believe that Tyrone could so suddenly undergo a change of heart as to throw all financial considerations to the wind—especially when, in both the scenario and the final play, he will shortly complain about the cost of a few burning light bulbs. O'Neill's handling of the sanitorium issue in the final play is, by contrast, both convincing and revealing. The first time Edmund mentions the state farm, Tyrone reacts with a scaled-down version of his scenario generosity: "Who said you had

to go to this Hilltown place? You can go anywhere you like. I don't give a
damn what it costs. All I care about is to have you get well" (p. 146).
Following his recitation of his youthful hardships, however, Tyrone is less
magnanimous: "You can choose any place you like! Never mind what it
costs! Any place I can afford. Any place you like—within reason" (p. 148).
As sentence by sentence Tyrone's offer becomes more qualified, we witness the struggle between his love for his son and his inescapable fear of
poverty. Even Edmund, whose fate is being decided, recognizes the
poignancy of his father's dilemma: "At this qualification, a grin twitches
Edmund's lips. His resentment has gone" (p. 149).

O'Neill did ignore one opportunity to bend audience opinion in Tyrone's
favor: the playwright could have developed brief note and scenario suggestions that Mary's childhood was less than idyllic, and that Mary was
aware of its flaws. These early notations indicate a more complex relationship between Mary and her parents than the published text acknowledges. *Journey* reveals almost nothing about Mary Tyrone's mother except
that she feared her husband would spoil their daughter and that Mary felt
guilty about preferring the nun Mother Elizabeth to her own parent.
Tyrone's manuscript comment that Mary's mother was "an ordinary, common-sense little Irish woman" (IV, p. 8) does not appear in subsequent
drafts. An early note describes Mary moving in her mind "back to loved—
admired father who cannot be admired because of his treatment of mother
whom she ought to have admired, loved, but really held in contempt."
Neither this contempt nor the "trace of scorn" in Mary's voice when she
laughs about her mother in the typescript (III, p. 13) survives in the final
Journey. It is interesting that this scorn for "an ordinary, common-sense
little Irish woman" parallels Sara Melody's feelings for her mother during
much of *A Touch of the Poet*, and Mary's ambivalence toward her mother
may well contribute to her own uneasiness with the maternal role.[69]

These early lines are even more significant with respect to Mary's father. In the published text, Mary never admits that he was anything but
perfect. Tyrone alone questions this view, telling Edmund that his maternal grandfather was an unremarkable man who declined into alcoholism.
Had O'Neill incorporated these note and scenario hints into the drama,
we would have less sympathy with Mary's claims that Tyrone took her
from a totally loving home and dropped her into a world of liquor and
dissension. We would see that Mary's father was, like her husband, a
hard-drinking man at times insensitive to his wife. Instead of developing

this parallel, O'Neill removed Mary's awareness of her father's failings and thus heightened—particularly in Mary's mind—the contrast between her childhood and her present situation. O'Neill's decision to delete the additional information about Mary's father seems motivated less by a desire to paint Tyrone darker (by comparison) than by a wish to show how Mary idealizes everything in her distant past.

The Tyrone family's financial situation was also more complicated in the scenario, where Mary reveals to the maid that her father "left me property—mother couldn't touch—I need to be independent about clothes, etc.—husband glad but resented" (IV, p. 4). If Mary had financial resources of her own, her husband's cheapness would be less momentous than it appears in the final play, which contains no mention of any inheritance. By omitting references to Mary's money, O'Neill underscored her entrapment and placed a greater burden of responsibility on Tyrone. On the other hand, the scenario implies that whatever money Mary once had is now gone, for she must pawn her jewelry to buy drugs (V, p. 6). The question of how Mary supports her habit never arises in *Journey*. The idea that she must sell her personal belongings to pay for her affliction is excruciatingly painful, and this reflects unfavorably on the tight-fisted Tyrone.

O'Neill's usual revision pattern was to present James Tyrone more favorably as work on *Journey* progressed. Particularly affecting in the published play are his accounts of his poverty-stricken childhood and his early acting days. The second story, in which Tyrone gains Edmund's and the audience's empathy by admitting how he ruined his chances for a great acting career, is missing from the scenario.[70] This moving speech obviously became very important in O'Neill's eyes, for he expanded it by more than seventy words when he revised the typescript. At this time he added Tyrone's tribute to his wife—"Her love was an added incentive to ambition"—as well as his explanation that he was first attracted to "the big money-maker play" not because of potential earnings but because the leading role "was a great romantic part I knew I could play better than anyone" (text, p. 150). To Tyrone's everlasting regret, the play ultimately destroyed his reputation instead of enhancing it.

Early drafts depict a depth of bitterness between the elder Tyrones that is not reached in the completed *Journey* even during the moments of greatest hostility, and the children (both dead and living) are frequently the subject of the conflict. For example, in the final play Tyrone never makes a serious attempt to tell Mary the exact nature of Edmund's illness. By the time he receives the diagnosis, he realizes she is in no condition to accept the situation rationally. One of the longest deletions from the manuscript involves Tyrone's attempt to speak to Mary on this subject. Her response is a torrent of abuse and condemnation. She claims that doctors lie because "curing a cold doesn't mean enough money for them," but her strongest attack is reserved for her husband:

> Don't tell me you believe it [the doctor's report]! You can't be so stupid! Unless there's a good reason why you want to believe it. Yes, I suspect that, but I know you'll never admit it. However, don't think you're going to send him away from me to a sanatorium, because you're not! I refuse to permit it, do you understand! You're up to your old jealous tricks but this time I'll never give in! Edmund is mine and I'm going to keep him! . . . [Tyrone interrupts and tries to soothe her. She continues] (more excitedly) The same old trick of using any excuse to send my children away, when they need me above all! Have you forgotten what happened to Eugene? Yes, because you didn't care! I remember now you showed hardly any sign of grief! But you were just as guilty of his death as I was! More! I didn't want to leave him! You used my love for you as an excuse! You made me leave him!   (III, p. 19)

Although in the final version Mary does charge Tyrone with being jealous of the children and partly responsible for the baby's death, her accusations do not reach this pitch of vituperation. She never accuses him, as she does here, of *wanting* Edmund to be ill or of being heartlessly unconcerned when the baby died. Further, early drafts place Tyrone's attitude toward their elder surviving son in a nastier light. Tyrone admits in *Journey* that only Mary's influence prevents him from evicting Jamie, but a canceled typescript passage depicts the familial triangle more harshly. Attempting to gain Jamie's sympathy, Mary argues: "If I hadn't taken your part against your father for years and years, he'd have thrown you out in the street. You know very well there have been times when I've even had to threaten I'd leave him, if he did. He'd let you sleep in the park and starve to teach you a lesson!" (II, 1, p. 9). While we may suspect that Mary is exaggerating, Jamie does not dispute her claim. He dismisses as "nonsense" her assertion that he is acting like her enemy, insisting that he is "grateful" for her intercession.

O'Neill also made a whole series of modifications and deletions that temper Mary's attitude toward the theater. Several excised passages re-

volve around Jamie's acting career. The fourth act of the scenario ends on
Mary's charge that Tyrone "forced" their older son to become an actor.
The thrust of her complaint is that her uneducated husband, "jealous" of
the young man's excellent school record and desirous of the "easy money"
acting offered, caused Jamie's dissipation by pushing him into a disreputable vocation (IV, p. 4). Mary insists in the manuscript that Jamie "always
hated the theatre. In that respect, at least, he's like me" (II, 2, p. 8).[71] The
manuscript also has Mary asserting that Jamie has been harmed by his
association "with the worst kind of cheap actress." She concludes: "I never
wanted him to go on the stage. I knew that would be the end. I remember
telling you I would rather see him dead" (III, p. 10). The effect of cutting
these lines is on the one hand to make Mary seem less unreasonably bitter
and on the other to remove from Tyrone the onus of a further betrayal.
Had Mary been as passionately opposed to Jamie's going on stage as she
appears to be in the scenario and manuscript, Tyrone's forcing the issue
would indeed have been a cruel action, whatever his motives. In the published play it is Jamie, rather than his mother, who complains that Tyrone
coerced him into an acting career, and even this discussion was modified
in the older man's favor. Originally Tyrone merely responded by saying
that Jamie "never wanted to do anything" (MS, I, p. 15). O'Neill added a
further explanation, which appears in the final *Journey:* "That's a lie! You
made no effort to find anything else to do. You left it to me to get you a job
and I have no influence except in the theater. Forced you!" (p. 32).
Whether or not Jamie accepts this argument, the audience sees its validity. The theater is almost the only world his father knows.

    As he edited, O'Neill changed numerous other references to the the-
ater. Gratuitous slurs on the acting profession, such as Mary's claim, "It's
so surprising that an actor should remain faithful to his wife" (MS, III, p.
6), disappear. This deletion, like most of the others, occurs in the third-act
scene between Mary and the maid, Cathleen. Where antitheater lines
were not canceled, they were frequently softened. In the first typescript,
when Cathleen asks why she never went on the stage, Mary retorts: "Can
you imagine me wishing to become a cheap actress?" (III, p. 4). This was
altered to the milder "I've never had the slightest desire to be an actress"
(text, p. 102). Similarly, Mary's "I've always hated the theatre" (TS, III, p.
4) was changed to "I've never felt at home in the theater" (text, p. 102).
These constitute but a small sample of the deleted or revised attacks on
the theater, actors, and actresses. Some lines were likely trimmed simply

because they were repetitious. In addition, O'Neill may well have felt guilty including, even from the mouth of a prejudiced character, such wholesale condemnations of the theater people to whom he owed so much. Although Mary's complaints about the theater remain in the published *Journey*, her objections are those of a convent-bred woman who could find no home in this alien milieu; the theatrical world is not by definition evil but rather the wrong place for her. Finally, O'Neill's changes moderate the portraits of both elder Tyrones. Mary's criticisms are far more restrained, and her husband is no longer stigmatized as a member of a wholly disreputable profession.

Part of O'Neill's shaping of James Tyrone's character involved clarifying to what extent he is an actor off stage as well as on. In the introduction to *Contour in Time*, Bogard contrasts the old romantic style of acting that held sway when O'Neill began to write with the Stanislavsky-inspired technique that was becoming popular in America in the 1930s. Bogard notes that O'Neill's late plays include characters who are themselves "actors" in the older manner: "In fact, O'Neill has incorporated into his cast characters who are concerned with role playing and who thus present themselves *as actors*. A large part of the characterization of both Cornelius Melody and James Tyrone rests in their being actors performing in the old, romantic tradition of O'Neill's father's theatre. Thus 'performance' becomes in the late plays an element of characterization and theme, totally incorporated into the context of the play."[72] Bogard could have added Hickey to the list, for the salesman is clearly a performer as (to a lesser extent) are Erie Smith in *Hughie* and James Tyrone, Jr., particularly in *A Moon for the Misbegotten*. O'Neill contrasts the actions and appearance of "Major Melody," a romantic poseur, with those of the crude Con Melody who emerges after his defeat by the Yankees and his killing of the mare. Similarly, Erie Smith attempts the role of the big-time gambler while Jim Tyrone fails miserably in his pose as the callous Broadway sport. The elder James Tyrone is an actor by profession, yet his histrionic qualities are suggested by his bearing and tone rather than by any sharp split between a part he plays and a more sincere intrinsic self. Early drafts do hint at such a division, however, and in a particularly unpleasant way. Mary tells Cathleen in the published *Journey* that her husband "never is worried about anything, except money and property and the fear he'll end his days in poverty. I mean, deeply worried" (p. 101). In the manuscript she continues bitterly: "But about anything else he doesn't really worry.

He has never been sensitive. He hasn't a nerve in his body. Of course, on the surface he can appear ⟨to be⟩ dreadfully ⟨disturbed at times—that is, by things which⟩ give him a chance to play a part. Don't let his acting fool you. If you'd been married to him thirty-five years . . ." (III, p. 4).[73] The first line was deleted from the manuscript; the rest was removed from the first typescript. While Tyrone remains an actor (on stage and off) in the final play, the charge that for him being an actor is synonymous with being insincere disappears. Like his fear of poverty, his despair over Mary's addiction is genuine, not a ham's imitation grief.

Edmund and Jamie, like Mary, are often harder on Tyrone in early drafts, more vehement in their claims that he is cheap, selfish, and even cruel. In the last act of the scenario, the Elder Son warns his brother not to let the Father "send you to State Farm to be killed off for him" and adds that the old man would like to see them all die (V, p. 5). In a moment of alcoholic exuberance the Younger Son declares, "I would not have another father for a million dollars!" (V, p. 5), yet a few minutes later he reproaches the Father: "You like to have him [the Elder Son] around to remind you of superiority, you like to be a master with dependents on your charity. But when I get well, I'll be free of you!" (V, p. 6). Although he is immediately ashamed of his words and quickly admits that his father does love the older boy, the depth of the Younger Son's antagonism is striking. In a passage cut from the manuscript, Edmund accuses Tyrone of sending Mary to take cures "when she got so bad that anyone who saw her could tell with one look—because that made you ashamed!" (IV, p. 11). His claim is that selfish pride rather than concern motivated Tyrone to seek help for his wife. All these accusations, and other less serious but similar ones, appear in early drafts but vanish before the published play. Tyrone remains a flawed individual, capable of unwittingly harming himself and others through his cheapness and shortsightedness, yet he is also a complex man who has suffered much and earned love as well as resentment from his family. The constant acrimonious condemnation of him in early versions of *Journey* was mitigated by O'Neill's revisions.

Even Jamie, perhaps the most maligned character, becomes through O'Neill's rewriting an individual worthy of compassion. As he developed the play, O'Neill did not radically alter the image of Jamie, but he did make two kinds of changes with respect to him. On the one hand, he removed suggestions that Jamie could still take hold of himself and begin a productive life.[74] Paralleling the changes he made in Mary and in the structure of the drama, O'Neill modified the portrait of Jamie to that of a man who has hit the end of the line, with no hope for a different tomorrow. As we shall see in Chapter 3, this is precisely the same change O'Neill made in Jim Tyrone in *A Moon for the Misbegotten*. Early versions of *Journey* suggest that Jamie has the potential to reclaim himself, and early versions of *Moon* hint that Josie's love may be able to save Jim. In the published texts of both dramas, James Tyrone, Jr., is beyond help. On the other hand, at the same time O'Neill was foreclosing Jamie's future, he was also moderating attacks on him by the other characters and even by Jamie himself.

In the typescript Tyrone optimistically says of his elder son: "Well, maybe I am too hard. Maybe he will turn out all right. God knows I hope so, and he has the brains to succeed, if he'd only use them" (I, p. 6). These lines, which come from a discussion that may have been added to the manuscript,[75] were cut from the typescript. O'Neill might have wished to temper the bleak presentation of Jamie but realized that the demands of the character he had created denied such an encouraging note. Personal motives as well as dramatic considerations could have influenced his revisions. O'Neill knew that the model for Jamie Tyrone, his own brother, never picked up the threads of his life except to weave them into his shroud. Insofar as Jamie Tyrone represents Jamie O'Neill, perhaps the playwright could not wrestle on stage with the haunting question: If Jamie was redeemable in 1912, why could his younger brother not save him?

O'Neill's removal of the typescript passage correlates with other revisions. In the scenario's last act, for example, the Father says that in spite of his son's past failures, "in spite of all he's done, I still hope—He's my oldest son—my name—and when he's sober—" (V, p. 6). By the final play, Tyrone is no longer hoping. Mary's feeble claim that Jamie will "turn out all right in the end, you wait and see" is said "without conviction," and Tyrone retorts: "He'd better start soon, then. He's nearly thirty-four" (text, p. 18). The sole time in the published *Journey* that Tyrone shows any confidence about Jamie's future occurs in the first act, when he tells his son, "You're young yet. You could still make your mark. You had the talent to become a fine actor! You have it still. You're my son—!" (p. 33). This hope is not based on Jamie himself but on the fact that he is Tyrone's son; the old man cannot accept the idea that his namesake will fail to augment the family reputation. His speech lacks even the limited optimism found in an early note, where Tyrone tells Jamie, "still chance for you, after summer up here—leave whiskey alone—beer—realize your own fault, make up mind— . . . go in something else, anything— . . . as long as you don't feel licked in yourself—you've got brains, etc." The Jamie that O'Neill ultimately portrays is "licked," and neither Tyrone nor anyone else has faith in his rehabilitation. Jamie is a poor actor with a bad reputation who despises his profession and lacks the interest and confidence to find another. Finally, there is a distinct irony in Tyrone's saying that Jamie can succeed because he is his son. Tyrone's last-act confession reveals that the success he achieved was a bitter one indeed.

Although Jamie's situation may be hopeless, his vices are partly redeemed by his honesty, his devotion to his mother, and the self-sacrificing love that goes hand in hand with his jealousy of Edmund. The Jamie of the early drafts has some of these qualities, but his own judgment on himself and his family's view of him are harsher than in the published play. The manuscript has Jamie telling Edmund that he "hated Eugene" and entered the baby's "room on purpose that time, hoping he'd get my measles. I was glad when he died" (IV, p. 25). In the final *Journey* Jamie admits to wishing secretly for Edmund's failure, but he never confirms Mary's hysterical accusation that he carried sibling rivalry to the extent of deliberately killing his infant brother.

Mary and Tyrone especially are more severe toward Jamie in early notes and drafts. One note includes an argument over Edmund's illness in which the Father accuses the Elder Son: "you hope he'll die—always jealous—waiting around for me to die—sponge on Mother—especially if she—." Despite Jamie's fears that his parents suspect him of harboring such thoughts, nowhere in the published *Journey* does Tyrone make such a vicious charge, accusing him of wishing his father and brother dead and being glad about his mother's readdiction because it makes her an easy mark for his sponging. Mary's withdrawal into her drug fog causes Jamie only anguish: a ready source of funds is no substitute for the mother to whom he is so fatally tied. "I'd begun to hope, if she'd beaten the game, I could, too" the drunken Jamie sobs (text, p. 162).

In the second act of *Journey*, Edmund responds to Tyrone's gift of a ten dollar bill with the cruel question: "Did Doc Hardy tell you I was going to die?" (text, p. 90). He immediately apologizes and his father is mollified. The manuscript, in contrast, has Tyrone blaming Jamie for Edmund's nasty remark. Tyrone claims that Edmund is not by nature cynical but has been influenced by his brother's "Broadway loafer's" attitude (II, 2, pp.

13–14). When Tyrone and Edmund enter in the third act of the published play, Mary notices Jamie's absence. She alleges that he won't "come home so long as he has the price of a drink left" and concludes that Jamie is "lost to" them but must not be allowed "to drag Edmund down with him" (text, p. 109). This anti-Jamie tirade is longer in the manuscript, for Mary is joined by her husband, who exclaims: "Good riddance! A lazy drunken hulk! He's no son of mine! Let him go his own road to ruin!" (III, p. 8). A few minutes later in the manuscript, when Edmund tells his mother how Jamie first informed him of her addiction, Mary responds "bitterly" that her elder son is "always believing the worst!" (III, p. 16). This too was cut.

The typescript shows similar revisions. Edmund's accusation that Tyrone caused Mary's addiction by hiring a cheap hotel doctor is answered with a stinging retort: "You're only repeating like a parrot lies you've heard from that poison-tongued brother of yours, who knows as little as you do—" (IV, p. 11). Tyrone's attack, which indicts Jamie for Edmund's antagonism, was deleted. Also in the final act of the typescript, Tyrone interjects in his appraisal of Edmund's work at sea, "It's more than your dead beat of a brother ever had the nounce to do" (IV, p. 16). This gratuitous insult was excised, and Jamie no longer figures in this particular discussion.

These comprise only a fraction of the many denunciations of Jamie that were modified or removed as *Journey* developed. Again O'Neill was certainly trying to eliminate unnecessary repetition, yet his revisions do have a perceptible effect on Jamie's characterization. First, the portrait of Jamie, like that of his parents, is softened. Cynical, dissipated, self-destructive, Jamie can still care enough about Edmund to warn his young brother to beware of him—an act of revelation and courage that tempers the bitter envy to which he confesses. Through his revisions, O'Neill slightly muted the others' antagonism to Jamie, thus suggesting that not all the young man's actions have been reprehensible and also according his positive qualities more attention. Second, O'Neill's revisions diminish Jamie's role somewhat: his name is not as constantly on everyone's lips as it is in early versions. Jamie is a significant figure, not merely a foil for the others, yet the very frequent references to him in preliminary drafts grant him more weight than the playwright wished. Perhaps O'Neill later felt that he had reduced Jamie's role too much, and wrote *A Moon for the Misbegotten* to give the character his due. *Journey* is about the Tyrone family, and while Jamie is a necessary piece in the family puzzle, he cannot be allowed to overshadow his kin—particularly his younger brother, Edmund.

EDMUND TYRONE is the most controversial character in *Long Day's Journey Into Night*. Critics often divide into two camps: those who believe he is as important as or only slightly secondary to Mary, and those who complain he is the weakest and least interesting figure in the drama.[76] Extraneous biographical considerations sometimes enter the discussion: Edmund is most important because he "is" the young O'Neill or, conversely, Edmund should be central and would be if O'Neill had been as biographically honest about this character as he was about the others. The biographical side of the argument is largely irrelevant; merely incorporating additional personal data would not have solved the problems O'Neill faced in defining Edmund and his place in the family tragedy. The dilemma is dramatic rather than biographical: like *Iceman's* Larry Slade, Edmund Tyrone's main function is to listen to, learn from, and gain compassion for the other characters. This role is basically a passive one, and all of O'Neill's considerable efforts to gain attention for Edmund could not overcome this fact.

Several issues surrounding Edmund concerned O'Neill as the play progressed: how closely connected he is to the other family members; how guilty he is of transgressions against himself and others; how serious his illness is; and what chance there is for him to escape from the circle of mistakes and betrayals that has entrapped his kin. While the playwright did not drastically change Edmund between the first notes and the published text, the subtle modifications he made are important.

O'Neill's first challenge was to bring Edmund out from under the shadow of the other characters, to make him an individual in his own right. *Journey* reveals that Jamie has deeply influenced his younger brother, but preliminary versions show a far stronger link between the two. Throughout the drafts Mary and Tyrone accuse Edmund of simply mouthing his brother's antagonistic sentiments; they imply that he, with little mind of his own, is scarcely more than a pale copy of Jamie. O'Neill not only canceled many of these accusations, he made other changes that weaken the ties between the Tyrone sons. In his third-act confession, Jamie tells Edmund, "Hell, you're more than my brother. I made you! You're my Frankenstein!" (text, p. 164). Jamie, making the common mistake of confusing Frankenstein with his monster, suggests that he has created Edmund.[77] Canceled typescript lines go even further, hinting that Edmund is not simply his older brother's creation but virtually a duplicate of him. Jamie asserts, "You're more my son, in a way, than Mama's or Papa's," and a few moments later adds, "You're me. I'm inside you!" (IV, p. 28). The manuscript's and typescript's final scenes have Edmund declaiming one stanza of Swinburne's tearful "A Leave-taking" while Jamie begins and ends the recitation with the second and sixth stanzas.[78] O'Neill subsequently gave all the verses to Jamie, thus separating the two brothers in the audience's mind—a necessary distinction as the drama draws to a close. It is Jamie's poem, an expression of his desolation; Edmund has his own lines in *Journey's* climactic scene.

O'Neill originally intended the dead baby Eugene to figure more prominently in Mary's ravings. An early note states: "Dead son becomes only child she loved—because living sons cause too much pain—." This idea is carried into the scenario, where Mary laments, "It is too bad [Eugene] could not have lived and we might have had one son we could be proud of" (IV, p. 4). This view of the dead Eugene, which implicitly links Jamie and Edmund as failures, disappears after the scenario. Through revisions O'Neill also weakened connections between Eugene and Edmund. In a deleted typescript passage, Mary complains to her younger son: "I loved you so much because you were you and you were Eugene, too. You took his place. I bore you into the world—in spite of my being so afraid, because I wanted you to take his place" (III, pp. 16–17). Once again Edmund is denied an identity of his own; he is a substitute for, almost a reincarnation of, his dead sibling. Jamie makes the same point in the manuscript when he charges, "You took Eugene's place" and adds that he is trying to ruin Edmund just as he killed the infant (IV, p. 25). Eugene does remain in *Journey* as a parallel figure to Edmund but, by deleting these passages, O'Neill blurs the bonds between the two. Mary and Jamie recognize Edmund as a separate person, not just a surrogate for the dead brother he never knew.

Before Edmund could stand alone as an independent character, the alliance between the young man and his mother also had to be diminished.[79] Early versions suggest that Mary's attachment to her younger son is stronger than the published text acknowledges. Throughout the drafts Mary proclaims her preference for Edmund, and this umbilical link seems almost certain to strangle him. The phrases "maternal solicitude" and "motherly solicitude," describing her attitude toward Edmund, occur more frequently in manuscript and typescript stage directions than in the final play. When Mary in the manuscript implies that Edmund's birth caused her misery, she is immediately contrite. "How could it be your fault?" she cries. "How could I blame you! Why, you are my baby still, you mean more to me than anyone, Dear!" Edmund responds with his own declaration: "And you are more to me, Mama" (I, p. 24). Later in the manuscript a furious Mary informs her husband, "Edmund is mine and I'm going to keep him!" (III, p. 19). These excised lines demonstrate both her stifling love for Edmund and her feeling that he is less a human being than a cherished possession. Mary's strongest statement of attachment in the published *Journey* comes when Edmund announces he must go to a sanatorium. She exclaims:

> No! I won't have it! How dare Doctor Hardy advise such a thing without consulting me! How dare your father allow him! What right has he? You are my baby! Let him attend to Jamie!
> *More and more excited and bitter*
> I know why he wants you sent to a sanatorium. To take you from me! He's always tried to do that. He's been jealous of every one of my babies! He kept finding ways to make me leave them. That's what caused Eugene's death. He's been jealous of you most of all. He knew I loved you most because—
> (p. 119)

Mary's anger and concern are passionately clear, but it is significant that Edmund cuts short her declaration of preference instead of responding in kind, as he did in the manuscript excerpt quoted above. Further, the typescript version of this speech is far longer and includes a more detailed explanation of Mary's feelings as well as a more virulent indictment of her husband:

> (Dazedly, as if this was something that had never occurred to her) Go away? (Violently) No! I won't have it! How dare Doctor Hardy advise such a thing without consulting me! How dare your father allow him! What right has he? You are my son, not his, even if he is your father! Let him attend to Jamie! I'm the one to take care of you! (More and more emotionally excited in her bitter accusations) But I see why he wants you sent to a sanatorium! To take you from me, that's why! He's always tried to do that. He's been jealous of you since the day you were born! He was jealous of every one of my babies! He wouldn't even let me take care of them. He insisted on hiring a nurse each time, and going to all the expense of having her travel with us all over the country—and you know how stingy he is about anything like that. I told him I didn't want a nurse, that I'd be so much less lonely if I did everything myself. But, of course, he wouldn't listen. And he kept finding excuses to make me leave my children. That's what caused Eugene's death. He's been jealous of you most of all because he knew I loved you the most of all. I loved

you so much because you were you and you were Eugene, too. You took his place. I bore you into the world—in spite of my being so afraid, because I wanted you to take his place. (Strangely now, as if she were talking more to herself than to him) I felt I wasn't worthy to be a mother again, after my desertion and neglect had killed Eugene, but at the same time I had a crazy hope that I could pay for him by having another baby—and then the Blessed Virgin and the Infant Jesus would forgive me.   (III, pp. 16–17)[80]

Past and present blend in Mary's tortured mind as she recalls her dead baby; to leave a child, or to allow him to leave her, is to kill him. No matter that Eugene was an infant and Edmund is a man of twenty-three: separation from the mother is a sentence of death. Mary's neurotic attachment to her younger son is much deeper here than in the later version, and the burden of responsibility she places on him is far heavier. Edmund is her dead baby as well as her living son. He is a peace offering to Christ and the Virgin, her last chance to prove her maternal capability. Unlike the milder published speech, this outburst makes painfully clear that Mary cannot let Edmund go, either literally or emotionally.

As he wrote, O'Neill gradually weakened what were initially very close connections between Edmund and Jamie, and Edmund and Eugene; and he decreased Mary's obsession with Edmund. The result is that the younger son emerges as a discrete individual similar to or strongly influenced by these three yet not overpowered by them. Moreover, by loosening the bonds between Edmund and the others, O'Neill introduces the suggestion that he may not be destroyed as they have been. Mary is an apparently hopeless emotional cripple, Jamie is ruined in spirit, and Eugene is dead. The often very close ties Edmund has to them in early drafts condemn him by association. Attenuating these ties raises at least the possibility that Edmund may be able to avoid the destructive family cycle.

Another way in which O'Neill suggested Edmund's individual integrity and distanced him from his family was by showing what he might be if he survived—a writer. The younger son is a particularly nebulous figure in the scenario because that draft barely hints at his literary ambitions or his potential to realize them. The scenario does reveal that Edmund has worked for a newspaper, and his interests are manifest in his debates with Tyrone over the "morbid" poetry he favors, but the quotations from Baudelaire and Dowson—which demonstrate how carefully Edmund has studied these poets—do not appear. Far more important, both Edmund's paean to the fog ("The fog was where I wanted to be") and his long tribute to his sea experiences are missing from the scenario. The fog speech is first mentioned in a post-scenario note; the sea speech occurs first in the manuscript. While, as Edmund himself readily admits, neither passage is great literature, they do show his love of words as well as his ability to put words together to create compelling descriptions.

Beyond the question of literary powers, the sea speech is also significant because it shows that Edmund has had a life of his own outside the family circle, a life he voluntarily pursued and which provided him with a sense of "belonging" he never found at home. "For a second you see—and seeing the secret, are the secret. For a second there is meaning!" he exults (text, p. 153). Finally, through both passages Edmund reveals an understanding that his mother, at least, never reaches. He clearly identifies his ecstatic experiences as escapes from the world and time. "I belonged, without past or future" (p. 153) he says of his shipboard reveries; he defines the fog world as one "where truth is untrue and life can hide from itself" (p. 131). Unlike Mary, however, who waits for the Virgin Mary to release her from more than thirty years of pain and guilt, Edmund realizes that such escapes are only temporary: "Then the hand lets the veil fall and you are alone, lost in the fog again, and you stumble on toward nowhere, for no good reason!" (p. 153). Edmund knows that one cannot hope to build a life on such transient revelations; one can, at best, hope to build literature on them.

Whether Edmund will live long enough to fulfill his ambitions is, of course, a major issue in *Journey*. He is suffering from consumption, a leading killer in 1912. While some critics, including Annette Rubenstein and Wolcott Gibbs,[81] believe that Edmund is destined to die of his disease, many of O'Neill's revisions undermine this assumption. Edmund's potential for survival is ambiguous: it is by no means certain that he has received an irrevocable death sentence.

According to early notes, O'Neill originally intended that the family know of Edmund's consumption before the drama begins. The note states: "The younger son has appointment p.m. with Doc. to hear results—the others already know because Father has talked with doc. over phone." In the scenario the diagnosis has apparently already been heard. No phone call comes from the physician, and Jamie's talk with Edmund before lunch includes the warning, "Well, from what the Old Man's hinted, you'd better be prepared for bad news" (II, p. 2). As with Mary's addiction, it is more dramatically compelling to create tension over Edmund's illness by placing the confirmation of consumption during the play. O'Neill does so in the manuscript.

One reason he may have originally wished to place the phone call before the curtain rises is that he was unsure exactly how to handle the reception of the bad news. In the final *Journey* (even more than in preliminary versions) the Tyrones are reluctant to acknowledge Mary's addiction and Edmund's consumption. The men's warnings to Mary to "be careful" are oblique, and the audience must wait until Act II before learning that she takes drugs. Likewise, the family members do not wish to state plainly what is wrong with Edmund. Guilt, fear, and pity prevent Tyrone and Jamie from telling the others what they have learned from the phone call. Early in the second act Jamie advises Edmund to be "prepared for bad news" (p. 55), but neither he nor his father reveals the diagnosis that is confirmed a half-hour later. Unless he is told during the ride uptown, Edmund hears the test results first from Dr. Hardy.

In the manuscript Tyrone devises an elaborate evasion about the doctor's call. He enters muttering vaguely, "He's found out what's wrong with you. It's nothing serious, if you take good care of yourself for a while." When Edmund asks, "What did he tell you? Not that I give a damn now," Tyrone responds: "(hiding behind irritation) Oh, you know, do you? Well, I say he didn't. He started to but I choked him off because he was using a lot of medical words that meant nothing to me. (He forces a laugh) Hardy is a great one to show off his learning, if you give him half a chance." Edmund spots the evasion yet merely says, "All right, Papa, stall along! But if you think I give a damn now what it is, you're a fool" (II, 2, pp. 2–3).

Tyrone's transparent lie was canceled in the manuscript, and Edmund's question is merely sidetracked by Mary's anti-Hardy tirade (text, p. 74). What is curious about the final version is that Edmund does not pursue the issue further. In the manuscript it is clear that such pursuit is pointless because Tyrone obviously will not admit that he was given the diagnosis. The published version places the emphasis on Edmund: he seems so depressed by his mother's readdiction that he does not even care what is wrong with himself. One could surmise that Edmund has already guessed the nature of his disease, but O'Neill's revisions suggest this is not so. Although both Mary and Jamie evidently fear consumption, Edmund does not appear to consider this possibility. The typescript has Jamie telling his father, "I have a hunch consumption is what he's been afraid of underneath" (II, 2, p. 7), yet this was deleted, and when cautioned by

Jamie that he may be seriously ill, Edmund mentions only that he suspects malaria (text, p. 55). There is no hint that the young patient is deliberately lying to spare his family. Rather, for someone who knows he is very sick, Edmund seems both imperceptive to the suspicions of those around him and curiously unconcerned about his malady.

How serious is Edmund's illness? O'Neill toyed with the question of fatality throughout his revisions, ending roughly where he began: although the family members fear Edmund's disease might kill him, neither the Tyrones nor the audience are certain he is doomed. Some changes move toward a more positive view. A scenario stage direction for the Elder Son reads: "shows he thinks Y[ounger]. S[on]. going to die" (V, p. 5). Jamie in the published *Journey* does dread this possibility and begs Edmund, "Don't die on me," but there is no corresponding stage direction to confirm Jamie's fear (text, p. 167). The manuscript has Edmund as well as Jamie accusing Tyrone: "Irish peasants think consumption is always fatal" (IV, p. 13). Jamie alone makes this charge in the final text. Edmund's fourth-act sea speech contains his claim that he is one "who must always be a little in love with death!" (text, p. 154). Although in the published play Tyrone objects only to the "morbid craziness" of the speech, the manuscript shows him responding more fully. Tyrone, assuming the death reference reflects Edmund's worry about his consumption, attempts to comfort his son by insisting, "You'll be completely cured in six months— that's what the specialist promised me, I swear to you" (IV, p. 18). Instead of being reassuring, this desperate assertion reminds the audience once again that death may be more than just a gloomy young poet's fancied escape from life's disappointments. O'Neill canceled Tyrone's words, so the old man no longer mentions Edmund's potentially deadly condition here. However, the playwright also included a new allusion a few lines later. Telling Tyrone that he will never be a poet but only a stammerer, Edmund adds "I mean, if I live" (text, p. 154)—a qualification apparently inserted during revision of the manuscript.

These examples suggest that O'Neill wished to present Edmund's illness in an ambiguous light. He was presumably aware the audience would know that Edmund's prototype, the playwright himself, did not die in the sanatorium, yet he was still concerned about how to dramatize the illness. Examination of the final text supports what the alterations suggest. Although Edmund is very sick, his condition is not medically hopeless. He is being sent to a semiprivate (if inexpensive) institution, rather than the state farm. He is a young man who has the potential for physical survival.

Physical survival alone, however, is not proof of survival in the larger sense explored in *Journey*. Although Jamie refers to himself as having a "part that's been dead so long" (text, p. 165), he, Mary, and Tyrone are literally alive. But O'Neill's revisions emphasize that all three are trapped by past mistakes, unrealized ambitions, and overwhelming guilt. O'Neill's development of Edmund, by contrast, moves tentatively in the opposite direction—toward the idea that he alone might have a constructive future. The playwright stressed that the guilt Edmund bears is painful yet not necessarily paralyzing: he has betrayed himself and his family, but not to the degree the others have. Further, the revisions clarify the fact that Edmund, unlike his parents and brother, has not made a mistake that will damn him. Mary's dependence on drugs, Tyrone's wasting his talents in a popular melodrama, Jamie's determined dissipation, are all past mistakes that limit the present and foreclose the future. Edmund, the youngest, has not yet made such a fatal error. Significantly, Edmund in the course of the play learns about the others' mistakes, and he is warned by their failures. Perhaps most important, Edmund gains understanding of and compassion for his haunted kin. This knowledge tempered by pity may well be his best hope for escape from the futile world of his family.[82]

The main charges leveled against Edmund are that his difficult birth caused Mary's original addiction, and that his present illness and lack of faith in his mother have led to her readdiction. To begin with the latter charges, we must refer again to the "notes for revision" quoted early in this chapter. The note reads:

> What really happened—she had been frantic—given in—gone to bathroom, spareroom—then, thinking of Edmund, for his sake had conquered craving which was brought on by continual worry about him—at end, she tells Edmund this—he wants believe but can't help suspecting—it is this lack of faith in him, combined with growing fear, which makes her give in—

Both Törnqvist and Tinsley cite this note, but both fail to acknowledge that O'Neill did not fully incorporate its implications into the play.[83] Never in the published *Journey* does Mary tell Edmund she had conquered her craving for his sake. Moreover, this note places the burden of Mary's readdiction squarely and solely on him, while the final text distributes responsibility among all the Tyrones. The crucial scene occurs at the end of Act I. Tyrone and Jamie have already had a discussion about Mary's nocturnal wanderings. The principal subject is the same in the later scene except that it is Mary and Edmund who talk about the preceding night. Mary senses her younger son's suspicions, but she includes in her accusation "your father and Jamie, too—particularly Jamie" (text, p. 45). A few moments later she cries: "Oh, I can't bear it, Edmund, when even you [suspect me]—!" Immediately she becomes nervous and "a strange undercurrent of revengefulness comes into her voice." Yet is is not Edmund alone who has set her off, as she acknowledges with her threat, "It would serve all of you right if it was true!" (p. 47). The blame for the injection she will soon take is to be shared by all of them, and by circumstances beyond their control. Further, Edmund's illness is only one factor contributing to her readdiction: she has been through many "cures" before and always returned to drugs, even when her younger son was healthy. Thus Edmund does not, as the note implies, have to suffer with the knowledge that he was solely responsible for his mother's failure to resist her morphine craving. He will be haunted only by his own share in the family's lapse of faith.

The other "crime" of which Edmund stands accused is that of being born. In the scenario Mary and Tyrone, upset because his birth caused Mary so much pain and because he has been "fired from college—ruined his health," wish that their younger son "had never been born" (III, p. 3). The harshness of these scenario lines is never reached in the published text. A canceled manuscript passage has Mary accusing Edmund of causing her drug problem:

> MARY (bitterly accusing) You should be the last one to remind me—considering—
> EDMUND (bitterly resentful in his turn) I see what's coming now! I know it by heart! Considering you were never ill a day in your life and didn't have a nerve in your body before I was born! So it's all [?] my fault! (I, p. 24)

Although Mary is immediately contrite, Edmund's response indicates that she frequently makes this charge. His "I see what's coming now" is reminiscent of his response to Tyrone's "How sharper than a serpent's tooth": both are family routines. In *Journey* Mary does blame her addiction on Edmund's birth, but there is little hint of the repeated litany this manuscript argument suggests.

Even the deletion of these lines, however, does not alter the fact that his parents and brother accuse Edmund of causing Mary's addiction by being born. Obviously Edmund had no control over his birth, yet this does not absolve him in the others' eyes. He must share the guilt with Tyrone, who hired the cheap hotel doctor to treat his sick wife, and with Jamie, who inadvertently or not caused the baby's death. In an essay on tragedy Richard B. Sewall writes: "Above all, the source of tragic suffering is the sense, in the consciousness of tragic man, of simultaneous guilt and guiltlessness."[84] This is Edmund's situation: he is both responsible and not responsible for his mother's addiction. What he is guilty of is original sin. As Helen Muchnic observes, for O'Neill "man is born guilty."[85] Mary laments Edmund's birth, saying, "He has never been happy. He never will be. Nor healthy. He was born nervous and too sensitive, and that's my fault" (text, p. 88). In a line cut from the typescript she states her point more bluntly: "He inherited my punishment" (II, 2, p. 12). The sins of the fathers and mothers are visited upon the children.

This notion of being born guilty pervades the O'Neill canon. From the earliest sea plays we find O'Neill's characters, by virtue of their human-ness, out of rhythm with a world more suited—in Edmund's words—to seagulls and fish. Billy Brown declares: "This is Daddy's bedtime secret for today: Man is born broken. He lives by mending. The grace of God is glue!"[86] Babies emerge from the womb with the curse of humanity on them, a curse that emanates from their position as intruders in a world whose harmony they disrupt. What better way to dramatize this than through a man whose very birth destroys the mother who bore him? O'Neill's late plays demonstrate little faith in the power of God's grace to make the individual whole again, but the concept of original sin informs them all. Larry Slade describes the inhabitants of Hope's bar as "mis-begotten," the term O'Neill includes in the title of his last play. Simon Harford in *More Stately Mansions* characterizes life as "a perpetual in-bankruptcy for debts we never contracted."[87]

All this does not mean that human beings are destroyed as soon as they are conceived. They are born with a burden of guilt, but they are still responsible for the shape of their lives. It is not original sin alone that condemns Mary, Tyrone, and Jamie: they have made mistakes which harmed others and, even more important, themselves. The past is para-mount in these dramas because any decision has future repercussions the individual cannot foresee. Moreover, additional forces—heredity, en-vironment, personality—complicate the decision. Mary (even more in the drafts than in the final play) is *Journey*'s most insistent apostle of deter-minism, asserting, "None of us can help the things life has done to us." Yet she qualifies this statement by adding: "They're done before you realize

it, and once they're done they make you do other things until at last
everything comes between you and what you'd like to be, and you've lost
your true self forever" (text, p. 61). Further, her repeated accusations
against her family suggest an only partially suppressed belief in individual
responsibility. How could she berate her husband, for example, if she
truly believed he had no control over his deeds? Tyrone, quoting Shakespeare, presents the argument for free will: "The fault, dear Brutus, is not
in our stars, but in ourselves that we are underlings" (text, p. 152).[88]
O'Neill's view lies between these two positions. Tyrone chose the role of
the Count and consequently lost forever his chance to be a great Shakespearean actor. Mary accepted drugs to ease her pain only to become a
victim of them. The choices they made were not entirely free. Fear of
poverty, physical suffering, feelings of guilt, even love, combined to push
them toward the wrong decision. But a choice was made. It is in this
sense of guilt and guiltlessness that O'Neill most closely approximates the
Greek idea of fate he hoped to translate into modern terms.[89] Biological,
psychological, and sociological forces—leavened with O'Neill's rein-
terpretation of a Christian notion, original sin—replace the gods of
Aeschylus and Sophocles. Human beings, however, are still held account-
able for their actions.

Bogard complains:

> Although O'Neill has been at pains to show what the past has made his
> parents and brother, it is unclear what the past has made Edmund. O'Neill
> perhaps understandably suppresses the fact of his brief marriage and his
> child and omits the crucial event in 1912 of his divorce. He mentions that
> Edmund has been to sea, and almost perfunctorily adds that he has lived in
> the sewers of New York and Buenos Aires and has attempted suicide. None of
> these events, except insofar as his having been to sea conditions his vision of
> belonging, bear heavily on what he is. He seems to be the victim of the
> family, unwanted, betrayed, led astray by his brother and, now, with tuber-
> culosis, suffering under his father's penuriousness.[90]

Surely Edmund is more than simply the victim of his family, for he has in
his own way—through his dissipation, his mistrust of his mother, his aca-
demic failures—contributed to the Tyrones' tragedies. To see him solely
as a victim is to accept Mary's deterministic claim that individuals cannot
control their fate. Yet Bogard may well be pointing toward an essential
difference between Edmund and his kin. Although O'Neill has created a

world in which past errors circumscribe and destroy the future, this does not mean he must present each character as having already made such an error. Perhaps O'Neill failed to give Edmund an ex-wife and a child not because he wished to suppress painful personal history but because he wanted to create one character who has yet to face life's crucial decisions. Through the young Edmund he could explore the possibilities of how one might avoid the web of mistakes in which the others are caught. Condemned to bear the guilt of his birth, of original sin, Edmund has still not betrayed himself as completely and finally as the other members of his family have betrayed themselves. When the curtain falls, the future lies before rather than behind him.

O'Neill designed the play very carefully so that Edmund hears the other characters' accounts of how they erred. He is on stage for all of the final act except the opening moments. He hears his brother and father tell how forces around them and their own blunders destroyed them, and he is warned. He is warned by Mary much earlier. In the second act's final scene, Mary tells him that some day she will be cured, "some day when the Blessed Virgin Mary forgives me and gives me back the faith in Her love and pity I used to have in my convent days, and I can pray to Her again—" (text, p. 94). These words show that Mary will not even try to help herself; she will merely wait passively for the Virgin's aid. In the notes O'Neill indicates his intention to move this speech to the very end of the play and, in fact, the final speech in the scenario is very similar to this. O'Neill wisely chose not to conclude *Journey* with this passage for several reasons: it focuses too sharply on Mary rather than on the family as a whole; it shows Mary aware of her present problem, an awareness she has lost well before the last scene of the published text; and it is a much less dramatic ending than the one he ultimately composed. O'Neill probably also left the speech in the second act because he wanted to emphasize that Edmund hears what his mother says. Edmund is alone with her here (as he is not at the play's conclusion) and he is neither drunk nor exhausted. Edmund does hear Mary, and what she is saying is that she will not, or cannot, attempt to help herself. The situation is beyond her control, and beyond Edmund's.

In the last act Edmund listens to Tyrone's tale about how he was ruined by the "big money maker" he starred in too long. After this speech Edmund tells his father, "I know you a lot better now" (text, p. 151). The emphatic "a lot" was added to the typescript (IV, p. 19).[91] He then, under protest, hears Jamie's confession, which ends with the admonition: "Only don't forget me. Remember I warned you—for your sake" (text, p. 167). Edmund has already shown that he knows the value of remembering. Early in the play he exhorts his mother to recall her previous drug episodes and warns: "it's bad for you to forget. The right way is to remember. So you'll always be on your guard" (text, p. 45). This is the advice Edmund must follow: to remember what Mary, Tyrone, and Jamie have told him.

The manuscript includes one curious scene absent from subsequent drafts, an appearance by Mary roughly one-quarter of the way into the final act. In the published text Edmund at this point fears "she's coming downstairs," but she retreats without being seen by the audience (p. 139). There are likely many reasons why O'Neill deleted this scene; the simplest explanation is that it serves virtually no purpose. Mary wanders about looking for "something I lost long ago—something I miss dreadfully now" and concludes "I could never find it here" (IV, p. 9).[92] These lines are confusing as well as unnecessary because, despite a reference by Mary to the convent, they might mislead the audience into believing that the object of her search is the wedding gown with which she appears at the drama's climax. What Mary seeks cannot be found in the attic any more than in the living room: it is her lost faith and childhood innocence. Further, this scene detracts from the stunning impact of the play's final moments when Mary, who has been absent from the stage for an hour, enters dramatically in a blaze of light. O'Neill's theatrical sense alone might have impelled him to eliminate the earlier appearance. Finally, surely one reason O'Neill canceled Mary's premature entrance was to keep the audience's attention on Edmund.[93] Up until the final act Mary dominates the play; during the first three acts of the published text she speaks more lines than do all the men combined. She is the dramatic focus of *Journey*, just as Hickey is the dramatic focus of *Iceman*. Deleting Mary's appearance at this point removes a distraction from Edmund's learning experience. He has already learned, in previous scenes, all that his mother's situation can teach him.

Like Larry Slade in *Iceman*, Edmund Tyrone learns the necessity for pity. Both characters are forced to listen to confessions they do not want to hear, and both are compelled to temper their cynicism with compassionate understanding. Edmund does try to quell fights throughout the play, but it is especially in the fourth act that he functions as peacemaker. When Tyrone and Jamie start to battle just before the final scene, Edmund refuses to join Jamie's attack on their father and attempts to squelch the argument. In the scenario, by contrast, Edmund's feelings for his father at this point are more equivocal. Although he is immediately ashamed of his words and tries to cover them with appeasing statements, Edmund's vicious attack on the old man—his claim that Tyrone likes to have a failure around so he can feel superior—occurs here. His anger has not been fully assuaged by the family's revelations. Shortly thereafter, in all drafts, Edmund defends Mary from Jamie's nasty tongue. In the scenario he orders his brother, "Stop it, damn you! Leave her alone," when Jamie cries "All hopped up. Our mother" and "mockingly" recites Kipling's "Mother o' Mine" (V, p. 6). His reaction is surer and swifter in the published text: he strikes his brother for his cruel comparison of Mary to Ophelia.

Even more than Larry Slade, however, Edmund is a character whose importance is difficult to convey on stage. He functions as the audience's touchstone: our perceptions grow as his do. The very structure of *Journey* forces us into a position analogous to Edmund's: he knew something was wrong with his mother long before he discovered the exact nature of her malady, just as we must wait through one and a half acts before her addiction is revealed to us. Like Edmund, we are witness to the wrenching confessions of the other Tyrones. Yet Edmund's sympathetic responses are relatively minor: he is never required to act as decisively on his newly acquired understanding and forgiveness as Larry is. His compassionate deeds—telling his father he knows him "a lot better now," intervening in family fights, protecting Tyrone and Mary from Jamie's verbal assaults— are small ones. Larry, on the other hand, must undertake a shattering dramatic action: the condemnation of Parritt. Jamie thanks Edmund for listening to his confession as Parritt thanks Larry for listening to and acting upon his. But it is Jamie himself who makes the greater sacrifice, who gives up his cherished self-image as his brother's protector to warn his brother that there is hatred in him as well as love.

When José Quintero first presented *Long Day's Journey Into Night* in 1957, he asked Jason Robards, Jr., who had made such a success as Hickey in the *Iceman* revival, to play the role of Edmund. Even though Edmund is the larger part (he is on stage longer and speaks more lines than his brother) Robards requested to play Jamie instead.[94] Reviewers of that production consistently praised the portrayal of the elder brother. Henry Hewes, among others, claimed that Robards stole the show.[95] Equally

consistently critics complained that Edmund is a less interesting character than his parents and brother, and gave more attention to the other
roles. It does not appear to be the performance of Bradford Dillman (who
played Edmund in the original production) that is responsible for this
judgment, since his acting was often praised. Walter Kerr, for example,
contended that Dillman handled his speeches "with swift, sensitive skill,"
yet he accorded Edmund and Dillman only half a sentence while spending three paragraphs discussing the other Tyrones and the actors and
actress portraying them.[96] In reviews of the movie version and of revivals,
critics continued to complain about the paleness of the younger son. An
anonymous *Time* reviewer, commenting on the movie, echoed many critics when he concluded that Edmund is "the weakest of the parts."[97]

We have seen how much care O'Neill gave to the portrayal of Edmund,
and how alterations in the various drafts help to focus attention on him as
a unique and important figure. But despite the effort expended on Edmund's characterization he is, on stage, less compelling than the others.
One clue may be found in the crucial last-act speeches. Tyrone's and Jamie's confessions are very personal, emotionally devastating admissions of
failure. While Edmund's sea speech is moving, there is little of the pathos
of personal pain and failure in it. One is as struck by the way he describes
his sea experiences as by the experiences themselves. Almost a set piece
on the miseries of any sensitive soul, it is not drawn from the torments of
individual defeat as are the words of his father and brother, and his mother's anguished ravings. Nothing in the logic of the play demands that Edmund have erred and suffered the same way the rest of the Tyrones have,
but the fact that he has not makes him a less emotionally affecting character.

The other problems are very similar to those O'Neill faced with *Iceman*. As Larry Slade must compete on stage with the flamboyant Hickey
and Harry Hope, so Edmund must compete for attention with two actors
and a dope-crazed Mary. By the very nature of the character O'Neill has
created, Edmund is less colorful and dynamic than the other family members. He is the quiet one. This contrast is further heightened because
much of Edmund's function, like Larry's, is to listen and learn—basically
passive, undramatic activities. It is only in his last play that O'Neill creates a character, Josie Hogan in *A Moon for the Misbegotten*, who as
sympathetic listener is as dramatically compelling as those with a tale of
suffering to tell.

CHAPTER THREE

A Moon for the Misbegotten

 "THE LIE OF A PIPE DREAM is what gives life to the whole misbegotten mad lot of us, drunk or sober."[1] So remarks Larry Slade in *The Iceman Cometh*, and in his last completed play O'Neill turned once again to the misbegotten, those who find themselves aliens in an uncongenial world. While *Iceman* shows how most people get by with a dream and a drink, *Moon* narrows the focus to a pair of special individuals for whom even these consolations will not suffice. Jim Tyrone is too haunted by guilt to fabricate a life-giving illusion and Josie Hogan, like Larry Slade, must abjure her fantasy world to help a tortured friend find the peace of death.

Like *The Iceman Cometh* and *Long Day's Journey Into Night*, O'Neill's final drama is based on people from the playwright's past. Phil Hogan is modeled after James O'Neill's feisty Irish tenant John Dolan, who was also the original for the off-stage Shaughnessy in *Journey*. In early Work Diary entries O'Neill referred to *Moon* as "S. play," the "S" presumably standing for Shaughnessy, and the scenario is entitled "Dolan play." John Henry Raleigh, among others, also sees Hogan as "a kind of final tribute to James O'Neill." Raleigh points out that Hogan and the elder O'Neill share "vitality," "survival powers," a penchant for "role-playing" and a large capacity for whiskey, as well as love for their families.[2] In a revealing line deleted from the typescript, Jim says: "Your esteemed Old Man would have made a hit on the stage, Josie. No kidding. He's a natural born actor—."[3] Also revealing is an August 11, 1936, diary entry in which Carlotta stated that O'Neill wanted to write "a *comedy* of his Father!" She added that it would be "A lovable, *kind* comedy!"

T. Stedman Harder (Harker in *Journey*) derives from Edward C. Hammond and Edward S. Harkness, two wealthy men with estates in and near New London. Hammond owned land adjoining the Dolan farm, while

Harkness was the son of a founder of Standard Oil.[4] In his 1914 verse "Upon Our Beach," O'Neill revealed his grudge against the millionaire Hammond, whom he labeled a "food-stuffed adorer of Mammon."[5] The maliciously satirical portrait of Harder also reflects another attitude O'Neill held all his life. Such early poems as "The Shut-Eye Candidate," "The Long Tale," and "Fratricide" accuse Standard Oil of fostering political corruption and war.[6] His distaste for the mammoth company is similar to that of the Hogans and Jim Tyrone in *Moon*, written thirty years later. In fact, their distaste is presented even more strongly in preliminary drafts than in the published play, for at least a half-dozen swipes at Standard Oil were cut from the typescript.

Jim Tyrone is, of course, based on O'Neill's older brother, James O'Neill, Jr. The first Work Diary entry about the play reads: "S. play idea, based on story told by E[dmund]. in 1st Act of 'L[ong]. D[ay's]. J[ourney]. I[nto]. N[ight].'—except here Jamie principal character & story of play otherwise entirely imaginary, except for J[amie]'s revelation of self."[7] "Jamie" obviously refers to both Jamie Tyrone of *Journey* and the playwright's sibling. The descriptions of James Tyrone, Jr., are nearly identical in *Journey* and *Moon*, with the alterations that eleven years necessitated (*Journey* is set in 1912, *Moon* in 1923). O'Neill added to the *Moon* manuscript (with a caret) the "Mephistophelian quality" he attributed to Jamie in the earlier drama. Although Jim tells Josie in *Moon* that he spent a period of sobriety with his widowed mother before her death, he appears as we would expect *Journey's* Jamie a decade later: even more dissipated, physically and emotionally; still jobless and aimless; still drinking very heavily. James O'Neill, Jr., was in even worse condition than Jim Tyrone in September 1923. Suffering from advanced alcoholism that rendered him nearly blind, he was confined to a New Jersey sanatorium, where he died in November.[8]

In the scenario and notes for *Moon*, and occasionally in the manuscript, James Tyrone, Jr., is called Jamie, as he was in *Journey*. Possibly O'Neill changed the name to Jim because that was the nickname by which Christine Ell, generally considered the model for Josie Hogan, called O'Neill's brother.[9] Christine, a friend of both O'Neill brothers, approximated the physical dimensions of Josie, although she was not quite as large. She was a warm, impulsive, motherly woman with whom Jamie had a brief affair a few years before he died.[10] According to Agnes Boulton, Jamie was wont to praise her hair and bosom,[11] the same features Jim

Tyrone appreciates in Josie. It seems clear, however, that although Christine was the inspiration for Josie, O'Neill cared little for biographical accuracy. She was scarcely a virginal Connecticut farm woman: O'Neill met her in Greenwich Village, where she had both a husband and a succession of lovers. Christine may well have shared with Josie an essential naïveté and goodness, but O'Neill demanded that his final heroine have purity of body as well as heart. Further, Jamie's "revelation of self," which O'Neill mentions in his Work Diary, was almost certainly made to the playwright rather than to Christine. It is probably neither accidental nor metaphorical that Josie calls Jim "my brother" in the *Moon* scenario (IV, p. 5).

A MOON FOR THE MISBEGOTTEN is first mentioned in the Work Diary on October 28, 1941. The following day O'Neill noted in the Diary, "this can be strange combination comic-tragic—am enthused about it." He finished the scenario on November 3.[12] Running somewhat over four thousand words, the *Moon* scenario is substantially shorter than that of *Journey* and only one-third as long as *Iceman*'s. It is even more shapeless than the scenarios of the other two plays: the focus is clearly on characters and their relationships rather than on plot or dramatic structure. Already O'Neill's plans for his last play seem limited, and his interest in the plot— the weakest part of this drama—minimal. There is no Act I in the *Moon* scenario. Instead, the first page consists of character notes, most about Josie Hogan, and a very brief synopsis of the Jim-Josie relationship as it will develop through the first three acts. Act II is covered by just a few lines; only Acts III and IV are fully treated in the scenario. This is the first indication of what later drafts will make apparent: the moonlight confessions and their effects engaged O'Neill's attention more fully than did the Irish victory over Standard Oil.

As with *Iceman* and *Journey*, various tentative titles are scribbled in the margins of the scenario. The moon, with its implications of reverie, peace, and femininity, recurs often. One proposed title, "The Moon of Other Days," has distinctly nostalgic connotations. Another, "The Moon Bore Twins," emphasizes the similarities between the misbegotten lovers— similarities more evident in the scenario than in the final draft. O'Neill eventually chose "Moon of the Misbegotten" as a "good title," subsequently revising this to "A Moon for the Misbegotten," which he considered "much more to point."[13] Although Work Diary entries show O'Neill

Josie: (defensively) That's not saying much. ~~I think~~
~~I know what you think you know~~ - (Forcing a contemptous laugh)
If it's that, ~~it's a lie and~~ you're a terrible ~~big~~ fool.

Tyrone: (teasingly) If it's what? I haven't said
anything.

Josie: You'd better not, or I'll die laughing at you~~,~~
~~and so would Father.~~ (She changes the subject abruptly)
"hy don't you drink up? It makes me nervous watching you
hold it as if you didn't know it was there.

Tyrone: I didn't, at that. (He drinks)

Josie: And have another.

Tyrone: (a bit drunkenly) Will a whore go to a picnic?
Real bonded Bourbon. That's my dish. ~~(He gets up) I warned~~
~~you you'd never get rid of me.~~ (He goes to the boulder for
the bottle. He is as steady on his feet as if he were com-
pletly sober.)

Josie: (in a light tone) ~~Who wants to get rid of you,~~
~~Jim darling? Not me. Not while out night lasts. Not till~~
~~the dawn at any rate.~~ Bring the bottle back so it'll be
handy and you won't have to leave me. I miss you.

Tyrone: (comes back with the bottle. ~~before he sits~~
~~down~~ He ~~stares~~ at her, ~~a cynical, wise-guy expression on his~~
~~face~~) Still trying to get me soused, Josie?

Josie: I'm not such a fool -with your capacity. ~~It's~~
~~water off a ducks back.~~

Tyrone: You better watch your step. It might work -
and then think of how ~~rotten and~~ disgusted you'd feel,
with my lying beside you, probably snoring, as you watched
the dawn come. ~~But you don't know -~~

Josie: (stiffens ~~resentfully~~ smugly) The hell I don't!

Tyrone: ~~(ignores this) You don't know.~~ But take it from
me, I know - ~~too damned well.~~ I've seen too god-damned many
dawns creeping grayly over too many dirty windows. ~~(He is~~
~~again talking as if to himself)~~

Josie: (insists ~~resentfully~~) I do know. Isn't that the
way I've felt with every one ~~of them~~ - after? ~~What do you~~
~~think I am,~~ anyway - an innocent virgin? ᴸut it would be
different with you. (Forcing a ~~teasing kidding tone~~) Sure, Aᴺᵈ
haven't I been head over heels in love ~~with~~ you ever since you
told me you loved me ~~for~~ my beautiful soul?. ~~Love would make~~
~~it different.~~

composing "notes" or "prelims" for *Moon* on four separate days in November, both before and while writing the manuscript, only two pages of notes from this period have survived.[14] Also extant is an undated sheet with two neatly executed drawings of the Hogan shack. The first sketch, crossed out, shows a building very slightly more prepossessing than the shack in the second drawing. The major difference is that the main body and front door of the first house, as well as Josie's bedroom, face forward. In the second sketch and the published play, the house is turned sideways and only Josie's bedroom directly faces the audience. O'Neill had used a similar arrangement before—the side rather than the front of the Cabot home is turned toward the audience in *Desire Under the Elms*—but he had a special reason for rotating the Hogan dwelling. In the second picture, visual emphasis is placed on Josie's door and steps: it is in her "territory" that the crucial third act confessions will take place.

According to the Work Diary, O'Neill began the first full manuscript of *Moon* on November 7 and completed Act I by November 26. He was pleased with his work and commented that he was "getting great satisfaction" from the play. After a few days of note-writing he plunged into Act II, on which he was working when the Japanese bombed Pearl Harbor. The attack, not unexpectedly, disrupted his writing and dampened his enthusiasm for the drama. Diary entries show that he was distracted by the war and illness while composing the third and fourth acts. He finished the draft on January 20, 1942, and complained in the Diary: "had to drag myself through it since Pearl Harbor and it needs much revision—wanders all over place."

Unwilling or unable to begin revising *Moon*, O'Neill spent most of the next year polishing the one-act *Hughie* (the only surviving drama from his "By Way of Obit" series), considering ideas for more short plays in this group, making notes for other dramas, and writing the final version of *A Touch of the Poet*. It was not until January 3, 1943, that he began in earnest to work on *Moon* again. After reading the first draft, he remarked in his Work Diary: "want to get this really written—real affection for it—can be fine, unusual play." He made a few more notes and three days later began "cutting, revising, etc." Most 1943 Diary entries include bitter complaints about the debilitating effects of his illness. According to Carlotta, her husband gave up the Work Diary, which ends on May 4, 1943, because he felt that her journal was "more complete" than his.[15] With the physical act of writing now so difficult, O'Neill was probably glad to avoid the effort even the brief Work Diary notations demanded. The pencil draft of *Moon*, labeled by the dramatist "2nd d.—still needs cuts & condensation," is dated May 17, 1943.[16]

O'Neill's revisions on the manuscript of *Moon* were extraordinarily extensive; in fact, he appears to have discarded and rewritten most of the original pencil draft. He began revising the first act, the portion with which he was most satisfied, in much the same way he had reworked the manuscripts of *Iceman* and *Journey*. Although there are relatively few minor corrections—canceled individual words or lines—there are several clues that more major alterations were made. Instead of simply deleting a sentence or passage, O'Neill removed and replaced whole pages. Some added sheets have fractional numbers. Some pages begin with dialogue that does not follow directly from speeches on preceding pages, indicating that O'Neill removed one or more sheets and substituted new material. He had done this with *Iceman* and *Journey*; he did it more often in the first act of *Moon*. Possibly more than one-half the original first act pages were rejected and replaced.

O'Neill was even more ruthless with the rest of *Moon*. While near the beginning of Act II there are a very few moderately edited sheets that may be part of the original manuscript, nearly all of this act appears to be new. Presumably O'Neill put aside the first manuscript and began composing afresh, probably keeping the original version by him as he wrote. In the Work Diary he refers to Acts II and III as "entirely" or "completely rewritten," and although he was still laboring on Act IV when the Diary concludes, he predicts that act also will need to be totally rewritten.[17] He may have been exaggerating very slightly about the second act, but not about the others. Unfortunately, the original Acts III and IV and the pages removed from Acts I and II have not survived. Moreover, because O'Neill did most of the revision as he rewrote, the new pages are largely free of obvious changes, deletions, and additions. We must depend primarily on the scenario and notes to elucidate O'Neill's earliest conception of *Moon*.

The revised manuscript was typed into the first typescript during the fall of 1943. The first typescript is labeled, in O'Neill's hand, "1st typed draft (typed by Cyn) with subsequent revisions made [?] at Hamilton Apts, San Francisco." For many years Carlotta had done most of her husband's typing, but a back ailment forced her to recruit her daughter Cynthia ("Cyn") to prepare the *Moon* typescript. Cynthia could not read

O'Neill's tiny handwriting, so Carlotta, sometimes lying flat on her back, dictated the script to her.[18] Given this strange arrangement, it is not surprising that errors abound in the typescript: Cynthia's spelling and typing skills were shaky, and Carlotta sometimes lost her place while reading aloud. Although in a note affixed to the published text O'Neill mentions "completing the play in 1943," final revisions must have been done the following year, for the playwright did not move back to San Francisco until February 1944. When inscribing the published play for his wife, O'Neill wrote "To darling Carlotta . . . This token of my gratitude and awareness—a poor thing—a play she dislikes, and which I have come to loathe—dating back to 1944—my last."[19] Illness, war, and the emotional effort expended on this very personal drama had spoiled the playwright's earlier affection for *Moon*.

The revision of the *Moon* typescript was also unusual. The first two acts and most of the third were heavily, in many parts very heavily, edited. Further, O'Neill was so dissatisfied with the last portion of the play that instead of simply revising the typescript he removed the last two pages of Act III and all of Act IV and rewrote this section by hand. Considering the advanced state of his tremor and the consequent difficulty in writing, this was a major effort and may in part explain his eventual loathing for the play. Luckily, the excised section of the typescript has been preserved and is filed at Yale with the scenario and notes.[20]

O'Neill's revisions on the first typescript were the last significant work he did on *Moon*.[21] Another typescript, called "2nd script" in the Beinecke Library Catalogue, shows only a few corrections. The Beinecke's proofs for the published *Moon* are unedited. Whoever was responsible for proofreading and seeing the script through to publication was rather careless; a small number of errors apparently made by typists or typesetters preparing the text were never rectified and appear in the book version. For example, fourth-act stage directions in the published text curiously note that Josie's "eyes are fixed on the wanton sky."[22] The correct reading, "eastern sky," was penciled into some typescripts but apparently never included in the script that Random House, publishers of *Moon*, received. Similarly, the third line of the section of Keats's "Ode to a Nightingale," that Jim recites in Act II—"While thou art pouring forth thy soul abroad"—appeared in the second typescript but mysteriously disappeared before the play reached print.

Like *The Iceman Cometh*, *A Moon for the Misbegotten* was produced during O'Neill's lifetime. The playwright gave Langner copies of *Moon* and *Hughie* early in the summer of 1944. Langner relates that "after some discussion, it was decided that it would be better to produce this play [*Moon*] before *The Iceman Cometh*, and we decided to go ahead immediately with the casting, and to endeavor to interest Dudley Digges in directing the play."[23] Casting difficulties arose, however, and the drama did not appear until after *Iceman*. "Above all," O'Neill wrote Langner in a letter dated V-J Day, postponing the premiere "will give you time to cast the woman right."[24] The following year the playwright settled on Mary Welch, who was suitably Irish if not suitably large.

In the same letter, O'Neill insisted: "I do not want, on thinking it over, any production except one that opens in New York, cold." His instincts were right but he did not get his wish; the production opened on February 20, 1947, in Columbus, Ohio, and closed before reaching New York. Cast problems and O'Neill's poor health, which prevented him from giving sufficient attention to the production, were probably most responsible for the play's failure to open in New York the following season,[25] since the out-of-town reviews were mixed rather than uniformly negative. Many critics complained that the work was static and repetitious, and several compared it (not always favorably) to the tremendously popular stage version of *Tobacco Road*. Some praised it highly: the *Columbus Dispatch* critic, Samuel T. Wilson, called *Moon* "an arresting and fine play." Among the negative voices was Florence Fisher Parry, who lamented in the *Pittsburgh Press*, "I was ashamed to have my mother's old ears assaulted by the profanity and vulgarity of this play."[26] Bitter must have been the irony for O'Neill when the Detroit police censor, Charles Snyder, objected to the fact that the words *mother* and *prostitute* occur "in the same sentence,"[27] for one of the drama's main points is that Jim Tyrone also cannot bear associating the two. In a passage deleted from the typescript, Jim thanks Josie for not naming his mother "in the same breath with the blonde whore on the train" (III, p. 82).

According to Mary Welch, "Mr. O'Neill was ill during most of the three weeks of rehearsals" and managed to attend only three. He did, she notes, "cut several sentences from his finished script" during rehearsals,[28] but this does not mean that all the revisions in the prompt script were made by him. Some changes were made by the Theatre Guild on the road to appease censors, and although they ostensibly had the playwright's approval,[29] it is unlikely he gave it willingly and very likely he was too ill to engage in long-distance wrangling. O'Neill would not permit a revival of *Moon* during his lifetime. In a draft of a 1951 letter to Elia Kazan, Lawrence Langner relates: "I discussed MOON FOR THE MISBEGOTTEN not once but several times at the beginning of the summer, and in every instance Gene refused to have this play done, not only on account of his health, but because he wanted to do some rewriting on it."[30] He never did this rewriting and, when financial pressures forced him to publish the play the following year, he added a note stating, "*A Moon for the Misbegotten* is published herewith with no revisions or deletions. It is an exact reproduction of the original manuscript which I delivered to Random House, Inc., on completing the play in 1943. . . . Since I cannot presently give it the attention required for appropriate presentation, I have decided to make it available in book form." Because it is impossible to ascertain which changes in the acting script were O'Neill's, and because he chose to ignore virtually all of them when he later published the drama, the book version of *Moon* is the only one that can be considered authoritative.

From the scenario through the finished play one point is evident: O'Neill's interest in Josie Hogan and Jim Tyrone and his comparative lack of interest in scenes not directly concerned with their relationship. In *The Iceman Cometh* a large group of "choral" figures shares attention with the major characters. Cast size decreases sharply in *Long Day's Journey Into Night*, but four of the five characters are of significant, if not equal, importance. In *Moon* the cast still numbers five, but the focus is almost solely on Josie and Jim. O'Neill expended little time on Phil Hogan and the entrapment plot, making changes that serve to minimize the number of extraneous characters and relegate Hogan to a secondary position. He labored both to particularize Jim Tyrone and to emphasize the qualities he shares with many previous male figures in the O'Neill canon. Finally, a study of the development of *Moon* indicates that Josie, the play's most complex figure, presented O'Neill with the most difficulties. She is both the logical culmination of and an important variation on the loving, maternal, earthy woman who figures prominently in numerous O'Neill dramas.

Eight characters are listed at the beginning of both the *Moon* scenario and the manuscript. The first five, with a few name changes,[31] are the figures who eventually appear in the finished play. The other three, according to the manuscript cast list, are "Simpson, superintendant of Harder's estate"; "Cassidy," the Harder "stableman"; and "Merlo, a gardener" on Harder's estate. These three characters were apparently intended to be part of the first-act scene with Harder, or the witnesses with whom Hogan returned at dawn, or both.[32] However, only two unnamed witnesses appear in the scenario, and (although they might have been included in the missing first manuscript draft of Act III) none of these individuals appears in the body of the extant manuscript. Hogan does not need witnesses, and the play does not need as elaborate a Harder scene as including these characters would entail.

In fact, the scene with Harder does not appear at all in the *Moon* scenario. Obviously O'Neill had it in mind when he composed the scenario, for the Standard Oil heir is mentioned in the character list. The incident in the published play follows fairly closely the story told by Edmund in *Journey,* and O'Neill did not bother working out the dialogue or dynamics in the scenario. Further, he apparently considered the Standard Oil scion so unimportant that in 1943, long after he had written the Harder scene, the playwright informed his older son that *Moon* had "only three characters."[33] He completely ignored Harder, as well as Mike Hogan.

The Harder scene does more than simply allow O'Neill a last jab at the plutocrats he always despised. During a rare appearance at a *Moon* rehearsal O'Neill complained, as he had similarly complained at an *Iceman* rehearsal, that the cast was "playing the tragedy of the work too early."[34] *Iceman, Journey,* and *Moon* all begin with laughter, a necessary contrast to the ensuing tragedy, and *Moon's* humor is the broadest. The comic battle between the vital Irish and their ineffectual wealthy neighbor is crucial evidence of the Hogans' zest for life. The Harder scene also permits O'Neill to set up the date between Josie and Jim (when she sends him to hide in her bedroom) and helps establish Hogan's plot by showing Josie and the audience that the Standard Oil heir has good reason to covet this poison ivy and milkweed farm. But this largely slapstick scene, absent from the scenario and only moderately edited in both manuscript and typescript, did not engage O'Neill's attention very long.

Because the first act does not appear in the scenario, Phil Hogan plays a significant role only in the last act of this draft. Act II, covered by a very few lines, omits the farmer's drunken performance on returning from the inn. Instead, at the beginning of the scenario's second act Jim comes to have dinner with Josie and Phil. Hogan then goes off to town and "says meaningly" that he "may not come home" (II, p. 2). How his hoax is set up is not mentioned at all here, although Hogan does reappear in the final act "with two cronies he has brought as witnesses" (IV, p. 6). O'Neill did not at this stage figure out the mechanics of Hogan's trick to bring the couple together. That kind of minor plotting could be done later.

Most of the changes O'Neill made regarding Phil Hogan in subsequent *Moon* drafts serve to minimize his role and clarify his position as an appealing yet secondary figure. O'Neill deleted several passages in which the farmer explains at length either his own motives or the feelings of other characters, especially Jim Tyrone. One reason for these revisions was surely to make the play more subtle and the characters more believable, but these changes do have a perceptible effect on the portrait of Hogan. For example, O'Neill cut from the first act Hogan's explanation to Josie: "It's happiness I want and wealth can't buy it" (TS, I, p. 20). Although this is apparent in the published play, Hogan's attitude is never baldly stated in such clichéd terms. In the fourth act of the manuscript and typescript Hogan recounts in minute detail why he laid the trap for the lovers:

> I thought, there's a beautiful sweethearts moon, I thought, let her start out mad with a bit of whiskey in her to help, and she'll be so brazen, he'll get mad at her and in the quarrel it'll come out he's not selling the farm at all, but he's leaving soon, and then she'll love him more, and she'll see he loves her as she is and still admit the truth that she's been lying about being a slut. And then, with that cleared up between them and no kidding left between them, and each knowing the other's love, well only good can come of it, no matter how far they go with it.   (MS, IV, p. 7)[35]

O'Neill drastically shortened this explanation when he rewrote Act IV; he was wise enough to know that Hogan need not explain at length something even the slowest readers and viewers could figure out for themselves. Further, Hogan's hopes and his trick, no matter how well meant, do not merit the attention they receive in the manuscript and typescript. The Hogan of the published *Moon*, in contrast to the earlier character, is less an interpreter of the action than an instigator of it, less a homespun philosopher than simply an individual with enough vitality to cope with the poison ivy life sends him.

O'Neill also removed from the typescript two speeches in which the farmer perceptively discusses Jim Tyrone's despair.[36] One is in the first act when Hogan, considering the possibility of pulling Mike's trick on Jim, notes that Tyrone would scarcely be terrified by threats: "But I know damned well this shotgun would never go with him. Sure, before he has a drink in the morning, or when be the black bitter fits he gets on him, if you came threatening him with a shotgun, he'd only offer you ten dollars to shoot him" (I, p. 17). In a similar discussion in the next act, Hogan reiterates that when Jim "has his sad bitter moods in him, he don't give a damn for death. He'd be grateful for it" (II, p. 64). Although Hogan does, in the final *Moon*, mention the different kinds of "queer drunks" Jim has, it is Josie alone who fully understands the depths of his anguish. Making Hogan too aware of Jim's troubled mind detracts from Josie's unusual perceptivity and from the unique relationship between the lovers.

Hogan's role was further diminished by several revisions that remove him, figuratively and sometimes literally, from center stage at important points, particularly curtain scenes. The final lines of Act I belong to Josie, in the manuscript and typescript as well as the published play, but early drafts give Hogan a larger role in his daughter's curtain speech:

> JOSIE . . . (From inside Hogan is heard pounding on a table and shouting angrily "Where's the grub, you lazy slut, you? I want me dinner!" She laughs) Will you listen to my mad father, losing his temper again. Come on in, Jim, and soothe him. (Tyrone follows her in, led by her hand.)
>
> (TS, I, p. 45)

In the published *Moon* Hogan is not heard during the final moments of the first act, and the conversation between Josie and Jim focuses on Josie's mothering of her young man.

The most massive change O'Neill made when he rewrote Act IV of the typescript was to split the encounter between Josie and Hogan into two scenes, forming a sort of frame around her more significant interchange with Jim. In all versions through the first typescript, Act IV begins with a scene between Josie and Jim, Jim departs before Hogan's arrival, and the play ends with a lengthy scene between Josie and her father. In the revised typescript, as in the final *Moon*, Hogan appears before Jim awakens, waits in the shack while Josie and Jim say their final good-byes, and reappears at the end for a brief scene of reconciliation with his daughter.

Mary Adrian Tinsley, one of the very few scholars who has studied the *Moon* typescript, suggests that postponing the scene between the lovers increases suspense, for we must wait through the first scene between Josie and her father before learning what Jim will remember of the moonlight confessions and how the act of confession has affected him. She also argues that "in the final version . . . the Josie-Hogan scene is split in order to create—artificially—a movement from separation to reconciliation" between Josie and her father.[37] Although both explanations, especially the first, are valid, there are even more important effects of O'Neill's rearrangement of confrontations in Act IV.

Splitting the Josie-Hogan scene places less emphasis on the farmer and more on the lovers. Even though when revising the final act O'Neill cut no more from the Josie-Hogan encounter than from the Josie-Jim scene, he moved the lion's share of the confrontation between father and daughter to the beginning of the act. In the final *Moon*, the very brief concluding scene between Josie and Hogan runs less than five minutes on stage. When revising *The Iceman Cometh*, O'Neill delayed Parritt's death and Larry's benediction so they would be strong in the audience's mind when the drama ended. Similarly, he here moved the crucial parting to a more dramatically salient point nearer the final curtain. As a man of the theater O'Neill was well aware of the importance of a play's closing moments. The reconciliation between Josie and her father, although significant, could not be allowed to overshadow the central relationship between her and Jim. O'Neill did not simply reverse the two scenes and end with the Josie-Jim parting because he wished to show the resiliency of his heroine. But he also made sure that the fate of her lover, and her sadness over his fate, are not obscured.

The scenario ends on a comic note that looks back to the first-act farce. Hearing Harder's car drive by, a "deeply satisfied" Hogan proclaims: "To hell with England, down with bloody tyrants, and God damn Standard Oil!" (IV, p. 6). His daughter adds an emphatic "Amen!" The manuscript and typescript conclude more somberly, yet the last speech still belongs to Hogan:

> May the blackest [curse] from the bottom of hell—(With startling suddenness he becomes calm again) What are you cursing, you old loon? Is it Jim? No, I know whatever happened, he meant well. Is it myself for a scheming fool? No, for I had the best intentions. Is it life? Sure, that's a fine waste of breath, if it does deserve it. (He sits on the boulder again, to wait for the call to breakfast)   (TS, IV, p. 114)[38]

Although much of this is retained in the published *Moon*, it appears slightly earlier. The curtain lines in the finished play are Josie's benediction: "May you have your wish and die in your sleep soon, Jim, darling.

May you rest forever in forgiveness and peace" (p. 177). *Moon* (like most of O'Neill's works) supports Hogan's judgment on life, but the playwright did not want to end his drama with either a jab at Standard Oil or the philosophical musings of a comic *raisonneur.* He replaced Hogan's curse with Josie's blessing, and Jim, even though no longer on stage, shares the focus because her prayer is for him. Instead of Hogan alone on stage, as at the end of the typescript, the published text has him already in the shack and Josie the sole object of audience attention. She turns and enters the house as the curtain falls.

While O'Neill was diminishing the importance of Hogan, he was also slightly softening the portrait of the wily farmer. The change is minor because Hogan is present only to a limited extent in the scenario, but there are a few rough edges on the character that do not appear in later drafts. In the scenario Jim is wary of the farmer and warns Josie: "Your father, now brother's gone, will make slave of you." She must order him: "Don't run down my father now. I like him" (III, p. 3). Good intentions clearly motivate Hogan's trick in the scenario as they do in the published *Moon;* he guesses that Josie loves Jim and this "is really what is behind his idea of framing Jamie" (p. 1).[39] Nevertheless Hogan does not, as in later drafts, leave the lovers to work out the problems themselves: he actually returns at dawn with two friends for witnesses and suddenly flings open the bedroom door. Unable to get a straight story out of Josie about what happened, he furiously threatens to go to Jim's father, who apparently is still alive in this version, and to sue (IV, p. 6). He is only appeased when Josie convinces him she is still a virgin. In subsequent drafts Jim's affection for the old man is clearer, and Hogan's anger, usually feigned, is never as virulent as it is in the scenario.

When editing the typescript O'Neill removed a large number of Hogan's blasphemous outbursts. However, he retained enough to give a vivid picture of the irreverent farmer, and it is probable that these deletions have less to do with his conception of the character than with his fear of unnecessarily offending his audience. (Based on the play's reception in Detroit and elsewhere, O'Neill's fear was well grounded and his cleanup efforts futile.) O'Neill had made similar modifications in *The Iceman Cometh,* although at a later stage in the editing. The other changes affecting Hogan are principally designed to modify the picture of Josie and only secondarily that of her father. Phil Hogan is not a negligible figure in *Moon* and he is, in at least one salient way, a typical inhabitant of the late plays.

While he shares with Josie an earthy vigor rarely found in characters in *Iceman* and *Journey* he, like them, presents a false front to the world. Pretending to be tough and mercenary, Hogan is in reality one of the kindest men and most loving fathers in the O'Neill canon—at least where his daughter is concerned. Nevertheless, both the time O'Neill spent shaping the character and the position he holds in the final drama indicate that Hogan is primarily present to serve the Jim-Josie story rather than to be himself a dramatic focus.

THE DEVELOPMENT OF JIM TYRONE through the stages of *Moon* is far more important. From a hazy figure philosophizing vaguely about the misery of life, Jim becomes a graphically realized example of a man tormented by personal guilt, trapped by past mistakes and present weaknesses, seeking only the love and forgiveness that will allow him to face death with some measure of tranquillity. The forces and events that shaped his predicament and the nature of his limited salvation are elucidated by O'Neill's revisions.

The Jim of the scenario, like the later Jim, "cannot feel flesh & spirit united—it must be one or the other—they are evil & good" (p. 1), [40] but the tales he tells about the source of his pain are curiously nonspecific. When Josie prods him to tell her about himself, he responds:

> Once upon a time a child was born of well-to-do but devout [?] parents—and the first thing he did was look around at the round earth and realize he'd been sent to the wrong planet and God had double-crossed him and so he began to curse and they slapped on the back, and he reached for a bottle of whiskey and said to himself, By God, I'll show you! Try and catch me now. And so he lived on cursing and drinking & being slapped on the back and no one ever caught him, and at last a lucky day dawned and he died and returned to his real home. That's all. And please don't slap me on the back.
>
> (III, p. 2)

This speech is reminiscent in sentiment if not in language of Edmund's "sea speech" in *Journey*. Both passages are about being misbegotten: Edmund says he was born the wrong species ("I would have been much more successful as a sea gull or a fish"), [41] and Jim contends that he was sent to the wrong planet at birth.

Later, when Jim refuses to talk further, Josie continues his story for him: "There was once a boy who loved goodness and honor and kindness and purity and God with a great quiet passion inside him." Jim, with a cynicism worthy of Jamie in *Journey,* picks up the tale: "All right. He was still wet behind the ears—a sucker, a sap, a fall guy, but he soon got wise to himself—all in the bag, etc." (III, p. 3). Finally, however, he relents. Josie insists that every individual possesses two conflicting dreams that war inside him. Jim describes one of his dreams: "kid stuff—dates back to school—catechism—the man who loves God, who gives up self & the world to worship of God and devotes self to good work, service of others, celibacy [?]—as he goes on contempt disappears and a note of hopeless yearning comes" (III, p. 4). Josie characterizes the cynical side of Jim as his "Lucifer dream," while this represents "a pure holy dream." "Here I've been trying to seduce a Saint," she muses "ruefully," claiming that his holy dream is the one he really loves.

The first of the quoted speeches may well express the most pessimistic side of O'Neill's vision: man is born a misfit and might just as well spend his days hiding from life in a bottle. Yet although the title and substance of the published *Moon* retain this notion of man's "misbegottenness," the Jim Tyrone presented there is too wrapped up in his own particular agonies to deliver such a broadly philosophical speech. Edmund in *Journey* is young enough and whole enough to speak of his pain in terms of sea gulls and fish; Jim is too broken to speak in anything but very personal terms of his experiences with his family. The last speech is both maudlin and unconvincing. *The Great God Brown* portrays Dion Anthony's duality in almost exactly the same terms used in the *Moon* scenario. As Dion's mask becomes increasingly demonic—Cybel at one point calls him "Kid Lucifer"—his real face comes to look like a "Christian Martyr's."[42] Virginia Floyd points out that Jim's conflicting scenario dreams "are similar to Satan's in 'The Last Conquest,' " the "duality of Man play" O'Neill worked on intermittently in the early 1940s while he was also composing *Moon.*[43] O'Neill ultimately chose, however, to present Jim Tyrone's duality in more believable ways. Saints in devils' garb might be suitable for a heavily stylized drama like *Brown* or the "spiritual propaganda play" *Conquest* was intended to be, but making Jim a holy man gone astray is pushing the notion of duality too far for a character cast in a largely realistic mold. The idea that Jim has much good in him that life has hidden and perverted is obvious in the final text, where his cynicism (hinted at in the Mephistophelian cast of his demeanor) wars with his need to love and be loved. Just as O'Neill could convey Mary Tyrone's complex nature without postulating "alien demons," so too he could show Jim's dividedness without resorting to "Lucifer dreams" and fantasies of martyrdom.

As we move into post-scenario versions of *Moon*, we find a series of revisions that play down Jim's past as an actor and his present penchant for theatrics. In part, O'Neill may have been removing inessential personal details about his brother. More likely, these changes were made for the same reason remarks concerning James Tyrone, Sr.'s acting were deleted from *Journey:* to eliminate the idea that the actor is simply a poseur faking his anguish. O'Neill removed from the manuscript character description the comment that Jim "can be a good actor—off the stage—when he wants to be. On the stage, he was always mediocre at best" (I, p. 20). The second line is clearly unnecessary; the first could mislead the reader into doubting Jim's sincerity. Similarly, among other cuts in the typescript description of Jim is the statement that "his fine voice is one of his charms, and he loves to recite poetry to show it off" (I, p. 26). By omitting this, O'Neill prevents the assumption that Jim recites Keats and Dowson simply to demonstrate his talents. Rather, he quotes their verses because they express feelings he shares.

A few deletions from the typescript dialogue also serve to de-emphasize Jim's acting, and these changes affect the viewer as well as the reader. One occurs at the very end of Act II, when Jim tries to light a cigarette while Josie is inside getting a bottle. The curtain lines of the typescript have Jim exclaiming to himself, "You lousy ham! You God damned lousy ham!" (II, p. 71). This was changed to "You rotten bastard!" (text, p. 107). Surely the sentiment of the line was not altered, but eliminating the word "ham" precludes the supposition that Jim is faking either his misery or his love for Josie. O'Neill also removed Jim's characterization of himself as "the old-fashioned parlor entertainer, that's me!" (rev. TS, IV, p. 111). His pathetic tales are not told for amusement.

Perhaps the most important change O'Neill made respecting Jim Tyrone concerns the possibility of a future for him, especially a future with Josie. Early drafts of *Long Day's Journey Into Night* contained hints that Jamie might somehow reverse his past errors and lead a constructive life. These hints were steadily excised until in the published *Journey* it is clear that there is no more hope for Jamie than for Mary or Tyrone: his mistakes have been too grave, his guilt is too powerful, it is too late for him to begin anew. O'Neill made very similar changes when writing *A Moon for the Misbegotten*, but the situation in the later play is more complex. There are two related questions: whether there is any chance at all for Jim to have a productive future, and whether Josie Hogan could be the impetus for and play a role in such a future.

In the scenario, hints that Jim is spiritually dead rarely appear before the final act. Although Jim mentions "loving death" and although he recites—as Jamie did in *Journey*—"Look in my face. My name is Might-Have-Been" (III, p. 4), his belief that his life has ended is less apparent here than in subsequent drafts. The manuscript and typescript, like the published play, show more strongly that Jim's fate is already sealed when *Moon* begins. All versions after the scenario imply that Jim's chances for a positive future have been destroyed by his longing for oblivion and by the causes of that longing.

O'Neill did modify the way in which Jim's yearning for death is expressed, but this has a relatively minor effect on the play. In all drafts up to the revised typescript, his death wish is often expressed metaphorically in terms of his love for Cynara.[44] As he awakens in the scenario's final act, Jim "quotes Cynara" with "sad cynicism" (IV, p. 5). The manuscript and typescript have Jim reciting verses from Ernest Dowson's poem about Cynara at the end of Act III and at the beginning of Act IV, where he declaims all six lines of the poem's second stanza (the same portion Edmund quotes in a *Journey* discussion of Jamie), including the last words: "I have been faithful to thee, Cynara, in my fashion." Hearing this, Josie concludes: "Well, at least I know now what Cynara is and I was right when I guessed it's a name for death—and the dead" (TS, IV, p. 105). References to Cynara were eliminated when O'Neill deleted the last mention of her from the revised typescript; only two lines of Dowson's poem, which do not include her name, remain in the text. There are sound reasons for this decision. First of all, Cynara is unnecessary: Jim's desire for death is obvious without being couched in metaphorical terms. Moreover, Jim's references to Cynara leave O'Neill with the awkward problem of explaining her significance to an audience that may be unfamiliar with both Dowson's poem and the Horatian ode which inspired it. Josie's guess that Cynara is a Latin word for death is a feeble ploy at best, and an improbably lucky guess for an uneducated farm woman. While Cynara does suggest "death—and the dead," this connotation comes not from the name itself but from its use by the two poets, especially Horace (whose Ode 4.13 is in part a lament for his dead beloved Cinara). The playwright simplified matters by removing a literary allusion that causes dramatic problems and serves little useful function. Egil Törnqvist is right when he argues that "in the play the symbolic Cynara figure is fused with the dead mother [even though] the name nowhere appears."[45] O'Neill need not explicitly name Cynara in order to show that Jim's longing for death is a longing for maternal comfort.

Jim Tyrone is a man in love with death, and O'Neill made a series of revisions that reveal even Josie cannot save him from self-destruction. It is only in early drafts that a new, shared life for the two seems conceivable. For example, in the scenario's fourth act, Jim tells Josie, "I—I'd like to marry you—but I've nothing to offer." Josie responds with an explanation of why such a union is impossible:

> Now, don't be foolish. . . . Sure you didn't seduce me, did you, there's no need to play the honorable gentleman, And even if you had, it's not marriage should be between us. Sure, in a month I'd lose patience with your coming home drunk & take the broom handle to you. No, it's nothing like that between us. It's a better thing. I can't describe it but you know & I know. It's the two of us in the world alone, two that do be dreaming, two born of the moon and the sadness of beauty, two in the dark night, two waiting in the dawn homesick for the land of heart's desire where only dreams come true.
>
> (IV, p. 5)

When Jim later says "I'll see you again before I leave," Josie refuses. The scenario implies it is she who rejects the idea that the two could wed and try to build a future together.

In the first act of the manuscript, when Hogan facetiously suggests that Jim has decided to give him the worthless farm, the younger man answers: "I have not. I'm saving this for a refuge in my old age. ⟨⟨Kiddingly⟩⟩ Josie and I are going to reform sometime and get married and settle down here. Aren't we, Josie?" (I, p. 25).[46] Josie, while puzzled by his remark, manages to respond jokingly: "Are we, indeed? And who said I'd have you?" Jim does speak "kiddingly," but there appears to be a kernel of seriousness beneath his jesting. This whole interchange was deleted from the manuscript, and no mention of a possible marriage occurs at this point in the published play.

At the end of the third act of *Moon*, Josie wonders: "Oh, Jim, Jim, maybe my love could still save you, if you could want it enough!" (p. 153). This is the last time in the final version that she entertains such a thought. The typescript fourth act, however, shows her experiencing a brief resurgence of hope. As he leaves, she repeats, "Oh, Jim darlin' maybe my love could still save you" and only at this point accepts the futility of such a wish (IV, p. 109). Further, while in the published text Jim never questions the necessity of their parting after their moonlight romance, earlier drafts hint that he is not quite resigned to a permanent separation. In a passage deleted from the typescript's third act, Jim tells Josie he came to her this night "because I knew I'd never see you again" (III, p. 93), yet his fourth act comments seem to contradict this:

JOSIE. . . That kiss was for goodbye.

TYRONE Goodbye? Why goodbye, Josie?

JOSIE Because that's my wish, Jim, for the sake of both of us. (Forcing a light reasonable tone) Sure, you'll only be here a couple of days more anyway, and if we met again it would drag out the parting and maybe spoil our memory of last night and the two of us together, and your sleeping in my arms.

TYRONE (sadly) All right. If you feel that way—It is all for the best, I guess.

(IV, p. 108)

Jim appears reluctant to depart, and consequently the burden of the decision is put on Josie. She rejects any further encounters and the possibility that something good might come from them.

Thus early versions of *Moon* seem to suggest that there is a chance for the lovers to create some kind of future together. It is only a hint—all versions except the scenario show Jim as one who has long been "dead"— yet a hint that is missing from the published play. The early drafts imply that perhaps Josie could save Jim, give him a new life with her, but *will* not do so. The published *Moon* makes it clear that she *can* not save him. Dion Anthony tells Cybel in *The Great God Brown*, "You've given me strength to die."[47] That is all Larry Slade can give Don Parritt, and all Josie Hogan can give Jim Tyrone. In O'Neill's dramatic world, merely being given the "strength to die" is a blessing.

There are several possible reasons why O'Neill felt compelled to foreclose on Jim Tyrone's future. Jim is modeled after Jamie O'Neill, and the change gives the play biographical validity: the playwright's brother died in late 1923.[48] Once again, as with *Journey*, the likelihood also arises that O'Neill could not face, even in the fictional guise of a play, the idea that Jamie was redeemable, for to do so would be to indict himself for his failure to aid his sibling. "He and I were great pals—once," Jim says of his younger brother in a line, deleted from the typescript (III, p. 96), that clearly refers to O'Neill's avoidance of Jamie during the latter's final months. However, O'Neill's plays, as well as his biography, suggest even more compelling reasons why the dramatist denied Jim a future. It is, interestingly, through an examination of autobiographical material removed from *Moon* during revision that we begin to see the most important reasons why Jim cannot survive: he has no life-giving illusion to protect him from a frightening world, and he has no means to cope with the loss of security and love that O'Neill sees as the inevitable consequence of adulthood. Jim has responded with anger to his loss, committing transgressions against himself and his mother that can be forgiven but not erased.

Several references to Jim's family, particularly to his younger brother, were excised during the editing of *Moon*. Many are simply passing allusions although a few are mildly hostile, such as Jim's exclamation: "Oh, to hell with the purple phrases book. That's my brother's yen. Let him have it" (TS, III, p. 92). These deletions are numerous—more than half a dozen in the typescript alone—and presumably were made largely because the material is not relevant to Jim's present situation. However, the lengthiest passage about his brother is intriguing for a number of reasons. In the published play, when Josie is briefly repelled by Jim's story of his life, he asks: "Don't want to touch me now, eh?" (p. 151). In the typescript he continues:

> Well, I don't blame you. Except you promised—No, forget that. You didn't know what you were letting yourself in for. My fault. I shouldn't have told you. Too rotten and horrible. Never told anyone before except my brother. He said "You dirty bastard"—then tried to excuse [me] because we'd always been such close pals—blamed it all [on] booze. He knows the booze game from his own experience—the mad things you do. All the same, he couldn't forget. He loved her, too. He's never felt the same about me since. Tries to. He's a pal. But can't. Makes excuses to himself to keep away from me. For another reason, too. Can't keep me from seeing that he knows what I'm up against, and that there's only one answer. He knows it's hopeless. He can't help wishing I were dead, too—for my sake. (Rousing himself, with a shrug of his shoulders—self-contemptuously) Nuts! Why do I tell you about him? Nothing to do with you.   (III, pp. 99–100)[49]

Much of this is irrelevant personal detail. Biographically the passage is fascinating and, as scholars have noted, reveals more about O'Neill's ambivalent attitude toward his brother than about his brother's feelings toward him.[50] Jim says his brother sees his condition as hopeless; O'Neill made certain in *Moon* that Jim's situation is presented as hopeless.

Significantly, the reactions this passage attributes to Jim's brother are similar to those of Josie, who is first repelled by his tale (his brother calls him a "dirty bastard") and then tries to make excuses for his actions. The brother wishes Jim dead, for Jim's sake, and in *Moon*'s final speech Josie compassionately hopes that her suffering lover will soon find the death he seeks. This remarkable similarity between Josie's words and deeds and an obviously autobiographical passage supports John Henry Raleigh's argument that Josie's benediction for Jim is O'Neill's also.[51] In a sense Josie Hogan, not Edmund Tyrone, is the last self-portrait O'Neill put on stage.

One salient difference exists, nonetheless, between Jim's brother and Josie. The published play does not suggest that Josie is making "excuses" to "keep away" from Jim; it is rather the typescript that leaves her open to the charge of wishing to avoid him in the future. O'Neill not only removed this passage, he changed Josie's actions so that they do not exactly match the actions attributed here to the brother. Unlike his brother, Josie helps Jim confront his ghosts, and she grants him the forgiveness he seeks. As with *Journey*, the process of composing *Moon* seems to have led O'Neill to a new sympathy for a character based on a member of his family. Through Josie Hogan, the playwright gave Jim Tyrone the unqualified pardon he could never offer Jamie O'Neill.

There are two other important reasons why O'Neill had to remove this long speech about Jim's brother. First, Jim's claim that he has told the whole story before mitigates the uniqueness of his confession to Josie. It is very likely that Jamie O'Neill did make to the playwright a revelation similar to the one Jim Tyrone makes to Josie, but dramatic attention must not be diverted from the lovers' relationship. Jim's confession would be diminished by the implication that it is a repeat performance. The second problem is that this passage, by focusing on Jim's brother at a crucial point in *Moon*, obscures the significance of Jim's mother.[52] Removing discussion of his sibling emphasizes that the overwhelming familial influence in Jim's life, as his obsessive talk about her reveals, has been his mother. Josie may well be a fictional representative for the playwright, but O'Neill took pains to show that her role in the drama is primarily maternal.

Jim's mother, and his grief and guilt over her death, play a curiously small role in the *Moon* scenario. O'Neill certainly had these in mind, for

the third act mentions "tale of mother's death—baggage car ahead—
sings." Josie responds as she does in the published text: "For moment she
is shocked, repulsed"; then she invites Jim to cry away his anguish in her
arms. Josie consoles him: "She had no right to die and leave you. But it's a
stupid thing to take revenge on the dead. They only smile at you for-
givingly!" (III, p. 3). What is surprising is that this exchange occurs fairly
early in Act III and, as the rest of the scenario unfolds, the focus shifts to
Jim's "twin dreams" of cynical debauchery and selfless sacrifice. O'Neill
may have failed to write out the "tale of mother's death" because his famil-
iarity with the story made such effort unnecessary, or perhaps he was
delaying a full confrontation with this painful episode from his past, yet
the absence of references to Jim's mother later in the scenario suggests
that the playwright did not initially envision Tyrone as a man fatally haunted by a maternal ghost.

The mother's influence grew as *Moon* progressed, gradually enveloping
almost the whole play. Indeed, Jim's mourning for his parent is mentioned
in the published text even before he himself appears. In the manuscript
and typescript, Hogan does not describe the "queer drunks" Jim experiences until Act II. When making revisions, O'Neill moved this description to the first act, thus introducing Jim's mother far earlier, for Josie
explains his quiet drunks by suggesting, "I think I know what comes over
him when he's like that. It's the memory of his mother comes back and his
grief for her death" (text, p. 33). [53]

The parent-child bond is a significant recurring element in O'Neill's
dramas, and Jim's relationships to his mother and Josie culminate a long
line of similar patterns in the playwright's earlier work. Psychologists,
critics, and biographers have had a field day with O'Neill's Oedipal feelings as expressed in his plays. What is of interest here is not the writer's
personal psychological makeup but rather a series of motifs in the O'Neill
canon that reaches a logical conclusion in *Moon*. Bogard observes that
"after *Welded* in 1922, the dual wife-mother character becomes the dominant female personality" in O'Neill's plays.[54] *Welded*, actually finished in
1923, should be included, and Bogard's comment can be broadened to
encompass even more works. In thirteen of the seventeen dramas O'Neill
completed after 1922, there is either a male character closely involved
with his mother or a male-female relationship with parent-child overtones
even though the two people are not literally parent and child.[55] Some
works contain both configurations.

In a few cases, the love between a man and a woman assumes a father-daughter pattern. Juan in *The Fountain* is infatuated with the daughter of a woman who once loved him. At the end of *All God's Chillun Got Wings* Jim Harris prays to God: "make me worthy of the child You send me for the woman You take away!"[56] The "child" is his deranged wife Ella. In *Mourning Becomes Electra* Lavinia is attracted to Adam Brant largely because of his resemblance to her adored father. Charles Marsden, wanting the best of both worlds in *Strange Interlude*, views Nina Leeds as a possible substitute mother *and* daughter. Like Marsden, Elsa Loving in *Days Without End* has it both ways and claims she loves John "for he's become my child and father now, as well as being a husband and —."[57] Most often the relationship between lovers or spouses has overtones of a mother-son bond. When Eleanor and Michael Cape are reconciled at the end of *Welded,* she runs to her husband "with a low tender cry as if she were awakening to maternity" and a few minutes later calls him "my child."[58] The maternal Margaret is not sufficient for her husband Dion Anthony in *The Great God Brown,* so he seeks comfort from Cybel, who is so obviously an earth-mother figure she is virtually a caricature. She even has a player piano that features "a sentimental medley of 'Mother-Mammy' tunes."[59] Miriam in *Lazarus Laughed* grows older as her husband Lazarus grows younger. At her death, stage directions note that Lazarus looks "like a young son who keeps watch by the body of his mother."[60] Nina Leeds calls her husband by the nickname Sammy, as his mother did, and is wont to think of him as her "poor little boy!"[61] Despite wide variations in the personalities and circumstances of O'Neill's heroes, most seek a maternal woman for a mate.

Further, in four O'Neill plays other than *A Moon for the Misbegotten,* a son's powerful love for his mother is central. In *More Stately Mansions* Simon Harford is torn between his desire for his wife and his attachment to his mother, Deborah, and he even finds himself confusing the two in his mind. The drama focuses on the battle between the women for possession of Simon, a battle he instigates and encourages. An unpublished epilogue to *Mansions* shows Simon awakening after a year's bout with "brain fever." During his illness he acted "like a kid," called his wife "Mother," and was treated like a brother by his sons. Interestingly, Simon's recovery coincides with the death of his mother, but he has a ready replacement. In a monologue addressed to the sleeping Simon, his wife Sara promises, "I'm your mother now, too. You've everything you need from life in me!"—an almost exact repetition of the promise she made a year earlier when Deborah abandoned him.[62] Orin Mannon in *Mourning Becomes Electra*, overpowered by his yearning for his mother and guilt at contributing to her death, commits suicide in hope of meeting her beyond the grave. During most of *Desire Under the Elms* Eben Cabot is impelled by a wish to take revenge on his father for his dead mother's suffering. He is seduced by Abbie, his stepmother, in his mother's parlor, with her maternal "spirit" as witness. *Dynamo*'s Reuben Light never forgives his mother for betraying him nor himself for abandoning her, and is even driven to murder the young woman he believes has come between him and his beloved parent. He takes the dynamo as his new mother. In the play's final scene Reuben, crying "mother," embraces the "exciter" of the dynamo and emits a loud orgasmic moan that dissolves into a baby's crooning.

Long Day's Journey Into Night shows both sons, particularly Jamie, distraught when Mary forsakes them for drugs. In *The Iceman Cometh* Don Parritt's love-hate relationship with his mother destroys him. Thus it is apparent that in virtually every O'Neill play after 1922 a major source of pain and solace is the parent-child, and especially mother-son, bond. Either this is presented directly or a later relationship is shown to be a repetition of, or substitute for, this primal alliance.

Writing to the Theatre Guild's Robert Sisk, O'Neill complained about the reception of *Dynamo*:

> It certainly seems damn queer to me—although, knowing what most of the critics are, it shouldn't—that no one seems to have gotten the real human relationship story, what his mother does to the boy and what that leads to in his sacrifice of the girl to a maternal deity in the end—the girl his mother hated and was jealous of.—that all that was the boy's real God struggle, or prompted it. This all fits in with the general theme of American life in back of the play, America being the land of the mother complex.[63]

One must beware of interpreting the term "mother complex" too narrowly, for what O'Neill presents is something more than just an individual's lifelong attachment to a parent. There is in the recurrent mother-child pattern a larger implication that links together most of the O'Neill canon.

A clue to the dramatist's view is found in a note he made for *A Touch of the Poet* entitled "Thoreau in Simon." O'Neill had evidently been reading Genevieve Taggard's *The Life and Mind of Emily Dickinson*, and he was so impressed with Taggard's comments about Thoreau (part of a comparison of Thoreau and Dickinson) that he copied them into his notes.[64] Taggard says of Thoreau that "the thought of leaving home made tears roll down his cheeks." According to Taggard, Thoreau was pushed from home by his mother as a fledgling bird is pushed from the nest, and then found that nature was "his only friend." He hoped it would "flow in" to fill the "vacancy at center of himself. But N[ature]. would not." The poet tried various ways to achieve a union with the natural world, yet ultimately discovered that nature is "discontinuous with the self." Finally, Taggard concludes, when Thoreau "lay dying he wished that his sister could place his bed and its covers in form of a shell so he could curl up in it—his last attempt to make nest of life."

While the words are Taggard's, O'Neill's sympathy with them is clear. In this interpretation, after Thoreau was deprived of the close bond with his mother (as all adults must be) he sought in nature a substitute for the complete, unquestioning love and security the mother supplies the child. He never found another nest because there is no "belonging" equivalent to that of the child to the mother; there is no equivalent comfort and safety. Bogard asserts that in O'Neill's later plays the woman "is not only the destroying wife, but also the mother, in whose love the poet seeks to find forgetfulness, and the sense of home and unity with nature."[65] In fact, O'Neill implies that nature itself is only a substitute for the mother. Like Thoreau as Taggard and O'Neill see him, the male characters in O'Neill's dramas, both early and late, wander through life in search of a place, a faith, or a person to replace the mother, to be at least a temporary haven from the loneliness and fear that mark his dramatic world. Some O'Neill characters find such a substitute; some are more successful than others in adapting to the terrifying uncertainty of the world. Some, like Jim Tyrone, are totally unable to face life without the primal protection of the mother. Even if they do find a surrogate, she (or it) arrives too late to stop their determined march toward the final security, death. For the last irony, as Doris Falk and others have suggested, is that the quest for the womb is ultimately a quest for the tomb.[66]

When O'Neill in his last play created a character irrevocably destroyed by the loss of his mother's devotion, he was writing the extension and culmination of nearly all his previous work. Jim Tyrone cannot tolerate being deprived of his mother's unconditional love, and he seeks with Josie a similar mother-son relationship. Whether or not O'Neill was aware of it,

the chorus of the sentimental song from which Jim quotes two lines—
"But baby's cries can't waken her, / In the baggage coach ahead"—is not
primarily about a child's loss of a parent but about a husband's loss of a
wife. The chorus of the Gussie L. Davis work, called "In the Baggage
Coach Ahead," runs:

> While the train rolled onward
> A husband sat in tears
> Thinking of the happiness
> Of just a few short years,
> For baby's face brings pictures of
> A cherish'd hope that's dead,
> But baby's cries can't waken her,
> In the baggage coach ahead.[67]

Although this stanza focuses on the husband's mourning, Jim quotes only
the lines concerning the baby's grief. Even in his rendition of a sob song,
he views relationships in terms of mother and child. The song is particularly appropriate for a man who, as he tells Josie, rode cross-country in the
train that bore his beloved mother's body home.

"I HOPED MAYBE you could put yourself in her place—and tell me she
would understand it was all because I loved her so much and couldn't
forgive her for leaving me alone" (III, p. 24). In this canceled manuscript
line, Jim explicitly spells out Josie's function: the "she" is his mother, the
"you" is the young woman beside him. While in the final text Jim never
makes quite so overt a statement—"You're like her deep in your heart.
That's why I told you," he says (p. 151)—Josie's role as mother surrogate is
clearer there than in earlier drafts. When the playwright revised the end
of Act I in the typescript, he not only lessened the focus on Hogan but
introduced Jim's need for maternal solicitude where it had not previously
been mentioned. The excised conclusion contains no direct references to
mothers or mothering, except in the stage directions. The new ending,
which appears in the published play, foreshadows the relationship the
lovers will establish:

> TYRONE (*Sardonically*) That's right. Mother me, Josie, I love it.
> JOSIE (*Bullyingly*) I will, then. You need one to take care of you. (*They disap-
> pear inside the house.*) Curtain   (p. 68)

Moreover, in the fourth act Josie becomes not just a replacement for Jim's mother but a symbol of the archetypal mother, Mary. Two revisions, one minor and one major, emphasize this Christian allusion. In the typescript Josie tells her father: "And I'm a virgin still. But I became a mother, too, in the night, instead of a whore. (She smiles strangely) That's a queer switch, don't you think?" (IV, p. 112). When revising the typescript, O'Neill moved this virgin-mother reference to a more prominent position earlier in the act and changed the wording slightly. This time Josie says: "A virgin who bears a dead child in the night, and the dawn finds her still a virgin. If that isn't a miracle, what is?" (text, p. 160). A "queer switch" becomes a "miracle," and the identification between Josie and the Virgin Mary is strengthened.

The connection between the two women is further heightened by O'Neill's extension of the Pietà pose in the last act. Although some may doubt whether the birthday dinner in *The Iceman Cometh* is meant physically to copy "The Last Supper," few will deny that Josie holding the sleeping Jim represents a Pietà.[68] This image, and hence the linking of Josie and Mary, does appear in the manuscript and typescript, but it is far more prominent in the published *Moon*. The typescript parting scene between Jim and Josie occurs almost immediately after the curtain rises on the final act. The Pietà pose is held only through the first few moments of the act, as Josie muses aloud on what has passed between Jim and herself and how she hopes he will react when awakened. In the revised version, the couple's position is sustained for several minutes as Josie and her father argue. *Moon* is not a play that generally calls for extensive physical movement on stage, but the continued immobility of Josie and Jim is still extraordinary; obviously O'Neill wanted this picture strongly impressed on the audience's mind.

The Pietà which O'Neill accorded so much attention in *Moon* is particularly appropriate because it represents not simply a mother and child but the archetypal mother holding a grown son who has died. The playwright portrays Jim Tyrone as one who is spiritually dead, and Hogan remarks that the sleeping man "looks dead" (text, p. 158). Further, the Pietà tableau carries significant religious as well as maternal implications. Although in his last works O'Neill generally eschews the more conventional trappings of religion and even at times mocks traditional Christianity, religious symbols and allusions are vitally important in these secular dramas.

In his comments to Robert Sisk about *Dynamo*, quoted above, O'Neill noted that Reuben Light's relationship with his mother was his "real God struggle, or prompted it." Bereft of the comfort of the mother, O'Neill's characters sometimes seek an analogous peace in religion, another form of protection from the frightening world. Reuben confuses God and electrical forces with his female parent, praying to the dynamo as "Oh, Mother of Life."[69] In *Strange Interlude* Charles Marsden agrees "with a strange passionate eagerness" to Nina Leeds's suggestion that people should worship a maternal deity.[70] Significantly, the finding of a mother-surrogate is often given religious connotations. At the end of *Welded* Michael Cape's reunion with his maternal wife is symbolized by an embrace in which their arms form a cross. In *Days Without End* John Loving's decision to go to church and his wife's forgiveness of his adultery are simultaneous. Cybel, the earth-mother whore in *The Great God Brown*, resembles "an idol" as she cradles the dying Billy Brown. The two form a tableau not unlike the Pietà O'Neill used in *Moon* more than fifteen years later.[71] A Pietà virtually identical to that in *Moon* appears in the Epilogue to *More Stately Mansions*, which takes place at Simon Harford's "old cabin by the lake on the farm." Sara, like Josie, is described as "strong, firm and healthy"; her feet are bare and "she wears a cheap calico working dress."[72] As the epilogue draws to a close, Sara sits on the bench outside the cabin with Simon on the ground in front of her, his head resting against her breast. Simon dozes as she delivers the play's final speech, including her wish that her husband "rest in peace," and the curtain comes down on Sara cradling the sleeping Simon.

After *Days Without End* O'Neill never completed a play that treats institutionalized religion favorably.[73] Mary Tyrone's search for the lost faith of her convent girlhood is futile, Hugo's biblical willow trees grow only in a bottle of rotgut, and Mike Hogan's piousness is cause for ridicule. However, confessions and blessings, scattered throughout O'Neill's earlier works, take center stage in *The Iceman Cometh*, *Long Day's Journey Into Night*, and *A Moon for the Misbegotten*. Larry says a benediction for the dead Parritt, Josie for the departing Jim. Jamie blesses Edmund after confessing to him, and in the final act of *Moon* Jim gives Josie his blessing, thanks for the love and forgiveness she has shown. In many earlier dramas O'Neill had given religious connotations to secular actions; he carries this further in his final plays by directly translating religious forms into humanistic ones.[74] As Robert Brustein comments, "O'Neill's problem is the problem of the modern drama as a whole: how to bring a religious vision to bear on a totally secular world."[75] The solace given in these late plays is analogous to—often couched in terms of—specifically Christian consolation, but absolution and forgiveness are no longer the gifts of God and his priests; they are only to be gained from human beings who show the pity and love traditionally associated with Christian figures. It is singularly appropriate that O'Neill's last troubled hero finds comfort in the Pietà-like embrace of a motherly confessor.

Törnqvist points out that Josie's very name has Christian associations: Josephine is "the feminine form of Joseph."[76] O'Neill deliberately made "Holy Joseph" her favorite epithet. While in the typescript she exclaims "Oh, be God, I'm a wreck entirely" (IV, p. 105), the revised typescript changes this to "Holy Joseph, I'm a wreck entirely" (text, p. 166). Rolf Scheibler notes that Josie's "symbolic quality" is hinted at in "her blue dress, her oversize body and her earth-stained feet"[77]—a larger-than-life figure clad in the Virgin's color. The clearest example of O'Neill's translation of religious ritual into secular terms is the "confessional pattern," a dramatic motif that looms large in *Iceman, Journey,* and especially *Moon.*[78] Not surprisingly, Josie's role in this pattern is central. A comparison of the three dramas shows O'Neill working toward a confessional design that is completely fulfilled only in his last play—and only through the offices of Josie Hogan.

O'Neill had of course used confessions—or the desire to confess—in dramas written before *Iceman, Journey,* and *Moon.* Orin Mannon, for one, longs to unburden himself to the pure Hazel, and John in *Days Without End* similarly seeks forgiveness for his trespasses. His uncle, a priest, encourages him while his alterego, Loving, mocks his desire for purgation. The play's climax finds John on his knees in front of a large cross. Unlike *Days Without End,* however, none of the dramas discussed here contains a church, and there are no actual priests. Instead, the listeners are Larry Slade, whose face has "the quality of a pitying but weary old priest's,"[79] Edmund Tyrone, and Josie Hogan, whom Raleigh aptly calls "the priestess in the confessional."[80] The religious overtones of the confessions are clear but muted. O'Neill deleted from the *Moon* typescript a speech in which Jim sounds very much like the two halves of John Loving having an argument. Josie, thinking Tyrone has agreed to sell the farm to Harder, urges him to admit his duplicity. Jim assumes she refers to his sins against his mother and replies:

You're thinking of a Catholic hereafter, eh? Nuts with that bunk! That's what
you meant by confess, like—confess my sins to a priest? [Crap! (His manner
changes) I wish I could still believe in it, at that. It's grand stuff for the sucker
who can. Come and be forgiven.] I wish—(He recovers himself—
sneeringly) Nuts! I must have the DTs.   (III, p. 85)[81]

In the published play Jim never so blatantly identifies his confession as a
religious act, yet the religious implications remain.

The four major confessions in these works—Hickey's and Parritt's in
Iceman, Jamie's in *Journey*, and Jim's in *Moon*—are remarkably similar.
In each instance the one confessing is compelled to do so by the pressure
of his guilt. Hickey says he doesn't have to confess but then proceeds
compulsively to tell his story. Parritt cannot stop talking about what he has
done, Jamie feels he must tell Edmund the truth no matter how painful
for both, and Jim returns again and again to the blonde on the train.

Each man picks his listener (or listeners) carefully. Hickey must tell the
boys about Evelyn because their failure to respond to his "peace" movement has led him to question his own feelings. In fact, however, he is
confessing as much to the dead Evelyn as to the assembled drunks. Jamie
unburdens himself to Edmund, the one he feels he has wronged. Both
Parritt and Jim have betrayed their mothers, and each chooses a mother
surrogate—one the mother's former lover, the other a maternal woman—
to hear his disclosure. In all four cases the listeners are reluctant to hear
the tale to be told. Chuck speaks eloquently for the crew in Hope's bar
when he commands Hickey: "Aw, put a bag over it!"[82] Through three and
a half acts of *Iceman* Larry tries to avoid hearing Parritt's confession.
When Jamie begins telling how he deliberately harmed his brother, Edmund says "I don't want to hear,"[83] and Josie, when Jim's recital becomes
too horrifying, uses the exact same words (p. 150).

Finally, although confessing may bring relief, it does not bring a re-
newal of the will to live. Hickey proclaims his wish to go to the electric
chair, and Parritt heads gratefully for the fire escape. There is no indication Jamie will reform; instead, he warns Edmund to avoid him in the
future, for he will be waiting to sabotage his young brother again. Jim,
like Parritt, is given only peace to die. O'Neill's late plays present a bleak
world and the character who chooses to live in it is the exception, not the
rule. Hickey, Parritt, Jamie, and Jim may receive forgiveness and even
absolution, but without a protective illusion about themselves such as the

men in Hope's bar have, death is preferable to life. As Jim says in lines cut from the *Moon* typescript, "It's crazy to mourn for the dead. They have all the luck. They're through" (III, p. 98).

Eric Bentley observes that *The Iceman Cometh* and *A Moon for the Misbegotten* are very similar because each has "at its core a confession of guilt from a man who has wronged a woman."[84] This is true of both confessions in *Iceman*. Although *Long Day's Journey Into Night* differs slightly because Jamie's confession is not primarily about his transgressions against Mary, there are striking similarities between Jamie's revelation to Edmund and Jim's to Josie. Before each confession can take place a father, who has been talking to the one who will hear the revelation, must be removed from the scene. Tyrone retires to the porch to avoid confronting his older son; Hogan goes off to the inn to leave the lovers alone. Alcohol is the common lubricant: Jamie and Edmund have been drinking heavily; Jim has been drinking, and Josie joins him. Jamie tries to prevent his ailing brother from imbibing any more, and Jim knocks the glass from Josie's hand. Jamie and Jim may well be concerned about the damaging effects of liquor on the others, but they are probably more concerned about having sober if reluctant audiences for their tales. Jamie dozes and Jim falls asleep after confessing, an indication of the relief they feel and a symbol of the death they seek. Possibly the confessions are so similar because the two are based on an actual experience O'Neill had with his brother. Equally likely (and both hypotheses may be correct), when the playwright composed the later confession scene, he consciously or unconsciously took as his dramatic model the one he had created a few years previously.

The *Moon* confession does, in one major way, go beyond that in *Journey*: absolution is freely given by the listener. When Edmund remains silent after his brother's speech, Jamie says, "Know you absolve me, don't you, Kid?"[85] By contrast, Josie actively absolves Jim: she tells him, "I do forgive!" (p. 152), and attempts to comfort him. This absolution has a crucial effect on both central characters in *Moon*, and O'Neill's revisions emphasize the impact of Josie's compassionate response. In Act IV of the typescript, Josie is reluctant to let Jim recall all that happened the previous night. She pretends she also was too drunk to remember: "Faith, I may as well admit I was half seas over from the big drinks I took of that strong Bourbon and I might have drawn a blank myself at the end for I can't remember much until I was on the steps with you in my arms and your

head on my breast asleep, and me awake watching the waning of the moon"
(IV, p. 106). She does not encourage Jim to remember, and his acknowledgment that he feels different is very sketchy. Although he agrees that the
dawn is beautiful and says, "I seem to have a pleasant, dreamy, peaceful
hangover for once. I wish it could go on forever" (IV, p. 108), this is all that
indicates he feels changed, absolved.[86] In the published play, by contrast,
his recognition of absolution is much clearer and is couched in religious
terms. After telling Josie how good he feels this morning, he adds: "It's hard
to describe how I feel. It's a new one on me. Sort of at peace with myself and
this lousy life—as if all my sins had been forgiven— . . . Nuts with that sin
bunk, but you know what I mean" (p. 171). Despite the cynical qualification, his relief is obvious.

Jim's parting words in the typescript are equivocal: "I only want to kiss
you goodbye again and thank you—again for *everything*—especially for
the forgiveness we can't remember. (He turns away abruptly) And to tell
you I love you better than anything in the world (Starting for the road,
without looking back) Except death, of course. But I know you understand that" (IV, p. 109). Jim does vaguely remember being forgiven, but it
is unclear how much of what transpired he actually recalls. In the published *Moon* Josie finally pleads: "I want you to remember my love for you
gave you peace for a while." As Jim leaves he tells her, "I do remember!
I'm glad I remember! I'll never forget your love!" (p. 174). The full cycle of
confession-absolution, with the steps of a shack for confessional and a
mother-woman for priest, is completed.

AT THE SAME TIME O'Neill was clarifying Josie Hogan's symbolic significance and her role in the confessional design, he was also at great pains
to illuminate her very human needs and desires. As Scheibler argues,
"she remains a completely credible human being throughout the play."[87]
To have made her simply an emblem, a secular savior in a bleak adult
world, would have been to rob the play of much of its emotional power,
perhaps its greatest asset. The suffering here is not confined to Jim Tyrone
alone; Josie too must find a way to live in this imperfect world. In developing the character, O'Neill progressively defined not only her virtues but
the touchingly real vulnerability that evokes audience empathy.

The playwright's first task was to bring out Josie's womanly qualities, to
show that despite her strength and size she is both gentle and feminine.[88]
The initial description of Josie is heavily revised in the manuscript and

moderately edited in the typescript. Cut from the manuscript are stage directions suggesting physical coarseness, either innate or assumed: "Her face is as rugged as her body" and "her voice in her habitual mocking give-and-take raillery with men has a harsh, brazen vulgarity but its natural quality is low, deep-throated and musical" (I, p. 1). Early drafts, like the published play, state "there is no mannish quality about her," but they include a qualification: "although in her manner and way of speech with men does she show a rough free-and-easy camaraderie as if she wanted to be accepted on their own terms, as one of them, rather than as a woman" (TS, I, p. 4). O'Neill replaced this with the comment, "She is all woman" (text, p. 3). While the comfort Josie gives Jim is nonsexual and could theoretically be offered by a male, O'Neill is careful to define Josie as female. Larry helps Parritt find peace as she gives solace to Jim, and Larry is in a sense a surrogate for Parritt's mother as Josie is for Jim's, yet O'Neill obviously wished to stress that the source of love and understanding in *Moon* is particularly feminine. He associates Josie not only with the Virgin Mary but with the moon, traditional symbol of femininity.

Josie is rougher, verbally and physically, in early drafts than in the published play. The November 1941 notes have her telling Jim what she would do if he sold the farm to the Hogans' hated neighbor:

> Be God, if you did, I'd murder you. No, I wouldn't. I'd think you weren't worth murdering. I'd think the worse revenge would be to let you live with yourself dead & stinking in your own heart—to make you look at yourself in the mirror & you shaving each day, until you saw what was there & cut your own throat.[89]

This is an especially vicious speech, for Josie is well aware of Jim's self-loathing and self-destructiveness. In the published play, no matter how angry she is at him, she is incapable of uttering such a threat.

Throughout the typescript O'Neill removed numerous expletives, especially "damn well," from Josie's speech and otherwise tempered her language. He also decreased evidence of her penchant for physical violence. Cut from the typescript is Josie's remark about the departed Mike: "I should have knocked him flat on his back!" (I, p. 16). In the same draft she warns her father: "You know damned well I'll beat better sense in your skull if you lay a finger on me. I've done so often enough, God knows" (I, p. 12). O'Neill deleted both the "damn well" and the entire second sentence. Also in the typescript Jim protests, "For God's sake,

Josie, nix on that club stuff" when he hears Hogan ask whether she has
her broomstick handy (I, p. 37). Neither this line nor the club appears at
this point in the published *Moon*. Josie's broomstick is, as she herself says,
merely a prop to save her father's pride. It is not a dangerous weapon
habitually wielded by a female roughneck.

In addition to making Josie less combative and abrasive, O'Neill carefully justified her participation in the scheme to trick Jim into selling the
farm to the Hogans. Flimsy though it may be, the blackmail plot cannot
be ignored, and her role in it could leave her open to charges of greed and
deviousness. Through his revisions O'Neill shows that Josie, rather than
being the instigator of the plan, is one of its victims.

The very first scene of the published *Moon*—that between Josie and
Mike—does not appear in the scenario, although O'Neill presumably was
thinking of it since Josie's brother is mentioned in the list of characters.
This scene, reminiscent of the opening minutes of *Desire Under the
Elms*,[90] serves several purposes. Törnqvist recognizes one important
function: Josie's motherliness is established here. We learn that she has
raised Mike like a son, and we see her help him to escape even though she
has little use for her brother and his pious lectures. She sends Mike off to
life as she later sends Jim off to death, and she gives each what he needs:
Mike a few dollars to escape his father, Jim the peace to die.[91]

Further, this scene introduces the entrapment plot when Mike suggests
that Josie seduce Jim. One of the few substantial changes O'Neill made in
the extant manuscript was the addition of Mike's advice about tricking
Tyrone. A long canceled manuscript passage has Mike outlining, in a particularly nasty way, the benefits of ensnaring him: "he'll have plenty of
money and land, once his mother's estate is settled. There's just the two of
them to inherit, him and his brother, and Jamie can't live long before the
whiskey kills him" (I, p. 4). However, this speech contains few specific
ideas concerning how to execute an entrapment plan. O'Neill replaced
this with a rough version of what appears in the published *Moon*: Mike's
concrete recommendations about compromising Jim when he's drunk and
bringing witnesses for verification. Although Mike accuses Josie and his
father of already devising such a scheme, it is evident that the plan is the
creation of the young man's jealous, vengeful mind. Hogan does not come
up with the plan; he simply adapts it to his purposes. Thus this scene
allows O'Neill to introduce the entrapment idea without tainting either
Josie or her father.

Not only is the original conception Mike's, O'Neill made changes that show Hogan carefully manipulating his daughter until she has little choice but to cooperate with him. In the published *Moon* Josie shows scarce interest in tricking Jim until her father goads her into action; in the typescript she seems set on revenge even before Hogan intervenes.

The Act II scene between Josie and her father was heavily cut in the typescript. Although most of what was omitted is simply superfluous talk by Hogan—additional bemoaning of his fate and an unnecessarily elaborate account of what occurred at the inn—some deletions bear directly on Josie's involvement in the plot. O'Neill removed from Josie's opening soliloquy her threat against the absent Jim: "It's the last dirty trick you'll ever play on me, and I'll look for a chance to pay you back!" (II, pp. 46–47). She immediately voices her willingness to forgive him, but is angry a few moments later when Hogan returns from the inn and commiserates with his bitter daughter. She tells her father: "And I only wanted him to come because I was thinking over Mike's scheme—I mean, the first one—and I thought maybe I'd try it, if I could get him drunk enough. As for my staying up, I'd have stayed up anyway a beautiful night like this to enjoy the moonlight, if there wasn't a Jim Tyrone in the world" (II, p. 51). O'Neill removed everything before "I'd have stayed up," so Josie's unprovoked mention of Mike's plan disappears. Similarly when Hogan shortly thereafter tells her that Jim has been calling her a virgin and praising her hair and eyes, she replies mockingly: "I'm flattered, I'm sure. If that's true, it may come in handy yet" (II, p. 59). This too was cut. At the beginning of the published second act Josie does mention playing "a joke on" Jim (p. 83), but this remark is nearly all that remains of the several typescript threats.

O'Neill made further modifications at the point where the Hogans spot Jim coming down the road. In the manuscript and typescript it is Josie who comments on his tardiness: "(. . . resentfully) No, he's only two hours and a half late, that's all" (TS, II, p. 65). In the published play it is Hogan who mentions Jim's lateness, and the lines O'Neill added are clearly designed to goad the young woman into action: "Oh, the dirty, double-crossing bastard! The nerve of him! Coming to call on you, after making you wait for hours, thinking you don't know what he's done to us this night, and it'll be a fine cruel joke to blarney you in the moonlight, and your trusting him like a poor sheep, and never suspecting—" (text, p. 98). Josie does ultimately suggest they attempt to enact Mike's scheme, but it

is evident—as it is not in early drafts—that she must first be carefully
primed by Hogan. Her father proves a skillful psychologist, pointing out
how badly Jim has treated her and thus touching her sensitive ego. Hurt
and humiliated, Josie is trapped into trying to trap Jim.[92]

Josie may be duped into acting her part in the blackmail plot, yet far
more important is the role she has written for herself: that of tramp. Like
nearly every other character in O'Neill's last works, Josie has been using a
fantasy, a mask, to help her confront the world. Unaided by drink or
drugs, the favorite props in these plays, she has executed her performance so successfully that everyone except Hogan and Jim believes she
has slept with half the men in the neighborhood. There is a certain perverse logic in her choice of masquerade; a generous woman who longs to
"give of herself" to others, Josie pretends she has literally done so. But
her motives run even deeper, and the various *Moon* drafts show O'Neill's
attempts to explain the complex issue of Josie's role-playing, to clarify why
she behaves as she does.

Josie's loose woman pose is more fully developed in early drafts than in
the published *Moon*. O'Neill's decision to cut back on Josie's pretended
promiscuity helps solve a serious problem: how to show that she is very
involved with her role-playing while also making it evident that her wantonness is only a pretense. The audience must realize Josie is a virgin;
otherwise her confession of innocence will seem simply a convenient lie
rather than the admission of a painful truth. Josie's chastity is also significant because it makes her unusual in the O'Neill canon. Varying the stage
cliché he had used so often—the whore with the heart of gold—O'Neill
creates in his last play a pure woman with only the appearance of a
wanton.

The scenario states bluntly, as the later drafts only imply, Josie's dilemma. O'Neill devotes nearly the whole first page of the scenario to describing her and begins with this account:

> Josie—as a defense she builds herself up as a slut—bawdy & brazen carry-
> ing on with men—even her own brother believes she is promiscuous—the
> one person she doesn't fool is her father . . . he knows she is still a virgin,
> although he pretends to accept her version because he guesses the reason for
> it—she is the one thing on earth he loves—
>
> In her build-up, she knows the men she has kidded along won't admit she
> slaps them down when they try to seduce her—they all let it be thought
> they've had her—

> It is not morality but a pride in her that makes her reject them—they are
> animals who see nothing but animal in her—she saves herself for a man who
> will see that inside her is beauty—   (p. 1)

Josie in the published play fits this description quite closely; apparently
O'Neill had a good idea of this aspect of his heroine when he first began
writing *Moon*. Curiously, this portrait is not borne out in the scenario
itself as well as it is in the finished text. Later in the scenario Josie tells Jim
that she, like everyone else, has two opposing dreams. One of hers is to
be "the triumphant beautiful ruthless harlot who uses [?] men but never
loves, makes men her slaves." In her second dream she is a "virtuous
married woman whose joy is to be a slave to husband, children & house"
(III, p. 4). The first suggests that Josie at least in part genuinely wants to
be the whore she pretends she is. This contrasts with both the long scenario account quoted above and with the final text. Josie may be jealous of
Jim's Broadway tarts, but that does not mean she yearns to be one. This
dream, remarkably close to Deborah Harford's fantasy in *More Stately
Mansions*, reflects the darker side of O'Neill's view of woman: a heartless
creature who deliberately destroys the men who love her. Such desires
are obviously inappropriate for the innocent heroine of O'Neill's last
drama. The second dream will, as we shall see, recur in subsequent drafts
and finally disappear during revision of the typescript. Josie's maternal
feelings are evident in the published *Moon*, but they do not assume such a
domesticated tone.

Although the dream of being a harlot does not reappear, Josie's promiscuity is more strongly stressed in the manuscript and typescript than in
the final text.[93] There are more than a dozen places, primarily in the
typescript, where O'Neill moderated or deleted references to her sup-
posed activities. For example, in a line cut from the manuscript Josie
answers Mike's comment that she has "a kind heart" by noting, "That's
what all the men say. Too damned kind" (I, p. 3). She tells Hogan in the
published play, "I've a right to be free" (p. 19). In the typescript she is
more explicit: "I've a right to be free in the night to take my fun when and
where and how I like" (I, p. 14). The typescript also has Josie claiming that
McCabe will "make a good witness" for their confrontation with Harder
because the groom is a "tattle-tale" who has been spreading "scandal"
about her. "It's too bad it was true," she adds (I, p. 36). All this was omitted along with numerous other allusions to her purported sexual adven-

tures, most by Josie herself and a few by her father and brother.[94] The manuscript and typescript references are so numerous that O'Neill is in danger of convincing the audience the stories are ture. By lessening emphasis on Josie's whore pose, O'Neill prevents the misconception that she really is a loose woman. Although Nicola Chiaromonte sees her as "a hardened sinner" and David Sievers believes "Josie has been promiscuous,"[95] few other viewers fail to realize that her wantonness is only feigned.

Josie clings to the pose because it shields her from feelings of inadequacy and loneliness, gives her at least the appearance of being wanted by many men. As he developed the character, O'Neill revealed how deeply her pride is involved in this pretense. The scenario has Josie quite readily admitting her masquerade: very early in the third act she concedes that the moon is "a virgin like me" (III, p. 2). Only in the November 1941 notes, composed shortly after the scenario, do we begin to see how tenaciously she holds to her role-playing, how much effort Jim must expend to break down her façade. Her full anguish is displayed in the final text, where she "begins to sob with a strange forlorn shame and humiliation" when forced to acknowledge her chastity (p. 136). Moreover, her admission of innocence in the scenario has little effect on Jim, who in that version is not obsessed with having a pure surrogate for his idolized mother. The published *Moon*, by contrast, makes her confession crucial: Jim cannot truly begin *his* confession until she becomes the virginal figure he needs as listener. Finally, the scenario shows Josie still playing her role, albeit to a limited extent and without much seriousness, in the fourth act. When she compares herself to Jim's previous women, he objects: "Don't talk like that. You're not one of them." "Not for lack of trying," Josie answers (IV, p. 5). Before telling her father the truth about what happened during the night, she teases him by implying she has slept with Jim and adding, "He promised to send me twenty dollars." When Hogan mocks her claim, she replies: "Well, if I was a whore for nothing, I'm all the prouder!" (IV, p. 6). It is only later that she reveals the truth, and also informs him that she has never slept with anyone. Paradoxically, this banter about promiscuity in the scenario makes Josie's role-playing seem less rather than more important to her. If pretending to be sexually free was a significant psychological defense, she would not treat this pose so lightly after she was compelled to give it up. In the last act of the published *Moon* Josie does not and cannot jest about the protective mask she has dropped.

O'Neill presumably also omitted these last-act references to show that Josie, unlike the men in Harry Hope's bar, is not reverting to her old ways. Her fourth-act allusions to whores might mislead the audience into assuming she still needs her charade. For example, the following interchange appears in Act IV of the typescript:

JOSIE . . . You'll have to forgive me for waking you at dawn but I had to get you away from here before some farmer passed and saw the two of us on the steps to my bedroom. I know you wouldn't want that.

TYRONE No, I wouldn't. There's enough lousy lies about you already. I remember now we argued that out last night, didn't we, and you finally admitted you were only bluffing about—

JOSIE (without looking at him) I did. Yes. [To you.] Because it was what you wanted to help make the night different and beautiful for you.

TYRONE And because it's true.

JOSIE Yes. It's true. (Forcing a smile) But don't go telling anyone my secrets, and shaming me before the world. (IV, pp. 107–108)[96]

Josie does with a little prodding concede that Jim is telling the truth, but her asking him not to reveal her "secrets" suggests that she may continue to play the tramp. This supposition is not dispelled until later, when she tells her father that she no longer needs to lie and boast about being "the slut of the world" (IV, p. 113). When he rewrote Act IV of the typescript, O'Neill deleted both these discussions of Josie's promiscuity. In the published play, her failure to mention her alleged sexual activities at all in the last act shows implicitly what is here stated explicitly to Hogan: the pretense is not necessary anymore.

THROUGH THE CHANGES noted so far, O'Neill made Josie Hogan even more appealing than she was in earlier drafts. The same process of "gentling" which most of the other figures in the late plays underwent is evident here, and the result is striking: stripped of her yearning to be a "ruthless harlot," her rough edges polished, allied with Jim's mother and the Virgin Mary, Josie emerges as one of the most positive characters in the entire O'Neill canon. Her goodness is matched by her uniqueness, for she is the only individual in the last dramas who loses both a cherished pipe dream and a loved one yet does not wish for a swift end to her life. How she does react to her loss presented O'Neill with his final challenge, and *Moon*'s concluding act changed radically, in both structure and tone, as he wrestled with the question of Josie's fate.

The fourth act of the published *Moon* consists of a scene between Josie and Hogan, then the parting of Josie and Jim, and a final brief interchange between father and daughter. As noted before, earlier drafts have only two scenes: first the farewell of the lovers, then a concluding scene between Josie and Hogan. The father-daughter confrontation in the scenario is comprised largely of Hogan's questions and speculations about what happened during the night, Josie's evasive answers, and discussion of her future. There are noticeably few indications that Josie is deeply distraught about losing Jim. Rather, the most prominent emotions here are Hogan's anger and frustration at not being able to learn whether his daughter has slept with Tyrone.

Josie's suffering is shown in the manuscript and typescript, but not very forcefully. As in the published *Moon*, Josie weeps briefly when Jim departs. She is unnaturally subdued during much of the closing scene with her father, and at one point "her voice falters and trembles. She seems about to sob—forces it back" (TS, IV, p. 113). Although the last scene in the manuscript and typescript is far longer than that in the final text, the tone and movement of the scenes are very similar. We see Josie's sadness, yet we also see her beginning to regain the vitality and humor she possessed before her night with Jim.

What is missing from these early versions is the fury that Josie unleashes against her father in the published *Moon*. The original arrangement of the fourth act limits the extent to which O'Neill can show Josie's distress over losing Jim. For his sake she must hide her misery as best she can, so her pain could not be fully revealed in the parting scene. The curtain scene must show her inherent strength, her ability to begin reconciling herself to her loss; she "returns" to her father and the farm. Thus here too the playwright was constrained in the degree to which he could display her unhappiness. By allowing Josie an encounter with her father before the conclusion of the play, he gave himself an opportunity to portray her emotional state.

Josie's anger is the most prominent aspect of the scene O'Neill placed at the beginning of the rewritten fourth act. Five times the stage directions describe her expression or her tone as "bitter." She threatens to leave the farm, refuses to listen to her father's explanations of his actions, and banishes him to the shack. Surely O'Neill does not mean to suggest that Josie has a cruel streak that leads her to enjoy tormenting Hogan, nor are we meant to believe she actually thinks her father tricked her into joining his scheme because he coveted Jim's money. As she tells him later, she was well aware of his motivation. Finally, her claim that she wanted to "punish" Hogan for his trickery does not sufficiently explain her outburst. O'Neill needed a convincing way to show Josie's pain over the loss of Jim, and he did so by having her transform her distress and frustration into anger at her father. We see her berating Hogan, yet we know that the real source of her misery is not his perfidy but her inability to give Jim Tyrone the will to live; Hogan is the most convenient scapegoat. This anger shows the intensity of Josie's disappointment far better than does the quiet sadness she manifests in earlier versions.

During the first stages of composition, O'Neill apparently felt obliged to "tie up" the drama neatly by sketching in a future for Josie. Only as work progressed does he seem to have fully realized that such an effort was both unnecessary and demeaning to his heroine, suggesting that she could easily assuage her grief with a ready-made set of alternative plans. While early drafts hint that she will soon follow woman's traditional path to marriage and family—replace her love for Jim and her pretended promiscuity with respectable domesticity—the published text leaves the question of her intentions largely unanswered. Instead, O'Neill's revisions focus inward to illuminate what Josie has gained from her relationship with Jim, the new strength she has acquired with which to face whatever the future may bring.

In the final act of the scenario, Josie informs Jim that she is going to marry another man:

> Anyway, I'll have you know I'm an engaged woman from now on—accept Mackay [?] today—he's been begging me to marry him since he tried seduce me. I let him have a box on the ears that rattled his brains—he's a good enough lad, a bit free with the girls but I'll soon knock that out of him. He has ten cows and two fine horses and 20 pigs and a fine bit of land I can boss [?]—he'll give me children I can love—the first will be a son and I'll call him Jamie. (IV, p. 5)

It is unclear, however, whether she really intends to wed the young farmer or is just saying this to hasten Jim's departure and prevent his worrying about her. As Jim leaves she muses, "I'll never love another." Her subsequent conversation with Hogan does not clarify her intentions appreciably. The scenario reads: "She says she told J. going marry M.—'And are you?' He praises M. hopefully—" (IV, p. 6). A few moments later Josie declares that Jim asked her to marry him. When Hogan asks, "And you refused?" she responds enigmatically, "I did. I wouldn't marry if best [last?] man in world" (IV, p. 6). This statement can be construed two ways: she would not marry Jim Tyrone if he were the best man in the world, or she would not marry anyone, not even the best man in the world. The latter interpretation is supported by her comment to Hogan, similar to one she makes in the published play, "And don't waste time feeling sorry for me. Sure, I have you to manage and keep out of jail and that keeps me busy" (IV, p. 6). Although the confusion here may be attributable to the cryptic nature of O'Neill's scenarios, it may also reflect the playwright's uncertainty, for such a marriage is surely a mundane fate for this extraordinary heroine.

O'Neill toyed briefly with the marriage question in the notes he wrote shortly after the scenario. This time it is Hogan who suggests matrimony: "Marry Mackay [?]—children—'even if he's a fool, he might give you some children.'" Josie, reminding her father that she has him to care for and that he is "always in more trouble than ten children could be," dismisses the idea. She returns to it again in the manuscript and typescript, however, although now no specific husband is mentioned and her plans are more tentative:

> And maybe some day after I've lived down my bad reputation, I'll marry some decent man who's a hard worker and will be a help on the farm—and who'll give me children. For I know now I've a great love for children and I'll make a good mother. (She pauses—then adds) I mean, some day after Jim Tyrone is— (Her voice falters and trembles. She seems about to sob—forces it back. Hogan keeps his eyes on the ground. She gets control of herself) I never want to talk about this again, Father. (He nods assent without looking at her. A pause)   (TS, IV, p. 113)

As Tinsley asserts, such a resolution of Josie's plight is "hopelessly sentimental."[97] It reduces her to the level of a soap-opera heroine. She has lost her great love, but when he is dead she will hide her heartbreak by doing what every good woman must: marry and raise a houseful of kids.

There are many other problems with this speech. Josie's comment "I know now I've a great love for children" implies that she, like some critics, sees Jim Tyrone as simply a case of arrested development. Such a statement diminishes the relationship between the lovers by suggesting that her feeling for him is solely maternal. Josie's affection has a significant maternal component, but it is not mother love alone. Most important, this line undercuts a major O'Neill theme: maternal love is something far more than just an appreciation of kids, and adults as well as children seek this reassuring devotion as protection against a dismaying world. Finally, this passage looks beyond the Josie-Jim relationship to focus on what Josie will do in the future rather than on what she has gained from her time with Jim. As O'Neill worked on *Moon*, he paid careful attention to what Jim received from the moonlit night: forgiveness, absolution, and peace. Similarly, his revisions alter the picture of what Josie has received. Although O'Neill rejected the clichés of marriage and family for his heroine, he ultimately came to a very conventional male view of male-female relations. In the published play Josie's consolation for the loss of Jim is the knowledge that she has helped him, at least for a while. The act of giving solace becomes, for Josie, its own reward.

The conclusion of the scenario and post-scenario notes show a Josie who seems compelled to convince Hogan that Jim proposed to her. She tells her father, in the notes: "I could have married him. He asked me, that's truth." Josie's claim is valid, but it is obvious she must repeat this because it is evidence of Jim's love for her, evidence she sorely needs to bolster her sagging ego. Although she gains some comfort in the scenario from having given Jim a very special night, her remarks emphasize what he has done for her rather than what she has done for him. Because Jim proposed, she no longer feels unwanted. Again in the manuscript and typescript, Josie is proud of providing "love no other woman would give him!" (TS, IV, p. 113), yet she still must console herself with the thought that Jim found her physically attractive. She muses aloud, "Well, anyway, I've been beautiful myself for a while—for him—and that's some consolation" (TS, IV, p. 109). A few moments later she informs her father she will not play the wanton because "I don't need to, now I know I can be beautiful" (IV, p. 113). Both lines disappear.

In the published *Moon* Josie has no need to sustain herself with teasing references to her alleged sexual activities or claims about her beauty. Jim's recognition of her sacrifices for him is enough. As he is about to depart without fully acknowledging what has passed between them, Josie begs "*(Pleadingly)* I hoped, for your sake, you wouldn't remember, but now you do, I want you to remember my love for you gave you peace for a while" (text, pp. 173–174). This plea is squeezed into a tiny space in the handwritten part of the revised typescript, suggesting that O'Neill expanded it when

reviewing the final act. Now Josie will not settle, as she does in the typescript, for a less than complete recollection of what occurred the previous
night. She needs Jim's statement that she has given him peace, for in her
ability to do so lies her new and valid image of herself and hence the
strength to face the future. The act of commitment horrifies and nearly
destroys Larry Slade, but Josie is given new life by her sacrifice. Jim's
admission of how much she helped him gives her a sense of worth that
allows her to continue, although greatly saddened, even after the loss of
him and of her protective mask of promiscuity.

DESPITE THE EFFORT O'Neill put into *A Moon for the Misbegotten*, it
is weaker than either *The Iceman Cometh* or *Long Day's Journey Into
Night*. The notes and early drafts offer a clue to what happened. O'Neill
began *Iceman* and *Journey* with a wealth of ideas and potential themes; his
work on these plays was largely a sharpening and narrowing of focus. In
the case of *Moon*, he began with more limited material: the idea of expanding Edmund's Shaughnessy story in *Journey* and the desire to dramatize what the Work Diary calls "J[amie]'s revelation of self." His intentions
limited and his illness advancing, he filled out the skeleton with comic
scenes and a tired melodramatic plot uneasily yoking together the pigs-in-
the-pond episode and the lovers' conversation. O'Neill had material for a
superb short drama, but he chose to stretch it into a sometimes tedious
longer work. Although he did considerable revision, subordinating unimportant elements and clarifying the central Josie-Jim relationship, he never did enough. The result is a fine yet flawed piece.

Ironically, although *Moon* is less successful than either *Iceman* or
Journey, O'Neill overcame in this last drama a theatrical problem he could
not solve in the other works. Critics have many reservations about *Moon*,
but few have complained that Josie Hogan is not a fully realized character
on stage. Tom Donnelly speaks for many when, reviewing the 1957 revival
of *Moon*, he states that Josie "is the one big-scale portrait in the gallery,
painfully, throbbingly, hopelessly alive."[98] Edmund Tyrone is nearly overwhelmed on stage by the more vocal members of his family, while Larry
Slade must vie for audience attention with the histrionic Hickey and a
chorus of alcoholics. Josie holds her own. In this towering farm woman
O'Neill finally found a character to balance the lost soul pouring out his
saga of anguish.

POSTSCRIPT

D URING THE PERIOD 1939–1944, Eugene O'Neill created the one-act *Hughie*, gentle coda to *Iceman*; wrote a new draft of *A Touch of the Poet*, the only completed cycle play; and worked extensively on dramas he never finished.[1] *The Iceman Cometh, Long Day's Journey Into Night*, and *A Moon for the Misbegotten* were also composed during this span, while O'Neill was wrestling with the disease that would end his dramatic career. All three took shape quite rapidly. Even *Moon*, whose gestation period was interrupted by World War II and substantial time allotted to other plays, was completed only two and a half years after it was begun. Yet despite the relative speed with which O'Neill worked, perhaps spurred by the knowledge that his writing days were coming to a close, his attention to revision was great. The manuscripts are indeed overwritten, but O'Neill's careful editing demonstrates that he labored painstakingly to trim and modify his early drafts. The repetitions that sometimes annoy directors and audiences are the result of deliberate intention rather than carelessness, laziness, or an inability to revise.

O'Neill's composition process followed a characteristic pattern. The playwright first put his thoughts on paper in notes and scenarios. The scenarios allowed him to begin creating characters, composing dialogue, formulating themes, and blocking out action and dramatic structure. One can almost literally see the playwright becoming absorbed in work on the scenarios, his already-cramped handwriting growing progressively smaller as it moves down each page. The *Iceman* and *Journey* scenarios contain ideas that did not survive in the printed text; O'Neill started these dramas with a plethora of sometimes contradictory intentions, and his process of composition involved selecting from among these initial concepts. The scenario of *Moon* is sparser, and when he came to flesh out that play O'Neill relied not only on an opening scene suggested by *Desire Under the Elms* but on a Pietà tableau used earlier (if much less centrally) in *More Stately Mansions*. The narrow plans with which O'Neill began his last play help explain why it is slightly less complex than *Iceman* or *Journey.*

The typescripts of *Iceman, Journey,* and *Moon* are longer than the published texts, and the manuscripts are still longer, even though the playwright did not drastically cut any draft. While writing *Strange Interlude,* O'Neill informed the critic Joseph Wood Krutch: "My fear in writing a first draft is always of omitting something, so there are bound to be many repetitions. I usually have a first draft at least one-fourth too long—almost intentionally, for I've gotten so cutting is a labor of love with me and I get a keen satisfaction out of it second only to the actual creating."[2] Whether or not he loved his labor, O'Neill did it conscientiously.

Often the material O'Neill deleted was simply gratuitous or repetitious, but he also cut lines and speeches that obscure rather than illuminate the point he wishes to present. On the other hand, overly obvious statements of theme also disappeared as the playwright revised. "Love is so horrible" Mary Tyrone laments in the *Journey* scenario—an unnecessary statement in a play about the ways love can torment people and destroy their dreams. O'Neill regularly canceled or recast passages in which characters express their feelings, motives, and intentions too bluntly.[3] By changing blatant statements to indirect ones, he made the works more dramatically convincing and at least somewhat more subtle. In early drafts a character will frequently voice an awareness of his or her situation that is appropriate to the playwright alone. O'Neill's revisions erase this incongruity. Albert Rothenberg, a psychiatrist who has studied O'Neill's works, contributes another important observation: "Implication often gives an issue greater emotional impact than explicitness."[4] A less direct presentation is by no means a less powerful one. It should also be noted that the playwright evidently had readers as well as theatergoers in mind when he edited his late dramas, for stage directions received as much attention as dialogue did. Although there are still copious directions in the published texts, many confusing or unnecessarily explicit ones were pruned, usually at a late stage in the composition process.[5]

O'Neill's theatrical instincts are further reflected in his rearrangement of scenes and speeches. The scenarios are relatively flat, lacking careful scene patterning and speech placement, and even manuscripts and typescripts fall short of the dramatic tension that makes the finished plays so effective. O'Neill knew the theatrical value of a delayed entrance and a striking curtain. Thus an anticlimactic appearance by Mary Tyrone early in the final act of *Journey* was deleted, and the concluding scenes of *Moon* were reorganized to highlight the lovers' valediction. Similarly, he knew how to create suspense by withholding a piece of information—such as the nature of Edmund's illness—or postponing an event. George Pierce Baker had preached the virtue of suspense, and O'Neill had encountered it in his father's *Monte Cristo*, in the works of dramatists like Ibsen, and even in the detective stories he favored for light reading.[6]

The "shape" of a dramatic work depends also on the amount of attention accorded each character. As he revised, O'Neill diminished focus on minor figures, accentuated major ones, and occasionally removed such distracting or unnecessary characters as Buzy in *Iceman* and the witnesses in *Moon*. His revisions insure the secondary status of Jamie Tyrone (in *Journey*), and Phil Hogan while directing more attention to Larry Slade, Edmund Tyrone, and Josie Hogan. Part of the increased focus on these latter characters comes through a process of differentiation: Edmund was progressively distinguished from his relatives, Larry was set apart from the rest of Hope's gang, and Josie was more sharply contrasted with Jim Tyrone. For all his obvious efforts to spotlight these figures, however, O'Neill was not completely successful. On stage if not on paper, Edmund is often overshadowed by his more theatrical kin, Larry by Hickey and the raucous drunks. O'Neill was well aware of the problem he faced in trying to make basically passive characters the center of dramatic attention; his revisions go far toward solving this problem if not far enough. Only the oversized Josie, like Larry and Edmund primarily a sympathetic listener, is in no danger of being effaced by those with whom she shares the stage.

While O'Neill's method of editing all three plays is impressively consistent, even more striking are the similarities among the dramas themselves, similarities that grow out of those very revisions. Thematically and structurally, *Iceman*, *Journey*, and *Moon* are more closely allied in their published versions than in their early drafts. John Henry Raleigh points out a number of correspondences among the late plays, including the prevalence of liquor and drugs, the device of the "backward journey" through memory, the pattern of "beginning in laughter and ending in sadness and tears," the hot summer settings, the importance of offstage characters, and the adherence to classical unities.[7] Most of these common elements are already present in the three scenarios, but the parallels were

honed during rewriting: the opening-act comedy was expanded in both
Journey and *Moon;* Parritt's imprisoned mother and Jim's dead mother
grew increasingly influential; the time period covered in *Iceman* was compressed from four days to two, more nearly approaching the one-day span
of the other plays. Even more significant is the development of what I
have called the "confessional pattern," the revelation of a distressed soul
to a sympathetic listener, which O'Neill sharpened as he worked. Hickey
confesses to those assembled in the bar (and receives Larry's pity, although he is unaware of this), Parritt confesses to Larry, Jamie to Edmund, Jim to Josie. In O'Neill's world a dream and a drink keep most
people afloat. When even these no longer suffice, the commiseration and
forgiveness of another human being are the only solace. The playwright
made the confessional pattern an important part of *Iceman* and *Journey;*
he made it virtually the whole of *Moon.*

The sympathetic listener who plays a central role in this confessional
motif points to one of the most striking aspects of the revisions: the increasing compassion O'Neill revealed as these dramas developed. The
"deep pity and understanding and forgiveness" for the characters O'Neill
mentions in his dedication of *Journey* to Carlotta are sometimes difficult
to perceive in the early notes and drafts. As he shaped all three works,
O'Neill softened, to a greater or lesser degree, his treatment of every
major character, forcing the audience to see how even their most reprehensible actions could be the product of initially good intentions. Characters grew less calculating while more vulnerable; the cynical veneer many
affect was rubbed thin enough to expose the anguish underneath. A comment O'Neill made about *Iceman* applies equally well to *Journey* or *Moon:*
"there are moments in it that suddenly strip the secret soul of a man stark
naked, not in cruelty or moral superiority, but with an understanding
compassion which sees him as a victim of the ironies of life and of himself."[8]

We cannot peer into the playwright's mind to learn the progress of his
thoughts, but we can speculate about the causes of this change. Part of the
shift in characters results from O'Neill's attempts to diminish repetition.
An accusation made a half-dozen times is damaging; the same accusation
made two dozen times is damning. Further, his theatrical instincts were
obviously at work. O'Neill, a seasoned playwright when he created these
dramas, must have known that complex figures would engage his au-

dience more than villains would. It may well have been easier for him to create a Hickey or a Mary Tyrone with bold strokes at an early stage and later paint in the nuances that are the material of tragedy rather than of the melodrama he knew so well from his youth.

The characters in *Iceman, Journey,* and *Moon* are based on individuals O'Neill knew or knew about, and the names of many of the models can be found in notes and scenarios. Not surprisingly, the early versions of all three plays are in some ways more directly autobiographical than the finished dramas: what began in memory was transmuted by imagination. In *Iceman* (and occasionally in *Moon*) O'Neill changed real names to fictional ones as individuals like Terry Carlin and Tom Wallace evolved into Larry Slade and Harry Hope. As the playwright worked he deleted biographical material that is not immediately relevant to the drama at hand.[9] Numerous superfluous references to Jim Tyrone's brother vanished from *Moon,* and some details about the mother's family did not survive beyond the scenario of *Journey.* But in the case of *Journey* O'Neill also made minor chronological adjustments to insure that the published play more nearly accords with historical fact than early versions do.

Although *Iceman, Journey,* and *Moon* are dramatic fiction, not unfiltered autobiography, biographical questions must be addressed. Most of the inhabitants of Hope's bar were based on the playwright's friends and acquaintances, the Tyrones were extrapolated from the O'Neills, and even Josie Hogan was loosely modeled on a woman the playwright knew. Was O'Neill more honest in his original harsh portrayals, and do his revisions reflect his unwillingness to reveal all the horror he knew or to attack, even through fictional characters, those long dead? This is possible but unlikely. Anyone who has seen these plays on stage (or merely read them) has felt their searing power and shared the anguish that must have gone into the author's creation of a mother who abandons her family for drugs or of tortured men who desire only a peaceful death. Since the final plays contain so much that must have been acutely painful to the playwright, it is doubtful that his revisions grew out of conscious or even unconscious attempts to avoid acknowledging the traumatic. O'Neill's changes in Jamie Tyrone in *Journey* and his counterpart Jim Tyrone in *Moon*—changes that deny the character a possibility for growth—are perhaps the only ones in which we can detect the forces of repression at work during rewriting, and even here we cannot be sure. Was O'Neill implicitly justifying his own failure to save his brother or was he just darkening the pall that in early drafts was already spread over the character—and over so many other doomed figures in his canon?

Moreover, even when early versions contain more biographical details than later ones, this does not necessarily mean they are, in the deepest sense, more "truthful."[10] As O'Neill himself said, "Facts are facts, but the truth is beyond and outside them."[11] Truth is largely a matter of judgment and perspective, and these are what seem to have changed most during the composition process. As O'Neill developed *Iceman, Journey,* and *Moon,* he evidently came to appreciate more fully the difficult circumstances in which he had placed his characters as well as the tangled motives that might lie behind their actions. Just as Larry Slade, Edmund Tyrone, and Josie Hogan grew in empathy for others as the plays were rewritten, so too did O'Neill grow in empathy for his characters. The result is gentler handling of figures like the Tyrones, based on the playwright's immediate family, and of those like Don Parritt, with whose "model" O'Neill had no personal relationship.

It is inaccurate, of course, to say that any of these plays underwent a radical metamorphosis from early notes to finished drama. Most of the elements present in the final versions are there in the early ones as well: love tinged with or corrupted into hatred, loyalty alternating with betrayal, kindness coupled with cruelty. But *The Iceman Cometh, Long Day's Journey Into Night,* and *A Moon for the Misbegotten* are, in the forms we know them, more finely balanced than they were when O'Neill began writing them. Whether through his growing understanding of his characters O'Neill gained new appreciation for his long-dead family and friends is a question for a psychologist rather than a critic, although his dedicatory inscription to *Journey* suggests that he did. What matters to critics and audiences is that through the complex process of composition—a process at once physical, literary, theatrical, and emotional—O'Neill created three of the finest plays in the American dramatic canon.

NOTES

INTRODUCTION

1. Valuable discussions of O'Neill's late plays may be found in Travis Bogard's *Contour in Time: The Plays of Eugene O'Neill* (New York: Oxford Univ. Press, 1972); Jean Chothia's *Forging a Language: A Study of the Plays of Eugene O'Neill* (London: Cambridge Univ. Press, 1979); Michael Manheim's *Eugene O'Neill's New Language of Kinship* (Syracuse: Syracuse Univ. Press, 1982); John Henry Raleigh's *The Plays of Eugene O'Neill* (Carbondale: So. Illinois Univ. Press, 1965); Rolf Scheibler's *The Late Plays of Eugene O'Neill* (Bern: A. Francke, 1970); and Egil Törnqvist's *A Drama of Souls: Studies in O'Neill's Super-naturalistic Technique* (New Haven: Yale Univ. Press, 1969). Virginia Floyd's seminal *Eugene O'Neill at Work: Newly Released Ideas for Plays* (New York: Ungar, 1981) includes chapters on the notes and scenarios for *Iceman, Journey,* and *Moon* but does not consider full manuscripts and typescripts. Mary Adrian Tinsley's "Two Biographical Plays by Eugene O'Neill: The Drafts and the Final Versions" (Ph.D. diss., Cornell Univ., 1969), studies the typescripts of *Journey* and *Moon* with only occasional references to O'Neill's handwritten notes and drafts.

2. Kenneth Muir, *Shakespeare's Sources (I): Comedies and Tragedies* (London: Methuen, 1957), p. 254.

3. Except for a few production scripts, all manuscripts and typescripts of *Iceman, Journey,* and *Moon* discussed in this study are in the Beinecke's Eugene O'Neill Collection. The Beinecke does not usually permit readers to consult the easily smeared original pencil drafts, but photocopies of these are available, as are all typescript materials. Carlotta's diary, her letters to various correspondents, and the playwright's letters except those to Lawrence Langner are in the same collection; the Langner correspondence is in the Beinecke's Theatre Guild Collection. Although the original Work Diary is not available to readers, a transcription has been published: Eugene O'Neill, *Work Diary 1924–1943*, transcribed by Donald Gallup, preliminary edition, 2 vols. (New Haven: Yale Univ. Library, 1981). The Macgowan correspondence is published in Jackson R. Bryer, ed. *"The Theatre We*

Worked For": The Letters of Eugene O'Neill to Kenneth Macgowan, with introductory essays by Travis Bogard (New Haven: Yale Univ. Press, 1982). Production scripts of *The Iceman Cometh* (described in the Bibliography) are scattered among the Beinecke's O'Neill and Theatre Guild collections and the New York Public Library Theatre Collection at Lincoln Center.

4. Letter to Julian P. Boyd, Jan. 28, 1943, in the Princeton University Library's Eugene O'Neill Collection. See Louis Sheaffer, *O'Neill: Son and Playwright* (Boston: Little, Brown, 1968), p. 265, for a discussion of other possible reasons why O'Neill's handwriting is so small.

5. Carlotta relates in her diary (Aug. 30, 1940) that she went to the doctor seeking stronger glasses with which to read her husband's handwriting. After seeing a sample of O'Neill's penmanship, he advised her to get a magnifying glass. Carlotta at first thought that she wouldn't "bother much" with the glass she bought, but subsequent diary entries show that she did use it. Because O'Neill could neither dictate his plays nor compose on a typewriter, his career ended when his tremor rendered him unable to control a pencil.

6. George Pierce Baker, *Dramatic Technique* (Boston: Houghton Mifflin, 1919), pp. 426–27, 433, 449.

7. Lawrence Langner, *The Play's the Thing* (New York: Putnam, 1960), p. 100. Not all of O'Neill's early scenarios have arrowheads indicating entrances and exits, but those that don't often have lists in the margins showing which characters appear in each scene.

8. Letter to a Mr. Perlman, quoted in Louis Sheaffer, *O'Neill: Son and Artist* (Boston: Little, Brown, 1973), p. 164.

9. Floyd, *O'Neill at Work*, p. xiv.

10. Donald Gallup, in conversation, Feb. 1973.

CHAPTER ONE

1. Agnes Boulton, *Part of a Long Story* (Garden City, N.Y.: Doubleday, 1958), p. 31.

2. Cyrus Day, "The Iceman and the Bridegroom: Some Observations on the Death of O'Neill's Salesman," *Modern Drama* 1 (May 1958): 3–9. For other discussions of the biblical and sexual connotations of the title, see Arthur Gelb and Barbara Gelb, *O'Neill,* enlarged ed. (New York: Harper & Row, 1973), pp. 831–32; and Albert Rothenberg, "The Iceman Changeth: Toward an Empirical Approach to Creativity," *Journal of the American Psychoanalytic Association* 17 (April 1969): 557–58, 561, 579–80. Virginia Floyd argues that "in the first act [of the *Iceman* scenario] the fireman assumes the role the iceman will later play in the joking allusion to the lover of Hickey's wife." While I am less certain than she about the

word in question (O'Neill's handwritten scenarios are sometimes difficult to decipher), her interpretation is certainly plausible: one phrase may well read "the Fireman cometh," and a word that looks like *fireman* appears a few sentences earlier. Floyd adds that "it is highly unlikely O'Neill ever seriously entertained the possibility" of using *fireman* in the title of the play. *Iceman*, with its clearer connotations of death, is surely more appropriate. See her *O'Neill at Work*, p. 270.

3. Karl Schriftgiesser, "Interview with O'Neill," *New York Times*, 6 Oct. 1946, sec. 2, p. 3.

4. Eugene O'Neill, *The Iceman Cometh* (New York: Random House, 1946), p. 183. All future references to the printed play are to this edition and will be given in the body of the text.

5. Eugene O'Neill, *More Stately Mansions*, shortened from the author's partly revised script by Karl Ragnar Gierow, ed. Donald Gallup (New Haven: Yale Univ. Press, 1964), p. 180. Rothenberg, "Iceman Changeth," pp. 561, 579–81, also discusses this passage and its relationship to *The Iceman Cometh*.

6. Letter to George Jean Nathan, Feb. 8, 1940. George Jean Nathan Collection, Cornell University Library. Unless otherwise indicated, all letters to Nathan cited subsequently are in this collection.

7. See, for example, Doris Alexander, "Hugo of *The Iceman Cometh*: Realism and O'Neill," *American Quarterly* 5 (Winter 1953): 357–66, and *The Tempering of Eugene O'Neill* (New York: Harcourt, Brace & World, 1962), pp. 115–226 passim, 267; Gelb and Gelb, *O'Neill*, pp. 170–71, 186, 284–99, 368; Sheaffer, *Son and Playwright*, pp. 129–31, 325–38, 386, 424–25, and *Son and Artist*, pp. 62, 427–28; Winifred L. Frazer, *E.G. and E.G.O.: Emma Goldman and "The Iceman Cometh"* (Gainesville: Univ. Presses of Florida, 1974), pp. 1–99 passim; and Floyd, *O'Neill at Work*, pp. 260–68.

8. "H.H." could not refer to Harry Hope. In these early notes the bar owner is called "Tom W."

9. O'Neill, *Work Diary 1924–1943*. The relevant entry is dated June 6, 1939. Because the original Work Diary is not available for examination, all subsequent references are to Gallup's transcription. Entry dates rather than page numbers will be given.

10. Sheaffer, *Son and Playwright*, offers the fullest discussions of these individuals, although he fails to mention Major Adams. He believes that Cecil Lewis is based on an actual Captain Lewis whom James Byth described to O'Neill (pp. 130–31). O'Neill may well have used Byth's stories when creating this character, but the name "Major A." in the character list supports the Gelbs' identification (*O'Neill*, p. 170) of Cecil Lewis with Major Adams. Floyd (*O'Neill at Work*, pp. 262–63) provides a chart indicating character sources, and she also includes (pp. 260–61) a transcription of the character list discussed here as well as excerpts (pp. 268–80) from the notes and scenario. As subsequent discussions indicate, my character identifications and transcriptions sometimes differ from hers.

11. Eugene O'Neill, *Poems 1912–1944*, ed. Donald Gallup (New Haven: Ticknor & Fields, 1980), pp. 4–6. Gallup identifies Louis ("Lefty Louie") Rosenberg in a note on p. 6.

12. Alexander (*The Tempering of Eugene O'Neill*, p. 267) and Sheaffer (*Son and Playwright*, pp. 424–25) cite Jack Croak as the model for Mosher. The Gelbs mention Croak but argue (*O'Neill*, pp. 297–98) that Bill Clarke was the source for this character. In all likelihood O'Neill had both men in mind when he created Mosher, although his friendship with Clarke, with whom he kept in contact for many years, was the more substantial.

13. Day, "The Iceman and the Bridegroom," p. 7.

14. See Emma Goldman, "Judas," *Mother Earth* 10 (Dec. 1915): 347–48, and "Donald Vose: The Accursed," *Mother Earth* 10 (Jan. 1916): 353–57. Goldman says that Vose sometimes used the name Meserve, which was apparently his father's surname (Vose was his mother's). According to Frazer (*E.G. and E.G.O.*, p. 14) O'Neill owned a copy of Emma Goldman's autobiography *Living My Life*. Immediately following Goldman's account of the Donald Vose affair is a brief discussion of Bob Minor. One possibility is that O'Neill's memory confused the two men and that his later use of the name Don for his traitor was the result of his having reread the Goldman account and sorted out the two figures. See Goldman, *Living My Life* (New York: Knopf, 1931), 2:566–67.

Alternatively, O'Neill might have begun with the idea of using Minor as the model for Parritt, then switched to Vose as a more suitable model. Richard Drinnon in *Rebel in Paradise: A Biography of Emma Goldman* (Chicago: Univ. of Chicago Press, 1961), p. 254, quotes a letter in which Goldman says, "I was once told by Robert Minor that individual human life does not matter at all. I consider that an outrage of revolutionary ethics." Even she seems to have considered him a fanatic. Although obviously biased in the subject's favor, the fullest single source of information about Minor is Joseph North, *Robert Minor, Artist and Crusader: An Informal Biography* (New York: International Publishers, 1956). I am indebted to Winifred L. Frazer for directing me to relevant parts of this book. Finally, the Gelbs (*O'Neill*, pp. 367–68) note that Parritt's suicide may partly have its roots in the experience of Louis Holliday. Holliday, a friend of O'Neill's, died of a heroin overdose reportedly supplied by Terry Carlin.

15. Scenario, Act I, p. 1; scenario, Act I, p. 2. Except for certain production scripts (see subsequent discussion) all manuscript and typescript material relating to *The Iceman Cometh* is in the Eugene O'Neill Collection, Collection of American Literature, Beinecke Library, Yale University. Future references to the scenario, manuscript, and typescripts will be given in parentheses in the body of the text.

16. It is possible that the name Rosa is a nod towards Rosa Luxemburg, a Polish-born revolutionary who was murdered by her enemies in Germany in

1919. (O'Neill created another anarchist Rosa—Rosa Daniello—in his unfinished comedy "The Visit of Malatesta," begun immediately after *Iceman* was completed.) The correspondences between Rosa Parritt and Rosa Luxemburg are, however, very limited. O'Neill had almost certainly heard of the famous "Red Rosa," and this may have led him, consciously or unconsciously, to adopt her first name for the off-stage character.

17. Schriftgiesser, "Interview with O'Neill," p. 1.

18. Letter to Nathan, Feb. 8, 1940.

19. Letter to Kenneth Macgowan, Dec. 30, 1940. In Bryer, *"The Theatre We Worked For,"* p. 258.

20. Letter to Nathan, Feb. 8, 1940.

21. Letter to Macgowan, Dec. 30, 1940. In Bryer, *"The Theatre We Worked For,"* p. 258.

22. Sheaffer, *Son and Artist,* pp. 493–94.

23. Gelb and Gelb, *O'Neill,* p. 285. Michael Manheim, who argues that "the persons of O'Neill's immediate family may be seen beneath the real-life models in almost every case" in *Iceman,* does not mention *The Traveling Salesman* but does identify correspondences between Hickey and James O'Neill, Jr. He notes that Hickey displays Jamie O'Neill's "wit and vitality" and shares with O'Neill's brother complex "feelings toward the most important woman in his life." See *O'Neill's New Language of Kinship,* pp. 227n, 132–34.

24. Winifred L. Frazer agrees that O'Neill "was no doubt familiar" with Forbes's play. See "Hughie and the Traveling Salesman," *Players* 44 (April–May 1969): 152.

25. James Forbes, *The Traveling Salesman* (New York: Samuel French, 1908), pp. 52, 53, 62.

26. Ibid., p. 99.

27. Letter to Sinclair Lewis, Nov. 25, 1936. Beinecke Library, Yale University.

28. Helen Muchnic, "Circe's Swine: Plays by Gorky and O'Neill," *Comparative Literature* 3 (Spring 1951): 119–28.

29. Gerald Weales, "Eugene O'Neill: *The Iceman Cometh,*" in *Landmarks of American Writing,* ed. Hennig Cohen (New York: Basic Books, 1969), p. 366n. See also Vivian C. Hopkins, "*The Iceman* Seen through *The Lower Depths,*" *College English* 11 (Nov. 1949): 81–87; and Peter Egri, "*The Iceman Cometh:* European Origins and American Originality," pt. 1, *The Eugene O'Neill Newsletter* 5 (Winter 1981): 9–10.

30. Robert Brustein, *The Theatre of Revolt* (Boston: Little, Brown, 1964), pp. 339–40. See also Sverre Arestad, "*The Iceman Cometh* and *The Wild Duck,*" *Scandinavian Studies* 20 (Feb. 1948): 1–11; and Egri, "*The Iceman Cometh,*" pt. 1, pp. 7–9.

31. See, for example, George Jean Nathan's review of *Iceman* in *The Theatre*

Book of the Year, 1946–1947 (New York: Knopf, 1947), p. 94; John Mason Brown, "All O'Neilling," *Saturday Review,* 19 Oct. 1946, p. 27; and Richard Watts, Jr., *New York Post,* 10 Oct. 1946, p. 40.

32. According to the Work Diary, June 6, 1939, O'Neill had the "idea" for *Iceman* some time previously. That entry begins: "Read over notes on various ideas for single plays." *Iceman* was one of those plays. As the following discussion indicates, some aspects of *Iceman* appear as early as 1917 in O'Neill's short story "Tomorrow." However, the play itself probably did not begin to take shape until June 1939, leaving open the possibility of influence—especially on technique and form—from Saroyan's work.

33. William Saroyan, *The Time of Your Life* (New York: Harcourt, Brace, 1939), p. 7.

34. Ibid., p. 62.

35. Ibid., p. 64.

36. Ibid., p. 89.

37. Ibid., p. 189.

38. Leonard Chabrowe, *Ritual and Pathos: The Theater of O'Neill* (Lewisburg, Pa.: Bucknell Univ. Press, 1976), pp. 93, 73–99; Bogard, *Contour in Time,* pp. 413–14.

39. Eugene O'Neill, *Chris Christophersen* (New York: Random House, 1982), p. 5.

40. Floyd, *O'Neill at Work,* p. 21. We learn in *Chris* that Adams had "good schoolin'," as did *Iceman*'s Willie Oban, but there are few other correspondences between the two characters. Adams, like Hickey, is talkative, a good salesman, a freespender, and comes to the bar only when on a periodical drinking spree. Boulton, *Part of a Long Story,* p. 279; Sheaffer, *Son and Playwright,* p. 451; and Bogard, *Contour in Time,* p. 410n, mention the similarities between Adams and Hickey.

41. See Rothenberg, "The Iceman Changeth," pp. 559–60, for another comparison between "Tomorrow" and *Iceman.* Travis Bogard, William R. Brashear, and Peter Egri discuss similarities between O'Neill's "Tomorrow" and Joseph Conrad's earlier short story with the same title. See Bogard, *Contour in Time,* pp. 93–94; Brashear, " 'To-morrow' and 'Tomorrow': Conrad and O'Neill," *Renascence* 20 (Autumn 1967): 18–21; Egri, "*The Iceman Cometh:* European Origins and American Originality," pts. 2 and 3, *The Eugene O'Neill Newsletter* 6 (Spring 1982): 18–24; 6 (Summer–Fall 1982), 30–36. In 1919 O'Neill wrote a short play entitled *Exorcism* which, like "Tomorrow" and *Iceman,* takes place in a combination saloon-rooming house. Unfortunately, O'Neill destroyed all copies of the work (possibly because of its autobiographical nature). Judging by accounts of the play and a fragmentary outline, *Exorcism* differed considerably, in tone as well as plot, from both the earlier short story and the later full-length drama. See Bogard, *Contour in Time,* pp. 108–9, and Floyd, *O'Neill at Work,* pp. 7–8.

42. Work Diary, June 7, 1939.

43. The Jimmy of the *Iceman* scenario is even closer to the character in the short story than is the Jimmy who emerges in the published play. Both these Jimmys have recently acquired and lost jobs, and neither admits that he was relieved by his wife's defection, as the Jimmy of the published *Iceman* eventually does.

44. Eugene O'Neill, "Tomorrow," *The Seven Arts* 2 (June 1917): 166.

45. Ibid., p. 152.

46. Ibid., p. 154.

47. Carlotta O'Neill's diary, Feb. 25, 1934.

48. In two places in the scenario O'Neill writes that a scene will occur "as in notes." No notes for these scenes are extant.

49. The second list may be part of the scenario (the date is in the upper left hand corner, as are the dates on all the scenario pages). However, some of the names on this list are those used in the final play rather than the scenario. For example, the names Don Parritt and Willie Oban are on this list, while the names Potter and Morrie are used for the corresponding characters in the scenario. It is therefore logical to conclude that this list was written after the scenario.

50. McGloin is here given the first name Bill instead of Pat; Wetjoen is listed as Colonel rather than General; the bartenders' last names are switched; one bartender is called Chick instead of Chuck; and Hugo's last name appears to be Kapnar, not Kalmar. A few alternate names, e.g., "Egan" for Larry Slade, appear in parentheses or superscripts; none of these was ultimately used in the play. The policemen are dubbed Farrell and Schwartz. The fact that O'Neill took the trouble to change the names of these very minor characters (the second detective is called Gehrig in the manuscript) supports Egil Törnqvist's claim that the final names have symbolic significance. He associates Lieb with love and Moran with death. Törnqvist, "Personal Nomenclature in the Plays of O'Neill," *Modern Drama* 8 (Feb. 1966): 371. Floyd (*O'Neill at Work,* p. 263) believes that Farrell is identified in the list as a dishwasher, but the four letters following his name appear to read "dick" (slang for detective) rather than "dish."

51. Letter to Macgowan, summer 1923. In Bryer, *"The Theatre We Worked For,"* p. 37.

52. Letter to Nathan, Feb. 8, 1940.

53. Quoted in Schriftgiesser, "Interview with O'Neill," p. 3.

54. Letter to Macgowan, Dec. 30, 1940. In Bryer, *"The Theatre We Worked For,"* p. 256.

55. For a detailed discussion of the language in *Iceman*, see Chothia, *Forging a Language,* pp. 111–42.

56. Dorothy Commins, *What Is an Editor? Saxe Commins at Work* (Chicago: Univ. of Chicago Press, 1978), p. 47.

57. See the Bibliography for descriptions of *Iceman* publication material and production scripts.

58. Commins, *What Is an Editor?* p. 47. A second copy of the typescript was sent by Carlotta O'Neill to the Register of Copyrights in Washington. Carlotta's diary, Feb. 8, 1940.

59. In a letter laid into the *Iceman* publication material at Yale, Norman Holmes Pearson, a Yale professor, states that "all handwriting on the galleys etc is in the hand of Saxe Commins" because O'Neill's physical disability made writing very difficult for him. Pearson adds that "Commins has made what changes there are at Mr. O'Neill's direction and while sitting by him. In terms of scholarship, therefore, they may be regarded as Mr. O'Neill's own." Lawrence Langner was also worried about *Iceman*'s off-color language. In a note to Buford Armitage, the production's stage manager, Langner advised: "Use 'Gee' or 'Jees' for 'Jesus.' . . . Use 'Oh Hell' instead of something worse. . . . Use 'bum' or 'louse' instead of 'bastard.'" This note (in the Beinecke's Theatre Guild Collection) is dated March 14, 1947—five months into the run. Langner wanted these changes implemented immediately. Despite these precautions, *Iceman* was rejected by the Boston censor because of its "unclean" dialogue. See Gelb and Gelb, *O'Neill,* p. 885.

60. Lawrence Langner, *The Magic Curtain* (New York: Dutton, 1951), p. 405.

61. All subsequent references to the "second typescript" are to this one, revised for the production.

62. Langner placed a note in his copy of the script recounting his feelings about the cuts and O'Neill's response. He also recorded the incident in *The Magic Curtain,* p. 406.

63. Two of the Theatre Guild scripts were received by Yale in unbound form and subsequently bound by them. These are considered "unbound" scripts or promptbooks. The third was given to the collection already bound.

64. Mary Hedwig Arbenz, "The Plays of Eugene O'Neill as Presented by the Theatre Guild." (Ph.D. diss., Univ. of Illinois, 1961), p. 421.

65. Commins, *What Is an Editor?* p. 46.

66. Commins, quoted in John H. Stroupe, "Eugene O'Neill and the Creative Process," *The English Record* 21 (Oct. 1970): 74.

67. Letter from Carlotta O'Neill to Dudley Nichols, postmarked Oct. 18, 1946. Beinecke Library, Yale University.

68. O'Neill expressed his reasons for withholding *Iceman* in numerous letters, including ones to Dudley Nichols (Oct. 13, 1940), Robert Sisk (Aug. 3, 1940), Eugene O'Neill, Jr. (April 28, 1941), George Jean Nathan (dated by Donald Gallup "1939 summer–fall"), and Kenneth Macgowan (March 15, 1941). The first three letters and a copy of the fourth are in the Beinecke Library, Yale University. The last is in Bryer, *"The Theatre We Worked For,"* pp. 259–60.

69. Letter to Macgowan, Dec. 30, 1940. In Bryer, *"The Theatre We Worked For,"* p. 257.

70. Letter to Madden, July 27, 1941. Beinecke Library, Yale University.

71. According to Stroupe, "O'Neill and the Creative Process," p. 74, O'Neill

complained about the fact that authors had to pay for changes made after a play was set into type. This situation, however, is unlikely to have deterred O'Neill from making alterations in *Iceman* had he wished to do so. As noted earlier, even the minor changes O'Neill made in the *Iceman* plate proof necessitated the resetting of numerous pages, possibly at his expense.

72. See Nancy Reinhardt, "Formal Patterns in *The Iceman Cometh,*" *Modern Drama* 16 (Sept. 1973): 119–28.

73. O'Neill was inconsistent in his spelling of "begeeses," and Carlotta was equally erratic in her transcription of this term. Rather than regularize the spelling, I have simply attempted to ascertain as closely as possible the spelling of the epithet in each particular instance.

74. Letter to Macgowan, Dec. 30, 1940. In Bryer, *"The Theatre We Worked For,"* p. 257.

75. Virginia Floyd is more confident than I am that O'Neill originally conceived *Iceman* without Hickey. She argues that "Hickey was not originally an integral part of it; he was, rather, an afterthought." Her claim rests on three points: that "Hickey's name is not mentioned in the outline until the end of Act One," that his name "is not included in any dramatis personae," and that the character lists do not mention "the names of the two detectives—Moran and Lieb—whose sole purpose in the play is to arrest him at the end" (*O'Neill at Work,* p. 267). The first point is a slight overstatement. Less than two-thirds of the way through the scenario's first act, Rocky tells Bull that the latter is the worst drunk he's ever seen "except Hickey," and Bull's response appears to read "Hickey about due" (I, p. 3). Second, although Hickey's name is not on either character list, the fuller list may have been written *after* the scenario and the omission of Hickey's name could be an oversight (see above, note 49). Buzy appears in the first two acts of the scenario, yet his name is also missing from both character lists. Finally Schwartz, the neighborhood cop, is included on the fuller list, and "Farrell," as I've argued earlier, may be a detective. Schwartz and Farrell could have made the arrest together, or there could have been just one arresting officer. While all this does not refute Floyd's claim that Hickey was an "afterthought," the evidence is not quite as ironclad as she assumes.

76. Buzy is given no surname in the scenario, but "Buzy Garrity" appears on a long list of names—some used in the play—on a separate note page.

77. See Rothenberg, "The Iceman Changeth," pp. 577ff, for a psychoanalytic discussion of O'Neill's changes in references to infidelity in *Iceman.*

78. Weales, "Eugene O'Neill," p. 361.

79. The bracketed *you* was added by Carlotta when she typed this draft.

80. In a sentence cut from Act IV of the typescript, Hickey insists: "My line of hardware was as good as any other" (IV, p. 15). This last-ditch defense, however, does not negate the telling revelation in his statement about the wash boiler.

81. Eric Bentley, "Trying to Like O'Neill," in Oscar Cargill, N. Bryllion Fagin,

and William J. Fisher, eds., *O'Neill and His Plays: Four Decades of Criticism* (New York: New York Univ. Press, 1961), p. 340; Stark Young, "O'Neill and Rostand," *New Republic*, 21 Oct. 1946, pp. 517–18; Mary McCarthy, "Dry Ice," *Partisan Review* 13 (Nov.–Dec. 1946): 577.

82. Margie's speech appears twice—and is canceled twice—on the same page.

83. Brustein, *The Theatre of Revolt*, pp. 346–47.

84. In the manuscript's last act, Hickey's exit covers four pages: 16, 16½, 17, and 17½. The fractional numbers and the condition of the pages indicate that 16½ and 17 were later additions, inserted when O'Neill was revising the manuscript. (Some sheets must have been removed, for pages 18–21 also appear to be new additions.) Page 17½ apparently originally followed from page 16, although 17½ itself contains at least two variations on Hickey's exit, with which O'Neill seems to have been experimenting as he wrote the draft. Page 17½ is divided roughly into three parts: the first third is heavily edited, the second and third parts are separately bounded by pencil lines and each individually canceled with a large pencil X. What I consider the initial rendering of Hickey's exit begins on 16 and continues directly through the first two-thirds of 17½. The next version of the scene is that on the bottom of 17½. The interpolated pages 16½ and 17 contain what is apparently the third rendering.

85. I quote this version from the manuscript rather than the typescript (where it is revised into the final version) because Carlotta accidentally omitted a few words when she typed this scene.

86. Arbenz, "Plays of Eugene O'Neill," p. 450.

87. The critic Tom Donnelly, who saw *Iceman* in Washington after the New York run, compared the published and stage versions and concluded that viewers of the shortened scene would know that Hickey was never demented because O'Neill removed "the lines which created all the confusion." His argument is unconvincing, as is his claim that the full scene as printed in the published text was actually performed at the very beginning of the New York run. Tom Donnelly, "A Few Ice Cubes Are Missing," *Washington Daily News*, 2 April 1947, p. 44.

88. Manheim, *O'Neill's New Language of Kinship*, p. 138.

89. Törnqvist, *A Drama of Souls*, p. 227.

90. Raleigh, *The Plays of Eugene O'Neill*, p. 163; Robert C. Lee, "Evangelism and Anarchy in *The Iceman Cometh*," *Modern Drama* 12 (Sept. 1969): 184.

91. For other discussions of the on and off-stage women in *Iceman*, see Edwin A. Engel, *The Haunted Heroes of Eugene O'Neill* (Cambridge: Harvard Univ. Press, 1953), pp. 286, 291; Winifred L. Frazer, *Love as Death in "The Iceman Cometh": A Modern Treatment of an Ancient Theme* (Gainesville: Univ. of Florida Press, 1967), p. 17 passim; Robert J. Andreach, "O'Neill's Women in *The Iceman Cometh*," *Renascence* 18 (Winter 1966): 89–98; and Bette Mandl, "Absence as Presence: The Second Sex in *The Iceman Cometh*," *The Eugene O'Neill Newslet-

ter 6 (Summer–Fall 1982): 10–15. Andreach (p. 90) discusses the pattern identified above, in which a woman "enters a man's life calling upon him to become more than he is, but by so doing, she makes him feel guilty because he cannot." Frazer (p. 22) argues that "references to the absent or dead wives or mothers or lovers are foolishly sentimental or cold with hatred, and the only women characters in the play sell love to make their living," and Mandl (p. 12) concurs that "the revelations about women that emerge in the play are revelations of hatred." It must be noted, however, that it is the complex amalgam of hatred *and* love that breeds so much anguish in Hickey and Parritt.

92. Letter to Nathan, Aug. 2, 1940.

93. Bogard, *Contour in Time*, pp. 416–17.

94. Robert Bechtold Heilman, *The Iceman, the Arsonist, and the Troubled Agent: Tragedy and Melodrama on the Modern Stage* (Seattle: Univ. of Washington Press, 1973), pp. 72–114.

95. Floyd, *O'Neill at Work*, p. 298.

96. One minor revision does not affect Larry's implied feelings for Rosa but does change a link between Larry and Rosa to a link between Parritt and Rosa. In one of his very last speeches in the first typescript, Parritt says his death will give Rosa a "chance to play the great brave terrible mistress of the Revolution" (IV, p. 22). This was changed to "the great incorruptible Mother of the Revolution" (text, p. 248).

97. This speech appears on a handwritten page inserted into the first typescript. In the corresponding manuscript speech (which itself appears to be an addition), Larry remarks that he and Rosa were friends and that "she was a fine, brave woman," but no mention is made of her qualities as a parent nor does he emphasize his present admiration for her (I, p. 9½).

98. Eugene O'Neill, *Long Day's Journey Into Night* (New Haven: Yale Univ. Press, 1956), p. 19.

99. Bogard, *Contour in Time*, p. 416n.

100. O'Neill also cut Hickey's ambiguous remark to Larry concerning Parritt: "He seems to look on you as a sort of stepfather or something" (plate proof, p. 117).

101. Letter to Lawrence Langner, May 13, 1944. Theatre Guild Collection, Beinecke Library, Yale University.

102. Letter to me from Tom Pedi, Aug. 22, 1983.

103. If fear of offending was O'Neill's motive, he was probably being overly cautious. It must be noted, however, that he had had his share of difficulties with censors. More important, the religious aspects of his last new play, *Days Without End*, had provoked widespread controversy that annoyed and embittered him. See Gelb and Gelb, *O'Neill*, pp. 780–85; and Sheaffer, *Son and Artist*, pp. 423–34. O'Neill might have (correctly) guessed that many of the play's remaining re-

ligious references, such as the Last Supper allusion in Act II, would not be recognized by the average theater-goer.

104. Brooks Atkinson, "O'Neill Tragedy Revived," *New York Times,* 9 May 1956, p. 38.

105. See Winifred L. Frazer, "'Revolution' in *The Iceman Cometh*," *Modern Drama* 22 (March 1979): 1–8, for a discussion of the poem and the poet. Frazer surmises that O'Neill heard the poem recited by Hippolyte Havel, the model for Hugo Kalmar.

106. Day, "The Iceman and the Bridegroom," pp. 3–9. See also Egil Törnqvist, "Jesus and Judas: On Biblical Allusions in O'Neill's Plays," *Etudes Anglaises* 24 (Jan. 1971): 41–49. While Törnqvist too sees biblical references in *Iceman,* he disagrees with Day's assertion that the play is a repudiation of Christ's gospel. Törnqvist argues that "Hickey resembles Christ in certain respects, not because O'Neill rejects Christ but because he (partially) rejects Hickey."

107. Floyd, *O'Neill at Work,* pp. xxvii, 317–45.

108. Bogard, *Contour in Time,* p. 412n.

109. In O'Neill's early sketch of Act II, Larry is placed slightly off-center rather than in the exact middle. The minuscule size of this drawing—seventeen chairs and names are squeezed into less than three inches—probably made exact placement difficult. Pictures of the birthday party were used as publicity photographs for the first production, and these place Larry at the central table (seven tables, rather than the four specified in the text, have been pushed together). These photographs also put Parritt three places to Larry's right, roughly the location of Judas in Da Vinci's Last Supper, where John and the head of Peter—who is leaning over—intervene between Christ and Judas. (The early sketch has Parritt one seat farther away from Larry.) In most versions of this production photograph, depending on the shooting angle, Larry is framed in the open doorway, just as Christ is framed in a window or doorway in Da Vinci's work. The photograph that most strikingly resembles the "Last Supper" appears in *Time,* 21 October 1946, p. 71. Other variations of the photograph are reproduced in Gelb and Gelb, *O'Neill,* following p. 840, Chabrowe, *Ritual and Pathos,* p. 71, and Normand Berlin, *Eugene O'Neill* (New York: Grove Press, 1982), following p. 82. It is impossible to know what role O'Neill played in the photograph session, but it is reasonable to conclude that the actors assumed for the photographer the same positions they actually occupied when the scene was staged.

110. Scheibler, *The Late Plays of Eugene O'Neill,* p. 191.

111. Lee, "Evangelism and Anarchy," p. 184.

112. J. Dennis Rich offers a very similar reading of Larry's motives. See his "Exile Without Remedy: The Late Plays of Eugene O'Neill," in Virginia Floyd, ed., *Eugene O'Neill: A World View* (New York: Ungar, 1979), p. 270.

113. Letter to Macgowan, Dec. 30, 1940. In Bryer, "*The Theatre We Worked For,*" p. 257.

114. Nathan, *The Theatre Book of the Year, 1946–1947*, p. 96.

115. Barrett H. Clark, *Eugene O'Neill: The Man and His Plays*, rev. ed. (New York: Dover, 1947), p. 161.

116. Arthur Pollock, "Theater: Eugene O'Neill's *The Iceman Cometh*," *Brooklyn Eagle*, 10 October 1946, p. 16.

117. Joseph T. Shipley, "Iceman Cometh: Chill from the World Doom," *New Leader*, 19 October 1946, p. 6. (Shipley slightly misquotes the text, which says "the racket" rather than "their racket.") For other reviews that mention Larry's walking toward the exit and/or committing suicide, see Howard Barnes, "The Theater: *The Iceman Cometh*," *New York Herald Tribune*, 20 October 1946, sec. 5, pp. 1, 5; Harry Bull, "The Theatre: *The Iceman Cometh*," *Town & Country*, December 1946, pp. 117, 274; and Elliot Norton, "O'Neill's *Iceman*: Second Thoughts of a First-Nighter," *Boston Sunday Post*, 13 October 1946. John Chapman's review, although rather ambiguous, appears to suggest that Larry kills himself; see the *New York Daily News*, 10 October 1946. All these reviews are in the *Iceman* pressbooks, Theatre Guild Collection, Beinecke Library.

118. It should also be noted that Larry was stripped of his function as "narrator" in the first production. The men's stories, which he recounts to Parritt in Act I, were deleted, presumably because they are not particularly dramatic or necessary. While these deletions do not change the characterization of Larry, they do diminish the role somewhat. There were, of course, many other speeches by Larry that were cut for the production, but no more than were removed from other characters, and Larry's lines were virtually intact in the last act.

CHAPTER TWO

1. Scenario, V, p. 6. All manuscript and typescript material relating to *Long Day's Journey Into Night* is in the Eugene O'Neill Collection, Collection of American Literature, Beinecke Library, Yale University. Future references to the scenario, manuscript, and typescript will be given in parentheses in the body of the text.

2. Clark, *Eugene O'Neill*, p. 7.

3. Letter to Kenneth Macgowan, April 27, 1928. In Bryer, *"The Theatre We Worked For,"* pp. 177–78.

4. Floyd, *O'Neill at Work*, pp. 180–82. Floyd, who notes similarities between "The Sea-Mother's Son" and *Days Without End*, believes that *Days Without End* "replaces" "Sea-Mother."

5. Letter to Nathan, Nov. 12, 1929. The "trilogy" is *Mourning Becomes Electra*. Interestingly, the technique O'Neill outlines here is similar to that he considered for the one-act *Hughie*, written 1941–42. For a discussion of his *Hughie* plans, see Gelb and Gelb, *O'Neill*, p. 844.

6. "Sea-Mother" is mentioned in the Work Diary on July 21 and 23, 1931. The first entry reads: " 'The Sea Mother's Son' (notes—'Nostalgia' (?))." Presumably "Nostalgia" was the tentative title for one of the plays in the series.

7. Gelb and Gelb, *O'Neill*, p. 208, are among those who mention the similarity between the maid's name and that of O'Neill's first wife. Egil Törnqvist discusses parallels between Mary Tyrone and the unseen cook who bears O'Neill's grandmother's name; see *A Drama of Souls*, pp. 240–41.

8. Florence Eldridge, "Reflections on *Long Day's Journey Into Night*: First Curtain Call for Mary Tyrone," in Floyd, *World View*, p. 287.

9. Carlotta O'Neill's diary, Oct. 9, 1943. Although O'Neill never finished work on *More Stately Mansions*, he had written three drafts of the play prior to 1943. "A Touch of the Poet" was originally the title for the entire cycle rather than just a single play. By 1943 the cycle had been renamed "A Tale of Possessors Self-Dispossessed," but it is at least possible that Carlotta was using the old name "A Touch of the Poet" to refer to the whole cycle.

10. Letter to George C. Tyler, Dec. 9, 1920. In the Princeton University Library's William Seymour Theatre Collection. See Gelb and Gelb, *O'Neill*, pp. 451–52, for a brief discussion of O'Neill's consideration of a *Monte Cristo* adaptation.

11. Bogard, *Contour in Time*, p. 435.

12. Matthew Black, introduction to William Shakespeare, *The Tragedy of King Richard the Second* (Baltimore: Penguin Books, 1957), p. 20.

13. Travis Bogard, "Dreams of Joy, Dreams of Pain," in *Eugene O'Neill* (Milwaukee Repertory Theater Co., 1978), p. 14. This is a program distributed to audience members of the Milwaukee Repertory's midwestern and western tour of their productions of *Ah, Wilderness!* and *Long Day's Journey Into Night*. See also Grant H. Redford, "Dramatic Art vs. Autobiography: A Look at *Long Day's Journey Into Night*," *College English* 25 (April 1964): 527–35. Redford argues: "That the material used is more intimately autobiographical than that used in other of his plays should not confuse the difference between biographical materials and the artistic use made of them. O'Neill assigned himself the responsibility of writing dramatic art. Biography attempts to discover and record the details of the years. Dramatic art chooses details of the moment, to illustrate, to emphasize, themes" (p. 534).

14. Letter to Macgowan, April 8, 1921. In Bryer, "*The Theatre We Worked For*," p. 23.

15. The one exception is the dead baby, who is referred to by his "real" name, Edmund, in the scenario. Also, Tyrone and Jamie are occasionally designated "J" in the scenario.

16. This includes one set of notes and the scenario, at the beginning of which various names are tried even though in the body of the scenario the designations

are Father, Mother, etc. The notes in question are dated Feb. 22, 1940, just before O'Neill began writing dialogue for the manuscript. In these notes the elder Tyrone has no first name, but since the older son is called Edmund, Jr., Edmund is presumably the father's name also. Immediately below this character list is a new list that gives the names as they appear in the published text. In the character descriptions at the beginning of the manuscript the father is accidentally called Edmund (his name is James everywhere else in the draft); this mistake was apparently corrected by Carlotta when she prepared the first typescript.

17. See for example Gelb and Gelb, *O'Neill*, pp. 188–89; Sheaffer, *Son and Playwright*, p. 14, and *Son and Artist*, p. 512; and Törnqvist, "Personal Nomenclature in the Plays of O'Neill," p. 371.

18. In his notes O'Neill occasionally gave his characters ages that do not correspond to those of his own family, but these "errors" were subsequently corrected. All the ages given in the published text are accurate if we assume it is early August 1912. Ella Quinlan O'Neill turned fifty-five on the thirteenth of that month. For discussions of some of O'Neill's alterations of family history, see Gelb and Gelb, *O'Neill*, p. 15; Sheaffer, *Son and Playwright*, esp. pp. 241–43; and Raleigh, *The Plays of Eugene O'Neill*, pp. 88–95.

19. O'Neill, *Long Day's Journey Into Night*, p. 150. All future references to the published play will be given in the body of the text. In the notes, 1873 is given as the date Booth praised James O'Neill. Judging from the Gelbs' account, 1874 (the date added in the typescript) is the correct one.

20. The scenario is difficult to read at this point (and also when a subsequent reference is made to the same incident); the age may be five rather than four. However, it is almost certainly one of the two, and the argument holds either way. James O'Neill, Jr., was actually about six and a half when his brother Edmund died.

21. See for example Bogard, *Contour in Time*, pp. 21, 110–11, 424–45; Doris V. Falk, *Eugene O'Neill and the Tragic Tension: An Interpretive Study of the Plays* (New Brunswick, N.J.: Rutgers Univ. Press, 1958), pp. 179–201; John T. Shawcross, "The Road to Ruin: The Beginning of O'Neill's *Long Day's Journey*," *Modern Drama* 3 (Dec. 1960): 289–96; and Robert C. Lee, "The Lonely Dream," *Modern Drama* 9 (Sept. 1966): 127–35. Comparisons between *Long Day's Journey* and O'Neill's other plays may be found throughout Manheim's *O'Neill's New Language of Kinship*; comparisons between *Journey* and O'Neill's unfinished as well as completed plays may be found throughout Floyd's *O'Neill at Work*.

22. "Upon Our Beach," in *Poems 1912–1944*, p. 53.

23. Untitled poem in *Poems 1912–1944*, p. 72.

24. Eugene O'Neill, *Strange Interlude*, in *Nine Plays by Eugene O'Neill* (New York: Random House, 1941), p. 673. Timo Tiusanen makes the same comparison in *O'Neill's Scenic Images* (Princeton: Princeton Univ. Press, 1968), pp. 223–24.

25. The typescript of *More Stately Mansions* is in the Beinecke Library, Yale University. According to the opening scene and canceled lines later in the play (none of which appear in the published "shortened" version of *Mansions*), Nora retired to a convent after her husband's death in 1832. She wrote to her daughter that she was very happy there. Ella Quinlan O'Neill eventually overcame her drug habit during a stay in a convent.

26. Travis Bogard, introduction to *The Later Plays of Eugene O'Neill* (New York: Random House, 1967), pp. xxiii–iv.

27. These notes are in the Beinecke Library, Yale University. A transcription appears in Floyd, *O'Neill at Work,* pp. 241–42.

28. A very slightly different version of the diary entry appears in Seymour Peck, "Talk with Mrs. O'Neill," *New York Times,* 4 Nov. 1956, sec. 2, p. 1.

29. The scenario itself bears out the Work Diary dates with one minor exception. The first four pages are dated June 1939, the fifth July 1, 1939, and the sixth July 2 & 3, 1939. The fifth scenario page contains the first half of Act V which, according to the Work Diary, O'Neill did not begin until July 2. Most likely O'Neill simply wrote "July 1" at the top of the page and then decided not to begin actual work on Act V until the following day.

30. Letter to Nathan, Oct. 1, 1939.

31. Letter to Nathan, June 15, 1940.

32. Work Diary, June 26, 1940.

33. Letter to Lawrence Langner, July 17, 1940.

34. Work Diary, Sept. 29, 1940. As with *Iceman,* in the Work Diary O'Neill refers to the revised manuscript as the "second draft."

35. For discussions of these unfinished plays, see Floyd, *O'Neill at Work,* pp. 352–70, 256–57, 298–316, and 317–45.

36. April 1 is the last day work on *Journey* is mentioned in the Diary. The April 1 entry reads: "addition father's M.C. speech IV," a reference to Tyrone's speech about his career in the final act. "M.C." stands for *Monte Cristo,* the play in which James O'Neill starred; Tyrone's "great box office success" is never given a title in *Journey.* This speech appears in the manuscript but was revised and expanded in the typescript, hence O'Neill's reference to "addition."

37. All references in this chapter to "the typescript" are to the first typescript, the only one on which significant changes were made.

38. Gelb and Gelb, *O'Neill,* p. 838.

39. In the typescript "Mother" was changed to "Mama" and "calling" was canceled.

40. Sheaffer, *Son and Artist,* p. 560, says that O'Neill expressed the desire that *Journey* "never be performed." The Gelbs, *O'Neill,* pp. 861–62, drawing on statements by Bennett Cerf at Random House, report that on November 29, 1945, O'Neill brought the script to Random House's offices in New York, insisted that

the script be sealed with wax, and dictated the cover note banning its publication until twenty-five years after his death. The script was then placed in the publisher's vault. Sheaffer gives a similar account. Saxe Commins, O'Neill's Random House editor, says that O'Neill was not present when *Journey* was sealed, but his story is suspect. Commins implies that O'Neill was still in California on November 29, 1945; in fact, a letter from Carlotta to O'Neill's lawyer, Winfield Aronberg, indicates that the couple had already moved to New York by that date. Since O'Neill was in New York at the time, it seems likely—as Cerf claims—that he was present at the sealing. Commins's account appears in Dorothy Commins, *What Is an Editor?* pp. 56–57.

41. Sheaffer, *Son and Artist*, p. 634, says that "in 1955, two years after O'Neill's death, Carlotta directed Random House to publish *Long Day's Journey*, but Bennett Cerf, on reading the personal testament 'written in tears and blood' decided to abide by the playwright's twenty-five year interdict." Sheaffer's account seems accurate, although the incident apparently occurred in 1954. That is the date given by Saxe Commins who, a sworn foe of Carlotta's, gives a vitriolic account in which he implies that Carlotta deliberately persuaded O'Neill to cut his children out of his will so that she, as his sole heir, would have control of *Journey* after his death; see Commins, *What Is an Editor?* pp. 57–59. In her diary, Carlotta gives her own highly colored version of what happened. She records that on June 20, 1954, she gave Cerf permission to read *Journey*. Cerf, she claims later, was "horrified" by the play, a response that launched her into a diatribe against the publisher personally and against his firm's booklist. Carlotta does not mention that Cerf refused to publish the drama, insisting instead that she would not permit him to do so: "I can't allow Random House to publish 'Long Day's Journey Into Night'—they haven't the *understanding* or the *feeling* for such a book!" (Carlotta's diary, June 20, July 2, 4, 9, and 13, 1954.) For an account of the Stockholm premiere and how the Royal Dramatic Theatre obtained permission to perform *Journey*, see Tom Olsson, "O'Neill and the Royal Dramatic," in Floyd, *World View*, pp. 43–51. For an account of Carlotta's role in the American premiere, see José Quintero, *If You Don't Dance They Beat You* (Boston: Little, Brown, 1974), pp. 203–14.

42. Gelb and Gelb, *O'Neill*, p. 937; Sheaffer, *Son and Artist*, p. 634.

43. Letter to Nathan, Jan. 30, 1941.

44. Letter to Nathan, Feb. 13, 1941.

45. Eugene O'Neill, Jr., visited his father in August 1939, after the *Journey* scenario was written.

46. Commins, *What Is an Editor?* pp. 53–54. Sheaffer, *Son and Artist*, p. 635, quotes a letter from O'Neill to Cerf to this effect. Sheaffer also offers other evidence which casts doubt on Carlotta's claim that Eugene O'Neill, Jr., requested that *Journey* be suppressed.

47. Some additional notes apparently have not survived. One extant note page contains a brief outline of scenes for the last two acts. Since the extant page is numbered "2," presumably a similar outline of the early acts is missing. Floyd offers partial transcriptions of the notes and scenario in *O'Neill at Work*, pp. 281–97. As subsequent discussions indicate, my transcriptions sometimes differ from hers.

48. In the upper right corner of the scenario's first page, O'Neill has written "The Long Day's Insurrection" with "Retirement" and "Retreat" penciled just below the word "Insurrection." Presumably "The Long Day's" was also meant to go with "Retirement" and "Retreat." On a note page, what appears to be the word "What's" is written and then canceled before the words "Long Unforgotten."

49. Tinsley, in "Two Biographical Plays," p. 89, makes a similar point about revisions on the typescript when she writes that "in *Long Day's Journey Into Night*, O'Neill seems to be attempting to delete from the final version his working notes to himself."

50. See Chothia, *Forging a Language*, pp. 172–73, for a discussion of the use of euphemisms in *Journey*.

51. Edward Stephen Harkness was, in part, the model for the unseen Harker in *Journey* and for T. Stedman Harder in *A Moon for the Misbegotten*. Dolan, a tenant who rented land from James O'Neill, was the model for the off-stage Shaughnessy in *Journey* and for Phil Hogan in *Moon*.

52. Rolf Scheibler, *The Late Plays of Eugene O'Neill*, p. 140.

53. Törnqvist, *A Drama of Souls*, p. 96.

54. Tinsley, "Two Biographical Plays," pp. 116–18.

55. Törnqvist, *A Drama of Souls*, p. 98.

56. Tinsley, "Two Biographical Plays," pp. 117–18, finds the same pattern. Although she cites only changes made in the typescript, similar revisions, as discussed, were made in other drafts as well.

57. This line is squeezed into the left margin of the page. The full marginal addition reads: "M. (just at end—quotes strangely) Forgive us our trespasses as we forgive those who trespass against us."

58. Törnqvist, *A Drama of Souls*, p. 202.

59. Sheaffer, *Son and Playwright*, pp. 241–42.

60. According to Carlotta, "Gene insisted that if I published 'Long Day's Journey Into Night' I must *insist* that the 'inscription' be published also,—& no other 'foreword' or 'introduction' be used *in place of it* or *with it*. I did just that. He claimed the 'inscription' showed what his mood was when writing it—& what hell he went through!" Letter to Dudley Nichols, Nov. 6, 1955. In the Beinecke Library, Yale University.

61. The end of the first sentence, all of the second, and the beginning of the third—from "by an electric current" to "At moments"—were inadvertently omit-

ted by Carlotta when she was preparing the typescript; apparently she lost her place while typing. These words were not marked for deletion in the manuscript, but O'Neill surely would have cut them from the typescript when the passage as a whole was excised. Tinsley, "Two Biographical Plays," p. 95, quotes the typescript version and also notes that this description of Mary, which emphasizes the character's duality, is more negative than the description in the final play.

62. Letter to Eugene O'Neill, Jr., Jan. 27, 1937. In the Beinecke Library, Yale University.

63. See, for example, Raleigh, *The Plays of Eugene O'Neill*, pp. 148–49; Bogard, *Contour in Time*, pp. 425ff; and Manheim, *O'Neill's New Language of Kinship*, p. 100. Both Bogard and Manheim suggest that O'Neill handles the duality theme more subtly and realistically in the late plays than in the early ones.

64. Eugene O'Neill, *Abortion*, in *Lost Plays of Eugene O'Neill* (New York: New Fathoms, 1950), p. 24.

65. Eugene O'Neill, *Days Without End* (New York: Random House, 1934), p. 148.

66. Tinsley, "Two Biographical Plays," pp. 94–96, makes a similar argument.

67. Although the biographical question—how closely O'Neill's portrait of Tyrone in *Journey* resembles James O'Neill—is outside the scope of this study, one interesting point may be made. After quoting an autobiographical summary that O'Neill wrote while attending therapy sessions in 1926, Sheaffer concludes that "the play is more favorable, on the whole, towards James O'Neill than the summary"; see *Son and Artist*, pp. 509–12.

68. Floyd, *O'Neill at Work*, p. 289.

69. In her discussion of Mary Tyrone during a talk on O'Neill at the Modern Language Association's meeting of December 29, 1978, the actress Geraldine Fitzgerald made a strikingly similar comment about the character. Fitzgerald had never read these notes, but her acting of the role led her to conclude that Mary's discomfort with motherhood grew from her negative feelings about her own mother. A somewhat shortened version of this talk was published under the title "Another Neurotic Electra: A New Look at Mary Tyrone," in Floyd, *World View*, pp. 290–92.

70. Tyrone's first story—about the poverty of his youth—is not in the scenario, but there are indications that O'Neill had it in mind. Tyrone's line at this point reads: "I remember file shop, my mother, etc." (V, p. 5). The "etc." suggests that O'Neill simply did not bother to write out the account in full.

71. While the spelling *theater* appears in the published text, O'Neill used *theatre* in his drafts.

72. Bogard, *Contour in Time*, p. xviii.

73. Some lines, apparently a suggestion by Cathleen that Edmund might have consumption, were erased from the manuscript at this point. Mary dismisses this

possibility, repeats her claim that Tyrone fears only poverty (that fear is "genuine," she adds), then continues with the accusation I have quoted. All of this was canceled in the manuscript. It is interesting to note that Mary's charge that her husband is insensitive closely resembles an accusation Carlotta leveled against *her* husband. The obvious difference is that James Tyrone is an actor, while O'Neill was a playwright. On July 29, 1942, Carlotta complained in her diary: "I have never seen Gene *really* disturbed by any *human being.* That is, by sorrow, or loneliness for them (after 3 or 4 hours!) I feel certain he feels closer to the men & women *he creates in his plays* than to flesh & blood human beings he comes in contact with."

74. Tinsley, "Two Biographical Plays," pp. 75–77, identifies the same pattern.

75. The page on which these lines occur was obviously added to the manuscript, for only a half-dozen lines appear on this otherwise blank sheet. It is evident, however, that O'Neill removed as well as added pages here, so Tyrone's statement could have appeared on a sheet that was removed.

76. See for example Frederic I. Carpenter, *Eugene O'Neill,* rev. ed. (Boston: Twayne, 1979), p. 158. He argues that, while all four characters are important, "philosophically, the play focuses on the Transcendental idealism of Edmund Tyrone." Bogard, *Contour in Time,* p. 432, admits that Edmund "as a dramatic character, offers adequate material to an actor" but complains that he "is no more than an embittered adolescent."

77. See Bogard, *Contour in Time,* pp. 440–44, for a lengthy discussion of the Frankenstein image. Bogard too confuses Frankenstein with his monster. His heavily psychological interpretation, which he concedes "cannot be the truth of it," actually works somewhat better with the typescript version and its stronger suggestion of identification between the brothers. David McDonald implies that O'Neill deliberately had Jamie mix up Frankenstein and the monster. He argues: "Jamie, of course, has displaced his brother's identity, since it was Frankenstein who made the monster from pieces of the dead and, plainly, Jamie is the monster who sees himself as more dead than living. . . . Still, he sees Edmund as his creation, even as Edmund, through dispossessing their mother's love, is seen as 'making' Jamie the way he is." See "The Phenomenology of the Glance in *Long Day's Journey Into Night," Theatre Journal* 31 (Oct. 1979): 355.

78. In *Journey,* Jamie begins by reciting the second stanza of "A Leave-taking," then follows it with the first and sixth stanzas. This unusual order makes more sense in early drafts, where Edmund's recitation of the first stanza could be seen as a "correction"—a reminder to Jamie that he has skipped the opening lines of the poem.

79. One curious link between Mary and Edmund that disappeared as the drama developed was the idea that Edmund may have rheumatism, his mother's disease. Comforting Mary in the scenario, Edmund tells her: "I'm not really

sick—only meant worse than cold—rheumatism, probably" (I, p. 1). When Jamie and Edmund discuss the latter's illness in the second act of the scenario, Edmund avers, "It must be rheumatism or something, not just cold like Mama makes out" (II, p. 2). Obviously Edmund's symptoms do not indicate rheumatism, and the farfetched surmises that Edmund and Mary may suffer from the same condition do not appear in the final *Journey*.

80. The manuscript version of this speech is longer still. In the canceled manuscript lines Mary concedes that it was "kind of" her husband to insist that she have another baby because he knew she really wanted one. She then charges that Tyrone, having failed to persuade her to leave Edmund when he was an infant, convinced her to send the boy to boarding school when he was seven (III, pp. 16–17).

81. Annette Rubenstein, "The Dark Journey of Eugene O'Neill," *Mainstream* 10 (April 1957): 33; Wolcott Gibbs, "Doom," *New Yorker*, 24 Nov. 1956, p. 120.

82. Tinsley, "Two Biographical Plays," p. 67, makes a similar point when she refers to "the process by which Edmund has been freed to forgive."

83. Törnqvist, *A Drama of Souls*, p. 96n; Tinsley, "Two Biographical Plays," p. 74. Our transcriptions vary very slightly.

84. Richard B. Sewall, "The Tragic Form," in Laurence Michel and Richard B. Sewall, eds., *Tragedy: Modern Essays in Criticism* (Englewood Cliffs, N.J.: Prentice-Hall, 1963), p. 125.

85. Muchnic, "Circe's Swine," p. 127.

86. Eugene O'Neill, *The Great God Brown*, in *Nine Plays by Eugene O'Neill*, p. 370.

87. O'Neill, *More Stately Mansions*, p. 180.

88. This crucial Shakespearean quotation was added, with a caret, presumably during revision of the manuscript.

89. John Henry Raleigh similarly argues, "As in life itself, O'Neill's characters are both free and unfree, depending on one's angle of vision" (*The Plays of Eugene O'Neill*, p. 159). For perceptive discussions of determinism and free will in O'Neill's plays, see pp. 157–61 and 280–81.

90. Bogard, *Contour in Time*, p. 432.

91. Tinsley, "Two Biographical Plays," p. 108, similarly notes that this addition "heightened" the "reconciliation" between Tyrone and Edmund.

92. This section of the manuscript is difficult to decipher. O'Neill was apparently canceling and revising as he wrote this part, and a portion of the scene was removed. O'Neill seems to have been unsure, even as he was writing the manuscript, of the wisdom of bringing Mary on stage at this point.

93. Tinsley, "Two Biographical Plays," p. 102, makes the same point.

94. Jason Robards, Jr., "The Actor: Trust Yourself," in Howard Greenberger,

The Off-Broadway Experience (Englewood Cliffs, N.J.: Prentice-Hall, 1971), p. 49.

95. Henry Hewes, "O'Neill: 100 Proof—Not a Blend," *Saturday Review,* 24 Nov. 1956, p. 31.

96. Walter Kerr, "*Long Day's Journey Into Night,*" *New York Herald-Tribune,* 8 Nov. 1956, p. 20.

97. "A Serpent That Eats Its Tail," *Time,* 12 Oct. 1962, p. M15.

CHAPTER THREE

1. O'Neill, *The Iceman Cometh,* p. 10.

2. John Henry Raleigh, "The Irish Atavism of *A Moon for the Misbegotten,*" in Floyd, *World View,* pp. 231–33.

3. Act III, p. 79. All manuscript and typescript material relating to *A Moon for the Misbegotten* is in the Eugene O'Neill Collection, Collection of American Literature, Beinecke Library, Yale University. Future references to the scenario, manuscript, and typescripts will be given in parentheses in the body of the text.

4. Gelb and Gelb, *O'Neill,* pp. 91–92; Sheaffer, *Son and Artist,* pp. 208–9.

5. O'Neill, *Poems 1912–1944,* pp. 48–53. The "food-stuffed adorer of Mammon" is not mentioned by name but, as Gallup's footnote indicates, he is evidently Hammond. Hammond owned the beach referred to in the poem's title.

6. Ibid., pp. 21, 29–31, 43–46.

7. This Work Diary entry is on Oct. 28, 1941.

8. Gelb and Gelb, *O'Neill,* pp. 531–32; Sheaffer, *Son and Artist,* pp. 116–17.

9. Agnes Boulton, in *Part of a Long Story,* p. 22, reports that Christine Ell called O'Neill's brother "Jim." The Gelbs, *O'Neill,* pp. 362–64, and Sheaffer, *Son and Playwright,* pp. 330 and 435, cite Christine Ell as the source for Josie. According to the Gelbs, Jim was also James O'Neill, Jr.'s early childhood nickname (p. 65). They relate that the name Jamie was later adopted because the elder James was uncomfortable sharing his own nickname (Jim) with his son.

10. Sheaffer, *Son and Playwright,* pp. 330–31, 435.

11. Boulton, *Part of a Long Story,* p. 19.

12. Work Diary, Nov. 3, 1941. The scenario bears out the Diary dates. The first, second, and fourth pages of the scenario are dated October 1941; the fifth page is dated November 1, 1941; the third and sixth pages are undated.

13. "The Moon of Other Days" appears in the top margin of the scenario's third page; "The Moon Bore Twins" is written in the same place on the fifth page. "Moon of the Misbegotten" appears in the top margin of p. 1 but, according to the Work Diary, O'Neill did not conceive this title until November 3, when the scenario was completed. See Work Diary entries for November 3 and November 12,

1941. Floyd in *O'Neill at Work*, p. 372, states that the first proposed title is "The Man of Other Days," while I read the words as "The *Moon* of Other Days." Floyd's partial transcriptions of the notes and scenario, which sometimes differ from my own, are on pp. 371–83.

14. One page of notes covers Act III, the second covers Act IV. Both are dated November 1941, so presumably were written shortly after the scenario. One page containing a few lines of "Notes—rewritings" for Acts I and II, dated February 1, 1943, survives from a later stage in the composing process.

15. Carlotta O'Neill's diary, Feb. 25, 1943.

16. O'Neill had also called his revised manuscripts of *Iceman* and *Journey* "second drafts."

17. Work Diary, March 6, April 10 and 12, 1943.

18. The designation of the "Hamilton Apts" is confusing, for no biographer lists this as a place of residence for the O'Neills in San Francisco. Presumably O'Neill meant the Huntington Hotel, where he and Carlotta moved after a short stay at the Fairmount. Carlotta describes the typing process in her diary on Oct. 11 and 18, 1943.

19. Inscription on copy in Yale O'Neill Collection. Reprinted in *Inscriptions: Eugene O'Neill to Carlotta Monterey O'Neill*, ed. Donald Gallup (New Haven: Yale University Library, privately printed, 1960). Saxe Commins, O'Neill's editor at Random House, also states that *Moon* was not completed until 1944. His comments are in Dorothy Commins, *What Is an Editor?* p. 63.

20. Also filed there is one handwritten page, numbered 115, which contains a version of the last moments of the play that does not exactly match any other version. When O'Neill rewrote the last act of the typescript he apparently composed this ending, then rejected it in favor of the one that appears in the published play. This final page is very similar to the conclusion of the unrevised typescript.

21. See Bibliography for descriptions of the *Moon* typescripts and production scripts. Because the first typescript is the only typed draft on which significant changes were made, all references in this chapter to "the typescript" are to the first typescript. Page numbers given for the end of Act III and for Act IV of the typescript are to the original pages—the typed sheets that are filed with the scenario and notes. The added handwritten pages are designated "revised typescript" (rev. TS).

22. Eugene O'Neill, *A Moon for the Misbegotten* (New York: Random House, 1952), p. 160. All future references to the printed play are to this edition and will be given in the body of the text.

23. Langner, *The Magic Curtain*, p. 403. Olsson, "O'Neill and the Royal Dramatic," p. 42, quotes a letter from the actress Elizabeth Scott in which she states: "In 1946 I was rehearsed for the premiere of Eugene O'Neill's *A Moon for the*

Misbegotten, working with Mr. O'Neill and Dudley Digges on the part [Josie] until the Theatre Guild decided to shelve the play in favor of *The Iceman Cometh.*" Scott's claim is questionable; the date she gives is suspect and most likely she was auditioned rather than rehearsed for the role. Judging by Langner, *The Magic Curtain,* p. 404, the decision to proceed with *Iceman* rather than *Moon* was made in late 1945, not 1946. Digges was involved in the ultimately futile 1945 search for an actress to play Josie.

24. Letter to Lawrence Langner, Aug. 15, 1945.

25. Langner, *The Magic Curtain,* p. 409, relates: "*A Moon for the Misbegotten* closed in St. Louis and it was decided to reopen it later with a new cast. However, because of his illness, 'Gene asked us to defer this until he was feeling better." O'Neill's health continued to deteriorate and no new production of *Moon* was mounted during his lifetime.

26. Both reviews are in the *Moon* pressbook, Theatre Guild Collection, Beinecke Library, Yale University.

27. Armina Marshall, quoted in Langner, *The Magic Curtain,* p. 408.

28. Mary Welch, "Softer Tones for Mr. O'Neill's Portrait," in Oscar Cargill, N. Bryllion Fagin, and William J. Fisher, eds., *O'Neill and His Plays: Four Decades of Criticism* (New York: New York Univ. Press, 1961), p. 90.

29. See Sheaffer, *Son and Artist,* pp. 595–96, for varying accounts of what was cut at this time.

30. This document, identified as a "proposed letter in reply to Elia Kazan," is dated Sept. 6, 1951. It is in the Theatre Guild Collection, Beinecke Library, Yale University.

31. Josie's father is called Mike Hogan in the scenario character list and sometimes referred to simply as Dolan in the body of the scenario. Josie's brother is called Neddie in the scenario character list. James Tyrone, Jr., is called Jamie in the scenario character list and elsewhere in that draft; except in direct quotations I will use the name Jim to prevent confusion with the *Journey* character.

32. All three names are crossed out in the manuscript character list. The scenario list includes Simpson and Cassidy; the last man is identified simply as "Wop."

33. Letter to Eugene O'Neill, Jr., Feb. 20, 1943. O'Neill said exactly the same thing in an earlier letter to his son, written on Feb. 2, 1942.

34. Welch, "Softer Tones," p. 90.

35. I quote this passage from the manuscript rather than the typescript because the typist made a number of small transcription errors.

36. A third passage, in which Hogan explains that Jim sits "up all night alone in his room with a bottle" when depressed, was also cut from the typescript (II, p. 55). Mary Adrian Tinsley, who cites these passages in "Two Biographical Plays," argues that "presumably Hogan ought not to be making these statements to Josie

because of the melodramatic 'trick' he is about to try to work" (pp. 167–68). This is a plausible explanation, although apparently Hogan has not yet in the first act fully decided to play the trick.

37. Ibid., pp. 177–78.

38. The typist accidentally transcribed O'Neill's "curse" as "come."

39. Page reference only is given for the first sheet of the scenario because O'Neill did not label these notes "Act I."

40. Writing about Act III in the scenario and early notes, Floyd comments, "Here Jamie is not repelled by sex as in the published text" (*O'Neill at Work*, p. 373). Floyd supports her claim by quoting from the November 1941 notes, in which Jim says that he will sell the farm to the Hogans if Josie doesn't reject his "advances, so to speak." What she fails to mention is that later in the same notes Jim admits that he was "only joking with" Hogan when he said a night with Josie was the "price" of the farm. In the scenario, when Josie asks Jim whether he wants to go to bed with her, he replies: "Yes! You fool! But I don't want to want that" (III, p. 4). Jim's physical attraction to Josie is stronger and his horror of sex less pronounced in the earliest drafts than in the published *Moon*, but the difference between the first and last versions is not as great as Floyd suggests.

41. O'Neill, *Long Day's Journey Into Night*, p. 153.

42. O'Neill, *The Great God Brown*, pp. 330, 350.

43. Floyd, *O'Neill at Work*, p. 374n. Floyd also notes (pp. xxv–xxviii, 375) similarities between Jim in the scenario and earlier O'Neill characters, including Dion Anthony, Reuben Light, and John Loving.

44. Tinsley, "Two Biographical Plays," p. 182, also mentions "the personification of death as Cynara" in the typescript.

45. Törnqvist, *A Drama of Souls*, p. 246n.

46. The stage direction "kiddingly" was apparently added to the manuscript during revisions, suggesting that O'Neill originally intended Jim's speech to be delivered at least partly seriously.

47. O'Neill, *The Great God Brown*, p. 337.

48. Tinsley, "Two Biographical Plays," p. 135, offers the biographical argument.

49. The bracketed word *me* was added by the typist; the bracketed word *on* was incorrectly typed as *in*.

50. Bogard, *Contour in Time*, pp. 432–33; Tinsley, "Two Biographical Plays," p. 174.

51. Raleigh, *The Plays of Eugene O'Neill*, p. 18.

52. Tinsley, "Two Biographical Plays," pp. 173–74, reaches a similar conclusion.

53. Tinsley, ibid., p. 168, also notes the significance of O'Neill's moving this speech.

54. Bogard, introduction to *The Later Plays of Eugene O'Neill*, pp. xv–xvi.

Bogard also discusses "the search for the surrogate mother" in *Contour in Time*, pp. 436–40.

55. This list omits O'Neill's adaptation of "The Ancient Mariner" but does include *More Stately Mansions*, even though O'Neill never completely finished work on this play. The four exceptions are *Marco Millions; Hughie; A Touch of the Poet;* and *Ah, Wilderness! Poet* may not actually be an exception, for Nora Melody, who looks older than her years, could be said to "baby" the childish Con. The play also contains some hints of the Oedipal Simon-Deborah relationship but, since Simon never appears on stage and Deborah appears only briefly, the hints are slight.

56. Eugene O'Neill, *All God's Chillun Got Wings*, in *Nine Plays*, p. 133.

57. O'Neill, *Days Without End*, p. 65.

58. Eugene O'Neill, *Welded*, in *"All God's Chillun Got Wings" and "Welded"* (New York: Boni and Liveright, 1924), pp. 167, 169.

59. O'Neill, *The Great God Brown*, p. 329.

60. Eugene O'Neill, *Lazarus Laughed*, in *Nine Plays*, p. 459.

61. O'Neill, *Strange Interlude*, p. 590.

62. This epilogue is omitted from the published *More Stately Mansions*. The full manuscript is in the Eugene O'Neill Collection, Beinecke Library, Yale University. Sara's lines are quoted from p. 278. The fact that she speaks almost the same lines at the end of Act III and at the end of the epilogue is probably attributable to O'Neill's never having finished revisions on *Mansions*.

63. Letter to Robert Sisk, March 11, 1929. O'Neill canceled the word *symbolism* and replaced it with *theme*.

64. Genevieve Taggard, *The Life and Mind of Emily Dickinson* (New York: Knopf, 1930), pp. 229–31, 247. The O'Neills owned a copy of this book, which is now at the Beinecke Library. O'Neill's transcription is in a folder of notes for *A Touch of the Poet* in the Yale O'Neill Collection. I quote O'Neill's notes rather than Taggard; he condenses her discussion, omits her remarks about Dickinson and changes a few words, but his copy is otherwise accurate. Taggard attributes her comment about Thoreau's tears to an unnamed "writer." Her source is probably Henry S. Salt, *Life of Henry David Thoreau* (London: Walter Scott, 1896). Salt mentions the tears (p. 29) and also relates the story about the bed (pp. 145–46).

65. Bogard, introduction to *The Later Plays of Eugene O'Neill*, p. xv.

66. Falk, *O'Neill and the Tragic Tension*, p. 176.

67. In Sigmund Spaeth, *Read 'Em and Weep: The Songs You Forgot to Remember* (Garden City, N.Y.: Doubleday, Page, 1926), p. 175.

68. Probably the most famous (and acid) discussion of this image appears in Eric Bentley, "Eugene O'Neill's Pietà," *New Republic*, 4 August 1952, p. 18. Bentley describes the Pietà as "a giant virgin holding in her arms a dipsomaniac

lecher with a heart of gold." For more sympathetic discussions of the image, see Manheim, *O'Neill's New Language of Kinship*, p. 206; and Scheibler, *The Late Plays of Eugene O'Neill*, pp. 85–88. Scheibler, who comments on the extensive length of time Josie and Jim remain in the Pietà position, also believes that the image "is really there almost from the beginning of the moonlight scenes" when Jim first lays his head on her breast.

69. Eugene O'Neill, *Dynamo* (New York: Liveright, 1929), p. 127. Reuben's worship of the "mother-dynamo" proves fatal when he dies in the machine's embrace. In one early version of *Days Without End* mother worship nearly kills John Loving as well. Kneeling "before the altar of the Virgin and Child" in a church, John identifies his mother and wife with the Virgin, "himself with child." His "longing for reunion with them through Mother Goddess . . . lures him to point of suicide before statue of Virgin," although he is ultimately saved from self-destruction. See Floyd, *O'Neill at Work*, pp. 151 and 155, as well as pp. xxxvii and 328–31, where she discusses the deadly "Mother of the Savior of the World" in the unfinished drama "The Last Conquest."

70. O'Neill, *Strange Interlude*, p. 525. James A. Robinson argues that Nina's Mother God "displays Oriental characteristics" which contrast with the Father God's "Western features." Robinson, *Eugene O'Neill and Oriental Thought: A Divided Vision* (Carbondale: So. Illinois Univ. Press, 1982), pp. 152–55. Evidently the concept of a maternal deity deeply interested O'Neill, for Carlotta noted in her diary on Aug. 13, 1932: "Gene talks to me at great length of one of his favourite topics 'Mother God'—!"

71. O'Neill, *The Great God Brown*, p. 374. Manheim, *O'Neill's New Language of Kinship*, p. 206, also notes the similarity between the Pietà images in *Brown* and *Moon*.

72. The same setting is used in Act I of *The Calms of Capricorn* which, had O'Neill completed it, would have been the sequel to *Mansions*. See Eugene O'Neill, *The Calms of Capricorn*, a play developed from O'Neill's scenario by Donald Gallup, with a transcription of the scenario (New Haven: Ticknor & Fields, 1982), p. 131.

73. As Floyd reveals (*O'Neill at Work*, pp. 317–45), O'Neill did labor in the 1940s on "The Last Conquest," an ambitious religious work initially entitled "The Thirteenth Apostle." The plans for the play underwent numerous revisions and included Christ and Satan as well as scenes based on the Temptation on the Mount and the Last Supper. It may be, as Floyd suggests, that he failed to complete "Conquest" partly because he feared audiences would not understand it and partly because his health gave out before he concluded his task. Nevertheless, O'Neill managed to finish two dramas—*Hughie* and *Moon*—that were begun after "Conquest," and he did most of the work on *Journey* and the final draft of *A Touch of the*

Poet during the period he wrestled with the religious opus. He must at some level have been aware that his previous religious plays, *Days Without End* and *Lazarus Laughed,* had been among his least dramatically satisfying. Particularly telling are his Work Diary entries for November 19 and 20, 1942, which Floyd quotes. In the first entry O'Neill remarks that "Conquest" is a "fine idea" but laments that he has developed "some inner struggle about it that has held it up." The following day he writes: "The Last Conquest (notes—I think the inner conflict is because it is at its final curtain a declaration of faith by one who is faithless—like D[ays]. W[ithout]. E[nd]. —a hope for faith instead of faith—and also a futile feeling that no one will see the truth, not even the author)." Floyd states that, according to Dudley Nichols, O'Neill "was still deeply absorbed" in the project "as late as 1948." One may surmise, however, that already in November 1942 he knew his efforts would be futile.

74. Esther M. Jackson uses the same terminology. She writes that the playwright "attempted to translate essentially religious concepts into a secular language." See "O'Neill the Humanist," in Floyd, *World View*, p. 254.

75. Brustein, *The Theatre of Revolt*, p. 331.

76. Törnqvist, "Personal Nomenclature," p. 373. One may speculate further that Josephine was the most obvious choice for a name with Christian connotations. Using Mary, Jamie's mother's name in *Journey*, would be pressing the identification between these women too far. Christine is an unacceptable choice because it might imply that the character is more directly modeled on Christine Ell than is actually the case.

77. Scheibler, *The Late Plays of Eugene O'Neill*, p. 98.

78. For a splendid discussion of confessions in O'Neill's late plays, which also includes a brief historical overview of the role of confession in the Catholic Church, see John Henry Raleigh, "The Last Confession: O'Neill and the Catholic Confessional," in Floyd, *World View*, pp. 212–28.

79. O'Neill, *The Iceman Cometh*, p. 5.

80. Raleigh, *The Plays of Eugene O'Neill*, p. 19.

81. The bracketed words appear in the manuscript but were accidentally omitted from the typescript.

82. O'Neill, *The Iceman Cometh*, p. 226.

83. O'Neill, *Long Day's Journey Into Night*, p. 165.

84. Bentley, "Eugene O'Neill's Pietà," p. 17.

85. O'Neill, *Long Day's Journey Into Night*, p. 167.

86. Tinsley ("Two Biographical Plays," p. 181) similarly observes that there is little evidence of absolution in the typescript.

87. Scheibler, *The Late Plays of Eugene O'Neill*, p. 98.

88. Although she discusses only the typescript, Tinsley, "Two Biographical Plays," p. 157, makes the same point. She writes: "In the typescript Josie has more

masculine characteristics than she does in the final version, and she is associated more frequently with physical violence."

89. This speech is reminiscent of a somewhat milder one Sara delivers in *A Touch of the Poet*. She tells her father: "All I pray to God is that someday when you're admiring yourself in the mirror something will make you see at last what you really are! That will be revenge in full for all you've done to Mother and me!" Eugene O'Neill, *A Touch of the Poet* (New Haven: Yale Univ. Press, 1957), p. 105.

90. See Bogard, *Contour in Time*, p. 448. In *Desire* Eben Cabot gives his father's hidden money to his two half-brothers so they can leave the farm. In *Moon* Josie gives her father's hidden money to her brother so he can escape. There is considerable discussion of the two fathers, Ephraim Cabot and Phil Hogan, before they appear on stage. It is very possible that O'Neill had points he wished to introduce at the beginning of *Moon*—Josie's motherliness, the entrapment plot— and chose as a model a scene he had written long ago rather than compose an entirely new one. In fact, the idea of a son stealing money to escape from his father's tyranny appears even earlier in *The Rope*, written in 1918. Although the scene is not dramatized, Annie reminds her father that her half-brother Luke "stole your money and ran off and left you just when he was sixteen and old enough to help" on the farm. Eugene O'Neill, *The Rope*, in *The Long Voyage Home: Seven Plays of the Sea* (New York: Random House, Modern Library, 1946), p. 185.

91. Törnqvist, *A Drama of Souls*, p. 250.

92. John J. Fitzgerald offers a detailed explication of how Hogan maneuvers Josie, concluding that "throughout this scene, Phil makes his moves like a maleficent chess master." See "Guilt and Redemption in O'Neill's Last Play: A Study of *A Moon for the Misbegotten*," *Texas Quarterly* 9 (Spring 1966): 152–53.

93. Comparing the typescript to the published play, Tinsley, "Two Biographical Plays," p. 157, also notes that "O'Neill devotes more attention to her role as promiscuous slut" in the former version.

94. In one place in the manuscript, talk of Josie's activities was slightly increased. Banter about her bad reputation was expanded a small amount when O'Neill revised Mike's suggestion about the entrapment plot (I, p. 4).

95. Nicola Chiaromonte, "Eugene O'Neill (1958)," *Sewanee Review* 68 (July–September 1960): 498. W. David Sievers, *Freud on Broadway: A History of Psychoanalysis and the American Drama* (New York: Hermitage House, 1955), p. 130.

96. The bracketed "to you" was accidentally omitted by the typist.

97. Tinsley, "Two Biographical Plays," p. 186.

98. Tom Donnelly, "A Long Night's Moongazing," *New York World-Telegram and Sun*, 3 May 1957; reprinted in Jordan Y. Miller, *Playwright's Progress: O'Neill and the Critics* (Chicago: Scott Foresman, 1965), p. 164.

POSTSCRIPT

1. According to the Work Diary, O'Neill wrote *Hughie* during April and May of 1941; he gave it a brief "final going over" the following year. O'Neill worked on the new (and final) draft of *A Touch of the Poet* intermittently between February and November of 1942. Although he considered the new version finished on November 13, he may have made further revisions at a later date.

2. Letter to Krutch, July 15, 1927. In the Beinecke's Eugene O'Neill Collection. It should be noted that O'Neill did occasionally expand a portion of a play during revision. According to the Work Diary, September 29, 1940, revisions on the manuscript of Act I of *Journey* expanded that act to "28 pages now instead of [the original] 22."

3. Tinsley, "Two Biographical Plays," p. 190, similarly observes that "O'Neill habitually blurs, obscures, or deletes direct statements about feeling and motivation as he revises."

4. Rothenberg, "The Iceman Changeth," p. 586n.

5. Törnqvist also notes that stage directions in early drafts "tend to be bulkier" and quotes O'Neill's statement to George Jean Nathan that he "weeded out" stage directions when he "read proofs." In these three plays O'Neill usually began trimming the stage directions in the typescripts. See "O'Neill's Work Method," *Studia Neophilologica* 49 (1977): 53.

6. The Gelbs, *O'Neill*, pp. 644 and 821, mention O'Neill's fondness for detective stories.

7. Raleigh, *The Plays of Eugene O'Neill*, pp. 175, 196–238.

8. Letter to Lawrence Langner, Aug. 11, 1940. In the Beinecke's Theatre Guild Collection.

9. Tinsley also comments that in *Journey* and *Moon* "O'Neill works to 'objectify' his material—to remove irrelevant parts of himself." See "Two Biographical Plays," p. 190.

10. See for example Floyd, *O'Neill at Work*, p. 297. Writing about *Long Day's Journey,* she asserts that the playwright "presents a more truthful and complete portrait of the four O'Neills and their relationships in his early notes and scenario than in the final draft of the play; the most significant difference is the emphasis in the former on the dual-natured mother as the betrayer, 'the guilty one.'"

11. Letter to Kenneth Macgowan, April 8, 1921. In Bryer, "*The Theatre We Worked For*," p. 23.

SELECTED BIBLIOGRAPHY

UNPUBLISHED SOURCES

Notes, scripts, letters, and diaries. Unless otherwise indicated, all material is in the Eugene O'Neill Collection, Collection of American Literature, Beinecke Library, Yale University.

The Iceman Cometh

Scenario and handwritten notes, including drawings of the set. The scenario is dated June 1939. Some notes precede the scenario; some were written later.

Original pencil manuscript with a typewritten note by the author laid in. The note, dated February 24, 1943, reads: "Begun June 8th 1939—Finished November 26th 1939."

First typewritten draft, copy of revised manuscript, with O'Neill's handwritten revisions.

Second typescript prepared for publication. A note in Carlotta's hand, signed by O'Neill, identifies this as the "2nd typed draft from first corrected 'script."

Carbon of the above, used for setting type and prepared for the press in an unknown hand.

Galley proofs for the published text, with a few handwritten corrections. A note laid into the publication material, signed by Norman Holmes Pearson, states that revisions on this material are in Saxe Commins's handwriting but were made "at Mr. O'Neill's direction."

Plate proofs, with numerous minor revisions. These proofs are in a folder on which is written "rev pages / fdry / 8–2," which may mean that the plates were sent back to the foundry on August 2, 1946, so revised pages could be prepared from them.

Page proofs, prepared from revised plate proofs.

"Uncorrected proof for Advance Readers," number 7 of a set of twenty Random House had bound at the playwright's request.

Second typescript, copy of revised first typescript, with the author's handwritten revisions for the first production. (This is identical, page for page, to the second typescript prepared for publication; it was, however, prepared on a different typewriter.) This script has a dedication to Carlotta dated 1941. A note in her handwriting, dated November 1945, identifies this as "2nd draft with cuts made before rehearsal." More than 4000 words of dialogue and an additional 450 words of stage direction are marked for deletion. There are also two unrevised carbon copies of this script.

Typescript apparently prepared from a partly revised second typescript; it incorporates only a few of the alterations O'Neill made in the second typescript for production. This script bears a note stating "Cuts not in this Copy / K.N. / Aug. 3rd." "K.N." is presumably Karl Nielsen, the Theatre Guild's dramatic production manager. New York Public Library at Lincoln Center.

Typescript in Hart Stenographic Bureau cover labeled "Mr. O'Neill." Omitted from this is the material marked for deletion in the second typescript. The playwright has marked this copy with additional cuts and revisions; apparently these changes were made during rehearsals.

Copy of the above, without the playwright's additional revisions. This was Lawrence Langner's script and he marked it with numerous suggestions for cuts. O'Neill simply ignored most of these suggestions but wrote "yes" next to a few and "no" next to several. On the title page he wrote "THE HELL with your cuts!" Laid into this script is a letter from Langner dated October 18, 1946. The last paragraph of the letter reads: "Before the play opened, I told Mr. O'Neill it would be acted exactly the way he wanted it, even though I felt it was overwritten. On the night the play opened, I went to his home and told him I thought the play was a great success but that it would never be cut down to the right dimensions till after his death." Theatre Guild Collection, Beinecke Library, Yale University.

Copy of the above except new endings for Act III and Act IV are inserted. The ending of the third act reflects the revisions O'Neill wrote into his script. The new conclusion of the fourth act, from Hickey's exit to the end, incorporates some of the changes O'Neill penciled into his script and other changes as well. This heavily marked and soiled script is labeled "Rehearsal Record Sept 3rd 1946." It includes cues for actors and stage crew, pencil sketches of the set, working property plots for each act, names and addresses of actors, and other production information. This script was probably the copy used by the production's stage manager. Yale Theatre Guild Collection.

Script, in red Hart Stenographic cover, bearing Carlotta's signature. Omitted from this script is nearly all material marked for deletion in the stage manager's script. Many cues for the actors that are written into the stage manager's script are already typed into this version, and this script includes production data (property plots, etc.). The most important difference between this script and earlier ones is the ending, which is new. Where previous scripts conclude with Hugo's "willow trees" line, this script ends on Willy's "Sailor Lad" song. There are no handwritten revisions in this script.

Carbon copy of above, in Hart cover marked "Playing 'Script."

Same as above. Lincoln Center.

Same as above, with some additional scene plans. Bound with a copy of the play-bill for the first production. Yale Theatre Guild Collection.

Same as above except that the earlier ending—the one found in the "stage manager's script"—has been inserted. There are also some additional cues and a few dialogue revisions penciled in. Written on the title page in an unknown hand is "Produced by the Theatre Guild at the Martin Beck Theatre, New York, 9 October, 1946." Lincoln Center.

The Yale O'Neill Collection has a clipping file that includes reviews of the original production as well as reviews of some foreign productions and American revivals. There are also photographs from various productions and some of Robert Edmond Jones's costume sketches. The Theatre Guild Collection has two press-books for the premiere in addition to photographs and several files of casting memos, receipts, press releases, reviews, and letters, all relating to the original production. The New York Public Library at Lincoln Center also has clippings, photographs, and programs from various productions.

Long Day's Journey Into Night

Scenario. The first four pages are dated June 1939, the fifth July 1, 1939, and the sixth July 2–3, 1939.

Handwritten notes (filed separately from the scenario), including drawings of the set. Some notes precede the scenario; some were written later. One note, a description of Mary Tyrone's wedding gown, is in Carlotta's hand.

Original pencil manuscript dated September 20, 1940. Includes the dedication to Carlotta that is reproduced in the published text.

First typewritten draft, copy of revised manuscript, with the author's handwritten revisions. Inscribed by O'Neill: "Typed copy of First Draft with revisions into Second Draft."

Second typewritten draft, copy of revised first typescript, with a few handwritten corrections by the author and Carlotta.

Typescript labeled by Yale "3rd (1st professional) typescript." This may be one of those typed by O'Neill's Random House editor, Saxe Commins. The typescript has a dedication to Carlotta dated December 27, 1951: "To Carlotta, my beloved wife, this play written in blood and tears, is dedicated. She did the slavery on it, typing it twice, encouraging me, giving faith and love and making it possible for me to go on with work which daily broke my heart with poignant memory!"

Unmarked carbon copy of above.

Typescript, galleys, page proofs, and plate proofs for the posthumous publication of the play.

Large collection of reviews of American and foreign productions, as well as of the book and of the film version, in addition to several folders of photographs. The New York Public Library at Lincoln Center also has clippings, photographs, and programs from various productions.

A Moon for the Misbegotten

Scenario and handwritten notes, including drawings of the exterior of the Dolan house. The first, second, and fourth pages of the scenario are dated October 1941; the fifth page is dated November 1, 1941; the third and sixth pages are undated. Some of the notes were written immediately after the scenario; others were written later. Filed with the scenario and notes is the first typescript of the end of Act III and all of Act IV.

Pencil manuscript inscribed by O'Neill "2nd d[raft]. —still needs cuts & condensation," dated May 17, 1943. Several pages in Act I and a very few pages in Act II appear to be revised sheets from the first manuscript, written in late 1941. The rest of the pages date from 1943, when O'Neill rewrote most of the manuscript.

First typewritten draft, copy of revised manuscript, with O'Neill's extensive handwritten revisions. The last page of Act III and all of Act IV are handwritten; the original typescript version of this portion is filed with the scenario and notes. This typescript is labeled, in the playwright's hand, "1st typed draft (typed by Cyn) with subsequent revisions made [?] at Hamilton Apts., San Francisco."

Second typewritten draft, with copy of revised first typescript, with a few handwritten corrections by O'Neill and a few marginal notations in an unknown hand (probably Lawrence Langner's). The script has Langner's name on it and a poem about "an Irish agricultural girl" named "Mary Anne Malone" inserted after the title page.

Third typewritten draft, copy of corrected second typescript, prepared by Dorothy Evans, Theatrical Typing. This script is signed by Carlotta; her signature is dated 1947.

Typescript in a Hart Stenographic Bureau cover. This script bears the signature of J. M. Kerrigan, who originated the role of Phil Hogan, and is marked with some revisions. The language in this copy has been "cleaned up," with blasphemous words canceled and other potentially offensive terms changed; "whores on Broadway," for example, was changed to "dancers on the stage." Yale Theatre Guild Collection.

Same as above with almost identical revisions and with some directions for actor movement written in. This script is labeled "Prompt copy—K.N.," the initials presumably those of Karl Nielsen, the Theatre Guild's dramatic production manager. Yale Theatre Guild Collection.

Unmarked copy of above, bound with a playbill for the first production. Yale Theatre Guild Collection.

Unmarked copy of above. New York Public Library at Lincoln Center.

Several sets of uncorrected proof for the published text, prepared for advance readers.

The Yale O'Neill Collection has a clipping file that includes reviews of the original production as well as of some foreign productions and American revivals. There are also photographs from various productions. The Theatre Guild Collection has one pressbook for the premiere in addition to photographs and files of memos, press releases, reviews, and letters, all relating to the original production. The New York Public Library at Lincoln Center also has clippings, photographs, and programs from various productions.

Other Relevant Notes, Manuscripts, and Typescripts

One page of notes, written in September of 1934, for a proposed sequel to *Ah, Wilderness!*

Typescript of *More Stately Mansions,* copy of revised second (manuscript) draft, with extensive revisions by the author. According to the Work Diary, O'Neill wrote the manuscripts in late 1938; Carlotta then prepared this typescript. O'Neill spent much of January 1939 revising this typescript, but additional revisions may have been made at a later date.

Handwritten notes for *A Touch of the Poet,* including comments about books read for background information, character descriptions, brief plot summaries, and set sketches. This and other material relating to *A Touch of the Poet* and *More Stately Mansions* is available for examination. Notes for other planned plays in the "A Tale of Possessors Self-Dispossessed" cycle are "restricted" (not yet available for examination).

A typescript of *The Personal Equation* (originally entitled *The Second Engineer*) is among the O'Neill holdings at the Houghton Library, Harvard University.

Unpublished Letters and Diaries

The Yale O'Neill Collection has hundreds of letters from Eugene and Carlotta O'Neill to various correspondents. The most important letters for this study were those from O'Neill to Bennett Cerf, Barrett Clark, Russel Crouse, Joseph Wood Krutch, Sinclair Lewis, Richard J. Madden, Dudley Nichols, Eugene O'Neill, Jr., Lee Simonson, and Robert Sisk, and those from Carlotta to Dudley Nichols.

O'Neill's letters to Lawrence Langner are in the Yale Theatre Guild Collection. Princeton University's William Seymour Theatre Collection has letters from O'Neill to George C. Tyler, while the O'Neill–George Jean Nathan correspondence is in the Nathan Collection, Cornell University Library, Department of Rare Books.

Carlotta Monterey O'Neill's diaries for the years 1931–1944, 1954, 1959, 1960, 1962, and 1963 are in the Beinecke. In the late 1940s Carlotta sent her diaries to Yale for safekeeping; in 1954 she asked that they be returned to her temporarily. She felt it was important that these volumes be preserved, and on March 12, 1954, she wrote: "Years later, an old woman, I am *copying* his diaries & mine— because the ink is fading!" Donald Gallup, who has published a transcription of O'Neill's Work Diary, states that Carlotta did not copy these volumes—the Work Diary is in the playwright's handwriting. Carlotta apparently did copy over most of her own diaries at this time, and it is at least possible that she did some minor editing. The volumes for 1931–1943 and 1954 are identical "Daily Reminder" books written in the same ink.

PUBLISHED SOURCES

Adams, Graham, Jr. *Age of Industrial Violence 1910–15.* New York: Columbia University Press, 1966.

Alexander, Doris M. "Hugo of *The Iceman Cometh:* Realism and O'Neill." *American Quarterly* 5 (Winter 1953): 357–66. Reprinted in *Twentieth Century Interpretations of "The Iceman Cometh,"* edited by John Henry Raleigh, pp. 63–71.

―――. *The Tempering of Eugene O'Neill.* New York: Harcourt, Brace & World, 1962.

Andreach, Robert J. "O'Neill's Women in *The Iceman Cometh.*" *Renascence* 18 (Winter 1966): 89–98. Reprinted in *Eugene O'Neill: A Collection of Criticism,* edited by Ernest G. Griffin, pp. 103–13.

Arbenz, Mary Hedwig. "The Plays of Eugene O'Neill as Presented by the Theatre Guild." Ph.D. dissertation, University of Illinois, 1961.

Arestad, Sverre. "*The Iceman Cometh* and *The Wild Duck.*" *Scandinavian Studies* 20 (February 1948): 1–11.

Atkinson, Brooks. "O'Neill's Journey." Review of *Long Day's Journey. New York Times,* 18 November 1956, sec. 2, p. 1.

―――. "O'Neill Tragedy Revived." Review of *The Iceman Cometh. New York Times,* 9 May 1956, p. 38. Reprinted in *O'Neill and His Plays,* edited by Oscar Cargill et al., pp. 212–13; and (slightly abridged) in *Twentieth Century In-*

terpretations of "The Iceman Cometh," edited by John Henry Raleigh, pp. 33–34.

Atkinson, Jennifer McCabe. *Eugene O'Neill: A Descriptive Bibliography.* Pittsburgh: University of Pittsburgh Press, 1974.

Baker, George Pierce. *Dramatic Technique.* Boston: Houghton Mifflin, 1919.

Barnes, Howard. "The Theater: *The Iceman Cometh.*" *New York Herald Tribune,* 20 October 1946, sec. 5, pp. 1, 5.

Bentley, Eric. "Eugene O'Neill's Pietà." *New Republic,* 4 August 1952, pp. 17–18. Reprinted in Eric Bentley, *The Dramatic Event: An American Chronicle,* New York: Horizon, 1954, pp. 30–33; and *Eugene O'Neill: A Collection of Criticism,* edited by Ernest G. Griffin, pp. 136–38.

_____. "The Return of Eugene O'Neill." Review of *The Iceman Cometh. Atlantic Monthly,* 4 November 1946, pp. 64–66. Reprinted in *Playwright's Progress: O'Neill and the Critics,* edited by Jordan Y. Miller, pp. 125–30.

_____. "Trying to Like O'Neill." *Kenyon Review* 14 (July 1952): 476–92. Reprinted in Eric Bentley, *In Search of Theatre,* New York: Knopf, 1953, pp. 233–47; in *O'Neill and His Plays,* edited by Oscar Cargill et al., pp. 331–45; in *Twentieth Century Interpretations of "The Iceman Cometh,"* edited by John Henry Raleigh, pp. 37–49; and (in abbreviated form) in *O'Neill: A Collection of Critical Essays,* edited by John Gassner, pp. 89–98.

Berlin, Normand. *Eugene O'Neill.* New York: Grove Press, 1982.

Black, Matthew W. Introduction to William Shakespeare, *The Tragedy of King Richard the Second.* Baltimore: Penguin Books, 1957.

Bogard, Travis. *Contour in Time: The Plays of Eugene O'Neill.* New York: Oxford University Press, 1972.

_____. "Dreams of Joy, Dreams of Pain." In *Eugene O'Neill,* Milwaukee Repertory Theater Company, pp. 14–15, 18–19.

Boulton, Agnes. *Part of a Long Story.* Garden City, N.Y.: Doubleday, 1958.

Bowen, Croswell, with the assistance of Shane O'Neill. *The Curse of the Misbegotten: A Tale of the House of O'Neill.* New York: McGraw-Hill, 1959.

Brashear, William R. " 'To-morrow' and 'Tomorrow': Conrad and O'Neill." *Renascence* 20 (Autumn 1967): 18–21.

_____. "The Wisdom of Silenus in O'Neill's *Iceman.*" *American Literature* 36 (May 1964): 180–88.

Broussard, Louis. *American Drama: Contemporary Allegory from Eugene O'Neill to Tennessee Williams.* Norman: University of Oklahoma Press, 1962.

Brown, John Mason. "All O'Neilling." Review of *The Iceman Cometh. Saturday Review,* 19 October 1946, pp. 26–30. Reprinted as "Moaning at the Bar" in John Mason Brown, *Dramatis Personae,* New York: Viking, 1963, pp. 57–62.

Brustein, Robert. *The Theatre of Revolt.* Boston: Little, Brown, 1964.

Bryer, Jackson R. *Checklist of Eugene O'Neill.* Columbus, Ohio: Charles E. Merrill, 1971.

————, ed. *"The Theatre We Worked For": The Letters of Eugene O'Neill to Kenneth Macgowan.* Witn introductory essays by Travis Bogard. New Haven: Yale University Press, 1982.

Bull, Harry. "The Theater: *The Iceman Cometh.*" *Town & Country,* December 1946, pp. 117, 274.

Cargill, Oscar, N. Bryllion Fagin, and William J. Fisher, eds. *O'Neill and His Plays: Four Decades of Criticism.* New York: New York University Press, 1961.

Carpenter, Frederic I. *Eugene O'Neill.* Revised edition, Boston: Twayne, 1979.

Chabrowe, Leonard. "Dionysus in *The Iceman Cometh.*" *Modern Drama* 4 (February 1962): 377–88.

————. *Ritual and Pathos: The Theater of O'Neill.* Lewisburg, Pa.: Bucknell University Press, 1976.

Chapman, John. Review of *The Iceman Cometh. New York Daily News,* 10 October 1946.

Chiaromonte, Nicola. "Eugene O'Neill (1958)." *Sewanee Review* 68 (July–September 1960): 494–501.

Chothia, Jean. *Forging a Language: A Study of the Plays of Eugene O'Neill.* London: Cambridge University Press, 1979.

Clark, Barrett H. *Eugene O'Neill: The Man and His Plays.* Revised edition, New York: Dover, 1947.

————. *European Theories of the Drama, with a Supplement on the American Drama.* Revised edition, New York: Crown, 1947.

Clurman, Harold. *Lies Like Truth.* New York: MacMillan, 1958.

Commins, Dorothy. *What Is an Editor? Saxe Commins at Work.* Chicago: University of Chicago Press, 1978.

Day, Cyrus. "The Iceman and the Bridegroom: Some Observations on the Death of O'Neill's Salesman." *Modern Drama* 1 (May 1958): 3–9. Reprinted in *Twentieth Century Interpretations of "The Iceman Cometh,"* edited by John Henry Raleigh, pp. 79–86.

Donnelly, Tom. "A Few Ice Cubes Are Missing." Review of *The Iceman Cometh. Washington Daily News,* 2 April 1947, p. 44.

————. "A Long Night's Moongazing." Review of *A Moon for the Misbegotten. New York World-Telegram and Sun,* 3 May 1957. Reprinted in *Playwright's Progress,* edited by Jordan Y. Miller, pp. 163–64.

Drinnon, Richard. *Rebel in Paradise: A Biography of Emma Goldman.* Chicago: University of Chicago Press, 1961.

Driver, Tom F. "On the Late Plays of Eugene O'Neill." *Tulane Drama Review* 3 (December 1958): 8–20. Reprinted in *O'Neill: A Collection of Critical Essays,* edited by John Gassner, pp. 110–23.

Egri, Peter. "*The Iceman Cometh:* European Origins and American Originality." 3 parts. *The Eugene O'Neill Newsletter* 5 (Winter 1981): 5–10; 6 (Spring 1982): 16–24; 6 (Summer–Fall 1982): 30–36.

Eldridge, Florence. "Reflections on *Long Day's Journey into Night:* First Curtain Call for Mary Tyrone." In *Eugene O'Neill: A World View,* edited by Virginia Floyd, pp. 286–87.

Engel, Edwin A. *The Haunted Heroes of Eugene O'Neill.* Cambridge: Harvard University Press, 1953.

Falk, Doris V. *Eugene O'Neill and the Tragic Tension: An Interpretive Study of the Plays.* New Brunswick, N.J.: Rutgers University Press, 1958.

Fechter, Charles. "Monte Cristo (James O'Neill's Version)." In *"Monte Cristo" and Other Plays,* edited by J. B. Russak. Princeton: Princeton University Press, 1941.

Fitzgerald, Geraldine. "Another Neurotic Electra: A New Look at Mary Tyrone." In *Eugene O'Neill: A World View,* edited by Virginia Floyd, pp. 290–92.

Fitzgerald, John J. "Guilt and Redemption in O'Neill's Last Play: A Study of *A Moon for the Misbegotten.*" *Texas Quarterly* 9 (Spring 1966): 146–58.

Floyd, Virginia, ed. *Eugene O'Neill: A World View.* New York: Ungar, 1979.

———, ed. *Eugene O'Neill at Work: Newly Released Ideas for Plays.* New York: Ungar, 1981.

Forbes, James. *The Traveling Salesman.* New York: Samuel French, 1908.

Frazer, Winifred L. (Dusenbury). *E.G. and E.G.O.: Emma Goldman and "The Iceman Cometh."* Gainesville: University Presses of Florida, 1974.

———. "Hughie and the Traveling Salesman." *Players* 44 (April–May 1969): 151–54.

———. "King Lear and Hickey: Bridegroom and Iceman." *Modern Drama* 15 (December 1972): 267–78.

———. *Love as Death in "The Iceman Cometh": A Modern Treatment of an Ancient Theme.* Gainesville: University of Florida Press, 1967.

———. "'Revolution' in *The Iceman Cometh.*" *Modern Drama* 22 (March 1979): 1–8.

Frenz, Horst. *Eugene O'Neill.* Translated by Helen Sebba. New York: Ungar, 1971.

Gassner, John. *Eugene O'Neill.* Minneapolis: University of Minnesota Press, 1965.

———, ed. *O'Neill: A Collection of Critical Essays.* Englewood Cliffs, N.J.: Prentice-Hall, 1964.

Gelb, Arthur, and Barbara Gelb. *O'Neill.* Enlarged edition, New York: Harper & Row, 1973.

Gibbs, Wolcott. "Doom." Review of *Long Day's Journey. New Yorker,* 24 Nov. 1956, pp. 120, 122.

Goldman, Emma. "Donald Vose: The Accursed." *Mother Earth* 10 (January 1916): 353–57.

———. "Judas." *Mother Earth* 10 (December 1915): 347–48.

———. *Living My Life.* 2 vols. New York: Knopf, 1931.

Granger, Bruce Ingham. "Illusion and Reality in Eugene O'Neill." *MLN* 73 (March 1958): 179–86.

Greenberger, Howard. *The Off-Broadway Experience.* Englewood Cliffs, N.J.: Prentice-Hall, 1971.

Griffin, Ernest G. "Pity, Alienation and Reconciliation in Eugene O'Neill." *Mosaic* 2 (Fall 1968): 66–76.

———, ed. *Eugene O'Neill: A Collection of Criticism.* New York: McGraw-Hill, 1976.

Heilman, Robert Bechtold. *The Iceman, the Arsonist, and the Troubled Agent: Tragedy and Melodrama on the Modern Stage.* Seattle: University of Washington Press, 1973.

Hewes, Henry. "O'Neill: 100 Proof—Not a Blend." Review of *Long Day's Journey. Saturday Review,* 24 November 1956, pp. 30–31. Reprinted in *O'Neill and His Plays,* edited by Oscar Cargill et al., pp. 217–20.

Hopkins, Vivian C. "*The Iceman* Seen Through *The Lower Depths.*" *College English* 11 (November 1949): 81–87.

Jackson, Esther M. "O'Neill the Humanist." In *Eugene O'Neill: A World View,* edited by Virginia Floyd, pp. 252–56.

Kerr, Walter. Review of *Long Day's Journey. New York Herald-Tribune,* 8 November 1956, p. 20. Reprinted in Jordan Y. Miller, *Playwright's Progress,* pp. 136–37.

Langner, Lawrence. *The Magic Curtain.* New York: Dutton, 1951.

———. *The Play's the Thing.* New York: Putnam, 1960.

Lee, Robert C. "Eugene O'Neill's Approach to Playwriting." *Drama Critique* 11 (Winter 1968): 2–8.

———. "Eugene O'Neill's Remembrance: The Past Is the Present." *Arizona Quarterly* 23 (Winter 1967): 293–305.

———. "Evangelism and Anarchy in *The Iceman Cometh.*" *Modern Drama* 12 (September 1969): 173–86.

———. "The Lonely Dream." *Modern Drama* 9 (September 1966): 127–35.

Leech, Clifford. *Eugene O'Neill.* New York: Grove, 1963.

Long, Chester Clayton. *The Role of Nemesis in the Structure of Selected Plays by Eugene O'Neill.* The Hague: Mouton, 1968.

McCarthy, Mary. "Dry Ice." Review of the *The Iceman Cometh. Partisan Review* 13 (November–December 1946): 577–79. Reprinted in Mary McCarthy, *Sights and Spectacles 1937–1956,* New York: Farrar, 1956, pp. 81–85; and *Twentieth*

Century Interpretations of "The Iceman Cometh," edited by John Henry Raleigh, pp. 50–53.

————. "The Farmer's Daughter." Review of *A Moon for the Misbegotten. New York Times*, 31 August 1952, sec. 7, p. 7. Reprinted in Mary McCarthy, *Sights and Spectacles 1937–1956*, New York: Farrar, 1965, pp. 86–88; and *O'Neill and His Plays*, edited by Oscar Cargill et al., pp. 209–11.

McDonald, David. "The Phenomenology of the Glance in *Long Day's Journey Into Night." Theatre Journal* 31 (October 1979): 343–56.

Mandl, Bette. "Absence as Presence: The Second Sex in *The Iceman Cometh." The Eugene O'Neill Newsletter* 6 (Summer–Fall 1982): 10–15.

Manheim, Michael. *Eugene O'Neill's New Language of Kinship.* Syracuse: Syracuse University Press, 1982.

Miller, Jordan Y. *Eugene O'Neill and the American Critic: A Bibliographical Checklist.* 2d edition revised, Hamden, Conn.: Archon, 1973.

————. *Playwright's Progress: O'Neill and the Critics.* Chicago: Scott, Foresman, 1965.

Milwaukee Repertory Theater Company. *Eugene O'Neill.* Program distributed to audience members of the midwestern and western tour of *Ah, Wilderness!* and *Long Day's Journey Into Night.* Literary content supervised by Paul Voelker. 1978.

Muchnic, Helen. "Circe's Swine: Plays by Gorky and O'Neill." *Comparative Literature* 3 (Spring 1951): 119–28. Reprinted in *O'Neill: A Collection of Critical Essays,* edited by John Gassner, pp. 99–109. Reprinted (in revised form) as "The Irrelevancy of Belief: *The Iceman* and *The Lower Depths,"* in *O'Neill and His Plays,* edited by Oscar Cargill et al., pp. 431–42; and *Twentieth Century Interpretations of "The Iceman Cometh,"* edited by John Henry Raleigh, pp. 103–12.

Muir, Kenneth. *Shakespeare's Sources (I): Comedies and Tragedies.* London: Methuen, 1957.

Myers, Henry Alonzo. *Tragedy: A View of Life.* Ithaca: Cornell University Press, 1956.

Nathan, George Jean. "The Iceman Cometh, Seeth, Conquereth." Review of *The Iceman Cometh. New York Journal-American,* 14 October 1946. Reprinted (with additional material) in George Jean Nathan, *The Theatre Book of the Year, 1946–1947,* New York: Knopf, 1947, pp. 93–111. The latter version is reprinted (abridged) in *Twentieth Century Interpretations of "The Iceman Cometh,"* edited by John Henry Raleigh, pp. 26–29.

North, Joseph. *Robert Minor, Artist and Crusader: An Informal Biography.* New York: International Publishers, 1956.

Norton, Elliot. "O'Neill's *Iceman:* Second Thoughts of a First-Nighter." *Boston Sunday Post,* 13 October 1946.

Olsson, Tom. "O'Neill and the Royal Dramatic." In *Eugene O'Neill: A World View,* edited by Virginia Floyd, pp. 34–60.

O'Neill, Eugene. *Abortion.* In *Lost Plays of Eugene O'Neill.* Reprinted in *Ten "Lost" Plays by Eugene O'Neill.*

————. *Ah, Wilderness!* New York: Random House, 1933. Reprinted in *The Later Plays Of Eugene O'Neill,* edited by Travis Bogard.

————. *All God's Chillun Got Wings.* In *"All God's Chillun Got Wings" and "Welded."* New York: Boni and Liveright, 1924. Reprinted in *Nine Plays by Eugene O'Neill.*

————. *The Ancient Mariner,* edited by Donald Gallup. *Yale University Library Gazette* 35 (October 1960): 61–86.

————. *Beyond the Horizon.* New York: Boni and Liveright, 1920.

————. *The Calms of Capricorn.* A play developed from O'Neill's scenario by Donald Gallup. With a transcription of the scenario. Introductory note by Donald Gallup. New Haven: Ticknor & Fields, 1982.

————. *"Children of the Sea" and Three Other Unpublished Plays by Eugene O'Neill.* Edited by Jennifer McCabe Atkinson. Foreword by Frank Durham. Washington: NCR/Microcard Editions, 1972.

————. *Chris Christophersen.* Foreword by Leslie Eric Comens. New York: Random House, 1982.

————. *Days Without End.* New York: Random House, 1934.

————. *Desire Under the Elms.* New York: Boni and Liveright, 1925. Reprinted in *Nine Plays by Eugene O'Neill.*

————. *Dynamo.* New York: Liveright, 1929.

————. *The Great God Brown.* New York: Boni & Liveright, 1926. Reprinted in *Nine Plays by Eugene O'Neill.*

————. *Hughie.* New Haven: Yale University Press, 1959. Reprinted in *The Later Plays of Eugene O'Neill,* edited by Travis Bogard.

————. *The Iceman Cometh.* New York: Random House, 1946.

————. *Inscriptions: Eugene O'Neill to Carlotta Monterey O'Neill.* Edited by Donald Gallup. New Haven: Yale University Library, Privately printed, 1960.

————. *The Later Plays of Eugene O'Neill.* Edited and with an introduction by Travis Bogard. New York: Random House, Modern Library, 1967.

————. *Lazarus Laughed.* New York: Boni & Liveright, 1927. Reprinted in *Nine Plays by Eugene O'Neill.*

————. *Long Day's Journey Into Night.* New Haven: Yale University Press, 1956.

————. *The Long Voyage Home: Seven Plays of the Sea.* New York: Random House, Modern Library, 1946.

———. *Lost Plays of Eugene O'Neill*. Introduction by Lawrence Gellert. New York: New Fathoms, 1950.

———. *A Moon for the Misbegotten*. New York: Random House, 1952. Reprinted in *The Later Plays of Eugene O'Neill*, edited by Travis Bogard.

———. *More Stately Mansions*. Shortened from the author's partly revised script by Karl Ragnar Gierow. Edited by Donald Gallup. New Haven: Yale University Press, 1964.

———. *Mourning Becomes Electra*. New York: Liveright, 1931. Reprinted in *Nine Plays by Eugene O'Neill*.

———. *Nine Plays by Eugene O'Neill*. Introduction by Joseph Wood Krutch. 1932. Reprint New York: Random House, Modern Library, 1941.

———. *Poems 1912–1944*. Edited by Donald Gallup. New Haven: Ticknor & Fields, 1980.

———. *The Rope*. In *"The Moon of the Caribbees" and Six Other Plays of the Sea*. New York: Boni and Liveright, 1919. Reprinted in *The Long Voyage Home: Seven Plays of the Sea*.

———. *Strange Interlude*. New York: Boni & Liveright, 1928. Reprinted in *Nine Plays by Eugene O'Neill*.

———. *Ten "Lost" Plays by Eugene O'Neill*. With a foreword by Bennett Cerf. New York: Random House, 1964.

———. *"The Theatre We Worked For": The Letters of Eugene O'Neill to Kenneth Macgowan*. Edited by Jackson Bryer. With introductory essays by Travis Bogard. New Haven: Yale University Press, 1982.

———. *"Thirst" and Other One Act Plays*. Boston: Gorham, 1914.

———. *"Tomorrow." The Seven Arts* 2 (June 1917): 147–70. Reprinted in *The Eugene O'Neill Newsletter* 7 (Winter 1983): 3–13.

———. *A Touch of the Poet*. New Haven: Yale University Press, 1957. Reprinted in *The Later Plays of Eugene O'Neill*, edited by Travis Bogard.

———. *Warnings*. In *"Thirst" and Other One Act Plays*. Reprinted in *Ten "Lost" Plays by Eugene O'Neill*.

———. *Welded*. In *"All God's Chillun Got Wings" and "Welded."* New York: Boni and Liveright, 1924.

———. *Work Diary 1924–1943*. Transcribed by Donald Gallup. Preliminary edition. 2 vols. New Haven: Yale University Library, 1981.

Pallette, Drew B. "O'Neill's *A Touch of the Poet* and His Other Last Plays." *Arizona Quarterly* 13 (Winter 1957): 308–19.

Peck, Seymour. "Talk with Mrs. O'Neill." *New York Times*, 4 November 1956, sec. 2, pp. 1, 3. Reprinted in *O'Neill and His Plays*, edited by Oscar Cargill et al., pp. 92–95.

Pollock, Arthur. "Theater: Eugene O'Neill's *The Iceman Cometh*." *Brooklyn Eagle*, 10 October 1946, p. 16.

Prideaux, Tom. "Eugene O'Neill: Most Celebrated U.S. Playwright Returns to Theater." *Life*, 14 October 1946, pp. 102–16.

Quintero, José. *If You Don't Dance They Beat You*. Boston: Little, Brown, 1974.

———. "Postscript to a Journey." *Theatre Arts* 41 (April 1957): 27–29, 88. Reprinted in *Twentieth Century Interpretations of "The Iceman Cometh,"* edited by John Henry Raleigh, pp. 31–33.

Raghavacharyulu, D. V. K. *Eugene O'Neill: A Study*. Bombay: Popular Prakashan, 1965.

Raleigh, John Henry. "The Irish Atavism of *A Moon for the Misbegotten*." In *Eugene O'Neill: A World View*, edited by Virginia Floyd, pp. 229–36.

———. "The Last Confession: O'Neill and the Catholic Confessional." In *Eugene O'Neill: A World View*, edited by Virginia Floyd, pp. 212–28.

———. *The Plays of Eugene O'Neill*. Carbondale: Southern Illinois University Press, 1965.

———, ed. *Twentieth Century Interpretations of "The Iceman Cometh": A Collection of Critical Essays*. Englewood, N.J.: Prentice-Hall, 1968.

Reardon, William R. "O'Neill Since World War II: Critical Reception in New York." *Modern Drama* 10 (December 1967): 289–99.

Reaver, J. Russell. *An O'Neill Concordance*. 3 vols. Detroit: Gale, 1969.

Redford, Grant H. "Dramatic Art vs. Autobiography: A Look at *Long Day's Journey Into Night*." *College English* 25 (April 1964): 527–35.

Reinhardt, Nancy. "Formal Patterns in *The Iceman Cometh*." *Modern Drama* 16 (September 1973): 119–28.

Rich, J. Dennis. "Exile Without Remedy: The Late Plays of Eugene O'Neill." In *Eugene O'Neill: A World View*, edited by Virginia Floyd, pp. 257–76.

Robards, Jason, Jr. "The Actor: Trust Yourself." In Howard Greenberger, *The Off-Broadway Experience*, pp. 32–51.

Robinson, James A. *Eugene O'Neill and Oriental Thought: A Divided Vision*. Carbondale: Southern Illinois University Press, 1982.

Rothenberg, Albert. "Autobiographical Drama: Strindberg and O'Neill." *Literature and Psychology* 17 (1967): 95–114.

———. "The Iceman Changeth: Toward an Empirical Approach to Creativity." *Journal of the American Psychoanalytic Association* 17 (April 1969): 549–607.

———, and Eugene D. Shapiro. "The Defense of Psychoanalysis in Literature: *Long Day's Journey Into Night* and *A View from the Bridge*." *Comparative Drama* 7 (Spring 1973): 51–67.

Rubenstein, Annette. "The Dark Journey of Eugene O'Neill." Review of *Long Day's Journey. Mainstream* 10 (April 1957): 29–33.

Salt, Henry S. *Life of Henry David Thoreau*. London: Walter Scott, 1896.

Sanborn, Ralph, and Barrett H. Clark, eds. *A Bibliography of the Works of Eu-*

gene O'Neill together with the Collected Poems of Eugene O'Neill. 1931. Reprint New York: Benjamin Blom, 1965.

Saroyan, William. *The Time of Your Life*. New York: Harcourt Brace, 1939.

Scheibler, Rolf. *The Late Plays of Eugene O'Neill*. Bern: A. Francke, 1970.

Schriftgiesser, Karl. "Interview with O'Neill." *New York Times*, 6 October 1946, sec. 2, pp. 1, 3. Excerpted in *Twentieth Century Interpretations of "The Iceman Cometh,"* edited by John Henry Raleigh, pp. 25–26.

"A Serpent That Eats Its Tail." Review of film version of *Long Day's Journey. Time*, 12 October 1962, pp. 102, M15.

Sewall, Richard B. "The Tragic Form." In *Tragedy: Modern Essays in Criticism*, edited by Laurence Michel and Richard Sewall. Englewood Cliffs, N.J.: Prentice-Hall, 1963, pp. 117–29.

———. *The Vision of Tragedy*. New enlarged edition, New Haven: Yale University Press, 1980.

Shawcross, John T. "The Road to Ruin: The Beginning of O'Neill's *Long Day's Journey.*" *Modern Drama* 3 (December 1960): 289–96.

Sheaffer, Louis. "Correcting Some Errors in Annals of O'Neill." *Comparative Drama* 17 (Fall 1983): 201–32. Reprinted in two parts in *The Eugene O'Neill Newsletter* 7 (Winter 1983): 13–24, and 8 (Spring 1984): 16–21.

———. *O'Neill: Son and Artist*. Boston: Little, Brown, 1973.

———. *O'Neill: Son and Playwright*. Boston: Little, Brown, 1968.

Shipley, Joseph T. "Iceman Cometh: Chill from the World Doom." *New Leader*, 19 October 1946, pp. 6, 13.

Sievers, W. David. *Freud on Broadway: A History of Psychoanalysis and the American Drama*. New York: Hermitage House, 1955.

Sinha, C. P. *Eugene O'Neill's Tragic Vision*. Atlantic Highlands, N.J.: Humanities Press, 1981.

Spaeth, Sigmund. *Read 'Em and Weep: The Songs You Forgot to Remember*. Garden City, N.Y.: Doubleday, Page, 1926.

Stroupe, John H. "Eugene O'Neill and the Creative Process." *The English Record* 21 (October 1970): 69–76.

Taggard, Genevieve. *The Life and Mind of Emily Dickinson*. New York: Knopf, 1930.

Tinsley, Mary Adrian. "Two Biographical Plays by Eugene O'Neill: The Drafts and the Final Versions." Ph.D. dissertation, Cornell University, 1969.

Tiusanen, Timo. *O'Neill's Scenic Images*. Princeton: Princeton University Press, 1968.

Törnqvist, Egil. *A Drama of Souls: Studies in O'Neill's Super-naturalistic Technique*. New Haven: Yale University Press, 1969.

————. "Jesus and Judas: On Biblical Allusions in O'Neill's Plays." *Etudes Anglaises* 24 (January 1971): 41–49.

————. "O'Neill's Work Method." *Studia Neophilologica* 49 (1977): 43–58.

————. "Personal Nomenclature in the Plays of O'Neill." *Modern Drama* 8 (February 1966): 362–73.

Waith, Eugene M. "Eugene O'Neill: An Exercise in Unmasking." *Educational Theatre Journal* 13 (October 1961): 182–91. Reprinted in *O'Neill: A Collection of Critical Essays,* edited by John Gassner, pp. 29–41.

Walker, Roy. "The Right Kind of Pity." *Twentieth Century* 155 (January 1954): 79–86.

Watts, Richard, Jr. Review of *The Iceman Cometh. New York Post,* 10 October 1946, p. 40.

Weales, Gerald. "Eugene O'Neill: *The Iceman Cometh.*" In *Landmarks of American Writing,* edited by Hennig Cohen. New York: Basic Books, 1969, pp. 353–67.

Weissman, Philip. "Conscious and Unconscious Autobiographical Dramas of Eugene O'Neill." *Journal of the American Psychoanalytic Association* 5 (July 1957): 432–60.

Welch, Mary. "Softer Tones for Mr. O'Neill's Portrait." *Theatre Arts* 41 (May 1957): 67–68, 82–83. Reprinted in *O'Neill and His Plays,* edited by Oscar Cargill et al., pp. 85–91.

Wilkins, Frederick. "O'Neill in Repertory: A Chance—A Challenge." In *Eugene O'Neill,* Milwaukee Repertory Theater Company, pp. 26–27.

Winther, Sophus Keith. *Eugene O'Neill: A Critical Study.* 2d edition, enlarged, New York: Russell & Russell, 1961.

————. "O'Neill's Tragic Themes: *Long Day's Journey Into Night.*" *Arizona Quarterly* 13 (Winter 1957): 295–307.

Wright, Robert C. "O'Neill's Universalizing Technique in *The Iceman Cometh.*" *Modern Drama* 8 (May 1965): 1–11.

Young, Stark. "O'Neill and Rostand." Review of *The Iceman Cometh. New Republic,* 21 October 1946, pp. 517–18. Reprinted in Stark Young, *Immortal Shadows: A Book of Dramatic Criticism,* New York: Scribner's, 1948, pp. 271–74.

INDEX

Abortion, 85–86

Aeschylus, 107

Ah, Wilderness!, 17, 23, 68, 71, 84;
  planned sequel, 71

Alexander, Doris, 166 (n. 12)

All God's Chillun Got Wings, 70, 71,
  135

"Ancient Mariner, The Rime of the,"
  (Samuel Taylor Coleridge), 70–71

Andreach, Robert J., 172–73 (n. 91)

Anna Christie, 17, 24, 70

Arbenz, Mary Hedwig, 22, 40

Atkinson, Brooks, 56

Autobiographical elements in plays
  and drafts, 2, 20, 161–62. *See also
  The Iceman Cometh; Long Day's
  Journey Into Night; A Moon for the
  Misbegotten*

Baker, George Pierce, 4, 159

Barton, James, 56

Baudelaire, Charles, 100

Before Breakfast, 70

Beinecke Rare Book and Manuscript
  Library, Yale University, 3, 6, 19,
  22, 61, 118, 163–64 (n. 3)

Bentley, Eric, 34, 143, 188 (n. 68)

Beyond the Horizon, 15

Black, Matthew W., 68

"Blind Alley Guy," 72

Bogard, Travis, 17, 45, 51, 57, 68, 71,
  92, 107, 134, 137, 181 (n. 63), 182
  (n. 76), 182 (n. 77), 187–88 (n. 54)

Boulton, Agnes (second wife of
  Eugene O'Neill), 8, 113

Brustein, Robert, 15–16, 35, 140–41

Byth, James Findlater, 9, 18, 165 (n. 10)

"By Way of Obit," 72, 116. *See also
  Hughie*

"The Calms of Capricorn," 189 (n. 72)

Carlin, Terry, 9, 10, 55, 161, 166 (n.
  14)

Carpenter, Frederic I., 182 (n. 76)

Cerf, Bennett, 24, 178–79 (n. 40), 179
  (n. 41)

Chabrowe, Leonard, 17

Chiaromonte, Nicola, 150

Chris Christophersen, 17

Clark, Barrett, 3, 61, 63

Commins, Saxe, 21, 23, 73–74, 170
  (n. 59), 178–79 (n. 40), 179 (n. 41)

"Confessional pattern" in plays, 140–
  44, 160

Cornell University Library, 3

Day, Cyrus, 8, 10, 57

Days Without End, 20, 23, 24, 50, 86,
  173 (n. 103), 175 (n. 4), 189 (n. 69),
  189–90 (n. 73)

Desire Under the Elms, 70, 116, 136,
    146, 157–58, 191 (n. 90)
Digges, Dudley, 119, 185–86 (n. 23)
Dillman, Bradford, 111
Dolan, John, 77, 112
Donnelly, Tom, 156, 172 (n. 87)
Dowling, Eddie, 61–62
Dowson, Ernest, 100, 128; "Cynara
    poem" ("Non Sum Qualis Eram
    Bonae sub Regno Cynarae"), 129–30
Drinnon, Richard, 166 (n. 14)
Duality of characters, 84–86, 126–28
Dynamo, 136, 140, 189 (n. 69)

Eldridge, Florence, 66
Ell, Christine, 113–14, 190 (n. 76)
Exorcism, 168 (n. 41)

Falk, Doris, 137
The First Man, 70
Fitzgerald, Geraldine, 181 (n. 69)
Fitzgerald, John J., 191 (n. 92)
Floyd, Virginia, 5, 17, 47, 87, 127,
    164–65 (n. 2), 165 (n. 10), 169 (n.
    50), 171 (n. 75), 175 (n. 4), 180 (n.
    47), 185 (n. 13), 187 (nn. 40, 43), 189
    (n. 69), 189–90 (n. 73), 192 (n. 10)
The Fountain, 68, 135
"Fratricide," 113
Frazer, Winifred L., 10, 166 (n. 14),
    167 (n. 24), 172–73 (n. 91), 174 (n.
    105)

Gallup, Donald, 6
Garden Hotel, 9, 19
Gelb, Arthur and Barbara, 10, 14, 73,
    165 (n. 10), 166 (n. 12), 178–79 (n.
    40), 184 (n. 9)
Gibbs, Wolcott, 101
Goldman, Emma, 10, 12–13, 166 (n.
    14)

Gorky, Maxim, 15
The Great God Brown, 50, 86, 106,
    127, 131, 135, 140

The Hairy Ape, 47
Hammond, Edward C., 112–13, 184
    (n. 5)
Harkness, Edward S., 77, 112–13
Heilman, Robert B., 45
"Hell Hole" (Golden Swan), 9, 19
Hewes, Henry, 110
Hickey (Theodore Hickman, *Iceman*),
    7–27 passim, 41–43, 45, 47, 50, 51–
    53, 61, 62, 83, 109, 110, 156, 159,
    161, 168 (n. 40), 171 (n. 75), 172 (n.
    87); as false Christ figure, 8, 57, 174
    (n. 106); possible character models,
    13–14, 167 (n. 23); as "preacher,"
    14, 55–56; and Bull (Chuck), 28–29;
    sincerity, 30–34; sanity, 30, 32, 34–
    40, 172 (n. 87); confession, 31–32,
    34–40, 41, 54, 141–43, 160
Hogan, Josie (*Moon*), 94, 112, 115–34
    passim, 152, 159, 160, 161–62, 187
    (n. 40); compassion, 7, 111, 143–44,
    156, 162; Christine Ell as model for,
    113–14; maternal qualities, 123,
    146, 154–55; as mother surrogate,
    133, 137–39, 142, 151; associated
    with Virgin Mary, 139–41, 145, 151;
    name, 141, 190 (n. 76); feminine
    qualities, 144–46; and entrapment
    plot, 146–48; pretended
    promiscuity, 148–51, 155–56, 191
    (n. 94); future plans (in early drafts),
    153–54
Hogan, Phil (*Moon*), 121–26, 138,
    143, 146–48, 149, 152–55, 159, 186
    (n. 36), 187 (n. 40); John Dolan as
    model for, 112; James O'Neill as

model for, 112; and entrapment
plot, 120–21, 146–48
Hope, Harry (*Iceman*), 18–32 passim,
36–40, 50, 52, 53, 56, 57, 61, 62,
111; and Bessie, 8, 32–33, 42, 43–
44; Tom Wallace as model for, 9,
161; birthday party, 20, 55, 57, 84
Horace (Ode 4.13), 129–30
Hughie, 92, 116, 119, 157, 175 (n. 5),
191 (n. 1)

Ibsen, Henrik, 15–16, 159
The Iceman Cometh, 1–7, 68, 70, 73–
74, 83, 84, 109–11, 112, 114, 117,
118–19, 120, 124, 126, 140, 156,
157–62; first production of, 1, 7, 21,
22–24, 25, 27, 28, 30, 34, 35, 40,
44, 54, 56, 60–62, 170 (n. 59), 172
(n. 87), 175 (n. 118), 186 (n. 23);
dates of composition of, 3, 18–21,
71, 72; publication of, 7, 21–22, 23–
24; biblical allusions in, 8, 10–12,
55–57, 140; relations between men
and women in, 8, 15, 31, 38, 41–44,
48–49, 136, 172–73 (n. 91);
autobiographical elements in, 9–12,
20, 41, 47, 49, 51–52, 161–62, 167
(n. 23); character models, 9–14, 165
(n. 10), 166 (n. 12), 166 (n. 14), 166–
67 (n. 16), 167 (n. 23); anarchism in,
10–13, 41, 46–49; and *The
Traveling Salesman*, 14–15; and *The
Lower Depths*, 15; and *The Wild
Duck*, 15–16; and *The Time of Your
Life*, 16–17, 168 (n. 32); and
Lazarus Laughed, 17; and *Chris
Christophersen*, 17; tentative titles
of, 17–18; and "Tomorrow," 17–18,
70, 168 (n. 41), 169 (n. 43); language
in, 21–22, 24–25, 34–35, 125;
comedy in, 25, 27, 30, 121; isolation
of characters in, 25–26; violence in,
26–27; Bull (Chuck), 26, 27–28;
drug addict (Buzy) in scenario, 29–
30, 159, 171 (n. 76); and "The Last
Supper," 55, 57, 139, 173–74 (n.
103), 174 (n. 109); 1956 revival of,
56, 73–74, 110. *See also* Hickey;
Hope, Harry; Parritt, Don; Slade,
Larry
"In the Baggage Coach Ahead"
(Gussie L. Davis), 137–38

Jackson, Esther M., 190 (n. 74)
Jenkins, Kathleen (first wife of Eugene
O'Neill), 64
Jimmy the Priest's, 9, 17, 19

Kazan, Elia, 119
Keats, John, 118, 128
Kerr, Walter, 111

Langner, Lawrence, 3, 4, 22, 51, 72,
118–20, 163 (n. 3), 170 (n. 59), 186
(n. 23), 186 (n. 25)
"The Last Conquest," 57, 72, 127,
189–90 (n. 73)
Lazarus Laughed, 17, 58, 135, 189–90
(n. 73)
"A Leave-taking" (Algernon
Swinburne), 81–82, 97–98, 182 (n.
78)
Lee, Robert C., 43, 57–58
Lewis, Sinclair, 15
Long Day's Journey Into Night, 1–7,
14, 19, 20, 29, 43–44, 50, 52, 59,
62, 112, 113, 114, 117, 120, 121,
126, 129, 131, 136, 156, 157–62;
first American production of, 1, 73–
74, 110–11, 179 (n. 41); dates of
composition of, 3, 20, 71–73, 178
(n. 29), 178 (n. 36); dedication to
Carlotta, 7, 83, 160, 180 (n. 60);

Long Day's Journey (cont'd)
  autobiographical elements, 63–70,
    71, 82–83, 87, 94, 97, 107–8, 143,
    161–62, 181 (n. 67), 182 (n. 73); and
    "The Sea-Mother's Son," 63–64;
    character models, 64–69; character
    names, 68–69; Eugene Tyrone
    (dead infant), 69, 70, 90, 95, 98–
    100; fog, 70, 75, 100–101; and *All
    God's Chillun Got Wings*, 70, 71;
    and *Warnings*, 70; and *Strange
    Interlude*, 70; and "The Ancient
    Mariner," 70–71; and *Ah,
    Wilderness!*, 71; and *Ah,
    Wilderness!* sequel, 71; suppression
    of, 73–74, 178–79 (n. 40), 179 (nn.
    41, 46); publication of, 73–74, 179
    (n. 41); tentative titles of, 75, 180
    (n. 48); humor in, 76–77, 121, 160;
    determinism and free will in, 105–
    8. *See also* Tyrone, Edmund;
    Tyrone, James; Tyrone, James, Jr.
    (Jamie); Tyrone, Mary
"The Long Tale," 113
The Lower Depths (Maxim Gorky), 15
Luxemburg, Rosa, 166–67 (n. 16)

McCarthy, Mary, 34
McDonald, David, 182 (n. 77)
Macgowan, Kenneth, 3, 13, 20, 21,
    27, 60, 63, 68
Madden, Richard, 24
Mandl, Bette, 172–73 (n. 91)
Manheim, Michael, 41, 167 (n. 23),
    181 (n. 63), 188–89 (n. 68)
Minor, Robert (Bob), 12, 166 (n. 14)
Monte Cristo, 66, 159, 178 (n. 36)
A Moon for the Misbegotten, 1–7, 43–
    44, 72–73, 92, 96, 111, 157–62; first
    production of, 1, 7, 118–20, 186 (n.
    25); publication of, 7, 118, 120;

comedy in, 76, 121, 124, 160;
    autobiographical elements in, 112–
    14, 128, 131–33, 143, 161–62;
    character models, 112–14; T.
    Stedman Harder, 112–13, 120–21,
    124; Standard Oil, 113, 114, 124–
    25; dates of composition of, 114–18;
    composing process of, 114–18, 133;
    tentative titles of, 114, 184–85 (n.
    13); and *Desire Under the Elms*,
    116, 146, 157–58, 191 (n. 90);
    Cynthia's typing of, 117–18;
    inscription to Carlotta, 118;
    censorship of, 119; entrapment plot
    in, 120–22, 146–48; Mike Hogan,
    121, 140, 145, 146–47, 186 (n. 31);
    and Dowson's "Cynara," 129–30;
    Pietà image, 139–41, 158, 188–89
    (n. 68); and *More Stately Mansions*,
    140, 149, 158. *See also* Hogan,
    Josie; Hogan, Phil; Tyrone, James
    Jr. (Jamie)
More Stately Mansions, 8, 66, 71, 106,
    135–36, 140, 149, 158, 176 (n. 9),
    178 (n. 25)
Mothers and mother figures in the
    plays, 38, 41–44, 48, 66, 88, 95, 99–
    100, 119, 120, 130, 132, 133–41,
    142, 150, 154–55, 189 (n. 69);
    concept of Mother God, 140, 189
    (n. 69), 189 (n. 70); *See also* Parritt,
    Don, and mother; Tyrone,
    Edmund, and Mary; Tyrone, James,
    Jr. (Jim) and mother; Women
Mourning Becomes Electra, 23, 40,
    58, 135, 136, 141
Muchnic, Helen, 15, 106
Muir, Kenneth, 2

Nathan, George Jean, 3, 9, 13, 16, 20,
    45, 61–62, 64, 71, 72, 74

New York Public Library at Lincoln Center, 22, 61

Nietzsche, Friedrich, 59

O'Neill, Carlotta Monterey (Mrs. Eugene), 2, 7, 18, 22, 64, 71, 83, 112, 116, 160; as typist of husband's plays, 3, 6, 20–21, 72–73, 164 (n. 5); and Mary Tyrone, 66, 181–82 (n. 73); and publication and production of *Journey*, 73–74, 179 (n. 41), 180 (n. 60); and Mary Tyrone's wedding gown, 75; and preparation of *Moon* typescript, 117–18

O'Neill, Edmund (brother of Eugene O'Neill), 69, 176 (n. 15), 177 (n. 20)

O'Neill, Eugene: and composing process, 1–7, 83, 133, 157–62; handwriting of, 3, 4, 6, 20, 157, 164 (n. 5); scenario writing technique of, 4–5, 164 (n. 7); illness of, 5, 116–18, 157, 170 (n. 59)

O'Neill, Eugene, Jr., 3, 74, 85, 179 (n. 45)

O'Neill, James (father of Eugene O'Neill), 66, 69, 112, 161–62, 178 (n. 36), 181 (n. 67)

O'Neill, James, Jr. (Jamie, brother of Eugene O'Neill), 14, 41, 69, 113–14, 128, 131–33, 143, 161–62, 167 (n. 23), 177 (n. 20)

O'Neill, Mary Ellen Quinlan (Ella, mother of Eugene O'Neill), 41, 69, 161–62, 177 (n. 18), 178 (n. 25)

Original sin, O'Neill's concept of, 106–8

Parritt, Don (*Iceman*), 7, 26, 29, 34, 41, 51, 52, 62, 110, 131, 145, 162, 173 (n. 100); as Judas figure, 10–12, 44, 55, 57, 174 (n. 109); character

models, 10–13, 166 (n. 14); suicide, 13, 18, 42, 53–55, 57–58, 62, 124; confession, 35, 41–42, 142, 160; and mother, 38, 41–44, 48, 136, 142, 160; parallels to Hickey, 41–43

Parritt, Rosa (unseen character, *Iceman*), 41–44, 45, 46, 47–50, 58, 160; Emma Goldman as character model, 10–13

Parry, Florence Fisher, 119

Pedi, Tom, 54

The Personal Equation, 17, 47

Pollock, Arthur, 62

Quinlan, Bridget (grandmother of Eugene O'Neill), 64–65

Quintero, José, 1, 66, 73–74, 110

Raleigh, John Henry, 43, 112, 133, 141, 159, 183 (n. 89), 190 (n. 78)

Random House, 1, 21, 73–74, 118, 120, 178–79 (n. 40), 179 (n. 41)

Redford, Grant H., 176 (n. 13)

"Revolution" (Ferdinand Freiligrath), 56

Robards, Jason, Jr., 56, 110

Robinson, James A., 189 (n. 70)

The Rope, 191 (n. 90)

Rothenberg, Albert, 158

Royal Dramatic Theatre (Stockholm), 73

Rubenstein, Annette, 101

Saroyan, William, 16

Scheibler, Rolf, 57, 78, 141, 144, 188–89 (n. 68)

Scott, Elizabeth, 185–86 (n. 23)

"The Sea-Mother's Son," 63–64, 175 (n. 4), 176 (n. 6)

Sewall, Richard B., 106

Sheaffer, Louis, 10, 14, 74, 82–83, 165 (n. 10), 166 (n. 12), 178–79 (n. 40), 179 (n. 41), 181 (n. 67)

Shipley, Joseph T., 62

"The Shut-Eye Candidate," 113

Sievers, W. David, 150

Sisk, Robert, 136, 140

Slade, Larry (*Iceman*), 8, 15, 16–17, 18, 26–40 passim, 40–62, 85, 106, 112, 124, 131, 141, 145, 156, 159, 173 (n. 100), 175 (n. 118); compassion, 7, 50–58, 62, 83, 97, 109–11, 156, 160, 162; Terry Carlin as model for, 9, 55, 161; and Rosa Parritt, 45–46, 47–50, 173 (n. 96), 173 (n. 97); and anarchism, 46–47, 49; as Christ figure, 56–58, 174 (n. 109)

Sophocles, 107

Stram, Cynthia Chapman (Carlotta's daughter), 6, 117–18

Strange Interlude, 68, 70, 135, 140, 141, 158, 189 (n. 70)

Stroupe, John H., 170–71 (n. 71)

Taggard, Genevieve, 136–37

"A Tale of Possessors Self-Dispossessed," 18, 71–72

Theatre Guild, 22–23, 119, 186 (n. 23). *See also* Langner, Lawrence

Thirst, 82

Thoreau, Henry David, 136–37

The Time of Your Life (William Saroyan), 16–17, 168 (n. 32)

Tinsley, Mary Adrian, 80, 104, 123–24, 154, 180 (n. 49), 183 (n. 82), 183 (n. 91), 186–87 (n. 36), 187 (n. 44), 190 (n. 88), 191 (n. 93), 192 (n. 3), 192 (n. 9)

"Tomorrow," 17–18, 70, 168 (n. 41), 169 (n. 43)

Törnqvist, Egil, 42, 79–80, 81, 82, 104, 130, 141, 146, 169 (n. 50), 174 (n. 106), 192 (n. 5)

A Touch of the Poet, 26, 66, 71, 84, 88, 116, 136, 157, 176 (n. 9), 188 (n. 55), 190–91 (n. 89), 191–92 (n. 1)

The Traveling Salesman (James Forbes), 14–15

Tyler, George C., 66

Tyrone Edmund (*Journey*), 52, 59, 62, 63–86 passim, 87–88, 89, 93, 95, 97–111, 126–27, 129, 133, 141–43, 156, 159, 160, 183 (n. 80); compassion, 7, 83, 97, 104, 108–11, 162; illness, 63, 77, 78–80, 89–90, 101–4, 105; autobiographical aspects, 68, 70, 107–8; and Mary, 73, 79–80, 98–100, 104–6, 182–83 (n. 79); birth, 79, 104–6, 108; influence of Jamie on, 95–96, 97–98, 100; and Eugene, 98–100; potential as writer, 100–101

Tyrone, James (*Journey*), 7, 73, 77, 78, 80, 82, 96–111 passim, 143, 161–62, 181 (n. 67), 182 (n. 73), 183 (n. 80); career, 66, 69, 89, 95, 108; and Mary, 83–84, 88–93, 99–100; and sanatorium for Edmund, 87–88; childhood, 89, 181 (n. 70); sincerity, 92–93, 128

Tyrone, James, Jr. (Jamie, *Journey*), 7, 50, 73, 78, 83, 85, 87, 90, 99, 101, 102, 103, 104, 105, 109–10, 110–11, 136, 159, 161–62; and Eugene's death, 69, 95, 106; acting career, 91, 94–95; possibility of a future, 93–95, 128–29; parallels to Jim in *Moon*, 94, 113, 127, 128–29;

influence on Edmund, 95–96, 97–98, 100; confession, 108–9, 140–43, 160

Tyrone, James, Jr. (Jim, *Moon*), 7, 48, 92, 112, 114, 118, 120, 121, 122, 123, 124, 125, 145–56 passim, 159, 161–62; and Jamie in *Journey*, 94, 113, 127, 128–29; possibility of a future, 94, 128–32; name, 113–14, 184 (n. 9), 186 (n. 31); and mother, 119, 130, 133–34, 137–39, 142, 150; duality, 126–28; sincerity, 128; and Cynara, 129–30; confession, 141–44, 160

Tyrone, Mary (*Journey*), 7, 63, 75, 76, 82–83, 87, 94, 95, 96, 97, 101, 102, 107, 109, 110, 111, 136, 143, 158, 159, 161–62, 183 (n. 80); and Carlotta, 66, 181–82 (n. 73); lost faith, 70–71, 86, 108, 140; and Edmund, 73, 79–80, 98–100, 104–6, 182–83 (n. 79); resumption of morphine habit, 77–81, 86; awareness, 81–82, 86, 108; and James, 83–84, 89–93, 99–100; duality, 84–86, 127–28; and parents, 88–89; attitude toward theater, 90–92

"Upon our Beach," 113

"The Visit of Malatesta," 47, 72, 166–67 (n. 16)

Vose, Donald, 10–13, 166 (n. 14)

Warnings, 70

"The Waterways Convention, A Study in Prophecy," 9

Weales, Gerald, 15, 33

The Web, 29

Welch, Mary, 119

Welded, 134–35, 140

The Wild Duck (Henrik Ibsen), 15–16

Wilson, Samuel T., 119

Women: influence on male characters, 42–44, 48–49, 149; men's search for a maternal mate, 134–41; religious implications of search for a mate, 140–41. *See also The Iceman Cometh*, relations between men and women; Mothers and mother figures in the plays

Young, Stark, 34